1 2021

WE THOUGHT
WE KNEW YOU

WE THOUGHT WE KNEW YOU

M. WILLIAM PHELPS

KENSINGTON
PUBLISHING CORP.

www.kensingtonbooks.com

Some names have been changed to protect the privacy of individuals connected to this story.

KENSINGTON BOOKS are published by

Kensington Publishing Corp.
119 West 40th Street
New York, NY 10018

All Kensington Titles, Imprints, and Distributed Lines are available at special quantity discounts for bulk purchases for sales promotions, premiums, fund-raising, and educational or institutional use. Special book excerpts or customized printings can also be created to fit specific needs. For details, write or phone the office of the Kensington special sales manager: Kensington Publishing Corp., 119 West 40th Street, New York, NY 10018, attn: Special Sales Department, Phone: 1-800-221-2647.

Library of Congress Card Catalogue Number: 2020943982

The K logo is a trademark of Kensington Publishing Corp.

ISBN-13: 978-1-4967-2881-4
ISBN-10: 1-4967-2881-5
First Kensington Hardcover Edition: January 2021

ISBN-13: 978-1-4967-2882-1 (ebook)
ISBN-10: 1-4967-2882-3 (ebook)

10 9 8 7 6 5 4 3 2 1

Printed in the United States of America

For Remington Jade and Kathleen Paige

Author's Note

In the past, I've opted to use CAPS to indicate text messages between people. Sometimes I've used a different style of font, or bold text to separate texting from actual dialogue. Because texting has become such an inherent, personal part of daily life—and the main source of communicating among most of us—in this book I am including text messages as normal conversational dialogue, mainly because a majority of us text to each other (sadly) more than we actually talk face-to-face. That said, frequently when I include a text conversation in this book, it will be qualified as such—i.e., "she/he texted."

Likewise, the use of written messages, such as love letters, or court transcripts and sheriff's reports, will be treated as quoted conversations when they are referenced in the text. They will only be italicized when presented in full or in an extracted form. These written pieces of dialogue will only be corrected for misspellings, grammatical difficulties, or problematic punctuation. In nearly all instances, they have been maintained to reflect what the participants said, and how they said it.

The more hidden the venom, the more dangerous it is.
—Marguerite De Valois

PART I

SHE'LL BE THE DEATH OF ME

1

BILL YODER DIDN'T NEED an alarm clock. On most days, the sixty-nine-year-old chiropractor was out of bed by 6:30 a.m. After washing up, he found his way to the exercise room inside his upstate New York home. As Bill spent the next hour getting his blood pumping, his sixty-year-old wife, Mary, rushed around the house getting ready for work.

Keys? Briefcase? Lunch?

"I generally stayed out of her way," Bill said.

After Bill finished his workout routine, a white towel slung over his shoulder, he made his way into the kitchen to rehydrate. At about the same time, Mary was ready to take off for her workday at the chiropractor practice they'd owned and operated for the past thirty years. The office was a fifteen-minute drive from their modest, upper-middle-class home. Bill generally kissed his wife, said good-bye, and told Mary to have a great day.

After Mary left, Bill had coffee with his usual morning reading. On certain days, he'd head over to the local Panera to write out "some thoughts" or "do some of my reflective reading." Other days, Bill puttered around the house doing "handyman work Mary needed me to finish." When he felt inspired, he'd tackle bigger projects in Mary's prized garden she'd assigned him.

With so many things going on at the same time, Mary Yoder was one of those people who forever ran a little bit late. She'd be on her way out the door and realize, *Oops, I* have *to do that before I leave.* And then off she went to accomplish what she presumed was a five-minute task that actually took twenty.

Bill would tease her about it.

"No, no . . . Bill. I used to be like that, but not anymore."

The Yoders' youngest child, and only son, Adam, was the practice's full-time office manager. Quite punctual, since starting in 2013, Adam was usually at the office by the time Mary arrived, opening the doors and completing a few duties in the quiet desolation of no one else being around. By the end of that year, however, Adam had returned to school and could no longer work full-time. So he asked his parents if his then-girlfriend, twenty-year-old Kaitlyn "Katie" Conley, could split the time with him. Both would work part-time, Adam explained to his parents. They would divide up office manager responsibilities. Rarely work the same hours.

Into early 2014, as school became more intense, Adam stopped working at the office altogether. He suggested Katie take over full-time office manager responsibilities herself.

Katie was pretty, in a girl-next-door way. Responsible. Smart. She had a royal look about her, like Kate Middleton: classy and businesslike, intelligent, sophisticated. She came from a family with deep roots in the Utica community. Many around town seemed to know a Conley. The house where she grew up and lived with her family sat on acres of land. They raised horses and livestock. Most who knew Katie would describe her as soft-spoken and shy, harmless, and wholesome.

Bill and Mary had gotten to know Katie fairly well as she immersed herself in the daily business of the practice. They liked her. Before that, they knew little about her. Adam had always been a private person, Bill explained, where his personal life was concerned.

"And he had been, from the time he started having relationships. So we didn't really know Katie until she came to work for us."

By all accounts, when they weren't fighting, Katie seemed to make Adam happy. There were bumps throughout the relationship, but Adam was unwilling to share exactly what was going on. The Yoders grew to love and trust Katie. However, the idea of Adam and Katie getting married one day was not something Bill and Mary thought much about.

"Simply because their relationship was too up-and-down at the time," Bill Yoder explained.

Still, Bill said, "We were reluctant [to hire her full-time] because we didn't want to have any relationship issues in the office."

A family-run business was difficult enough, even though Bill and Mary had figured it out. According to Bill, "Mary and I loved working together. We were grateful we could do it. There were no husband-and-wife difficulties where running the business was concerned."

But Adam had pleaded with his parents. It would be okay, he promised. Katie would focus on work while in the office. Their personal life would be left outside the door.

"We finally said okay," Bill remembered.

With Katie running the office, Adam pulled back even further when sharing anything about his and Katie's relationship. For good reason.

"Look," he told his parents not long after Katie started full-time, "you've got this work relationship with her. Our personal stuff should not have anything to do with how she's treated at the office."

Fair point.

The office hours were 8:00 a.m. to 5:30 p.m., Monday through Friday. The office closed between 12:30 and 1:30 p.m. every day for lunch.

Doors locked. OPEN/CLOSED sign flipped around.

Bill scaled back his hours as chiropractor almost completely during the summer of 2015, focusing on the books—taxes, accounting, payroll. He worked two days a week, Tuesdays and Thursdays, and a half-day wherever he could fit it in. He still saw patients, but less as his retirement seemed to be beckoning. Mary covered the other days of the week: Mondays, Wednesdays, and Fridays. So dedicated to her work, Mary often drove out to nearby Amish country on certain days after working hours to provide treatment to the Amish. The horse-and-buggy trip into Utica was too far. Likewise, it was too difficult to arrange rides from non-Amish neighbors.

"And that was Mary," said a friend and longtime patient. "She drove out to the Amish because they *needed* care."

An accomplished potter and avid gardener, Mary viewed both

hobbies as an extension of her life, not something she did to tinker around and pass time. She also became a Shaklee company rep, selling the products out of the office. According to the company, "Shaklee Corporation is an American manufacturer and distributor of natural nutrition supplements, weight-management . . . beauty . . . and household products."

Mary kept a "little shop in the back office," where she sold pottery, health-centered books, and herbal supplies, with lots of Shaklee inventory always on hand. She was passionate about organic products and food. Mary encouraged friends, family, and patients to give themselves the best chance at a healthy lifestyle. Within her own life, a default lunch for Mary on those days she had forgotten to bring one from home was a Shaklee protein shake. She kept a large cannister of Shaklee protein powder in the office refrigerator and mixed a smoothie when a craving hit. The simple recipe she favored never changed: almond milk and Shaklee powder.

As the summer of 2015 burned hot and humid in Oneida County, New York, Mary and Bill seemed to be on autopilot toward retirement. They were dividing the workweek, with Katie Conley running the office, and son Adam completely out of the picture. The Yoders had started to make plans earlier that year to sell the business and to travel.

"Life was as perfect as it could be," Bill said.

2

*C*UTTING THROUGH THE CENTER of New York State, Mohawk Valley has a combined populace of about 650,000. Situated between the Adirondack and Catskill Mountains, its aesthetic wonder is impossible to miss as you trek through the New York State Thruway.

That summer of 2015, Bill and Mary Yoder were actively looking to sell the practice. Every time the subject came up, however, step-by-step, behind-the-scenes process of the sale seemed daunting and exhausting. A sale would involve two years of bringing someone in—that is, after they found a qualified buyer with whom they were happy. Then they'd have to train the doctor, beyond making sure patients were comfortable with him or her. To Mary and Bill, the patients were their number one priority—people with whom they'd spent their careers building relationships.

"We were always too busy to do it," Bill said regarding a potential sale. They'd routinely begin a conversation about retirement and selling, then table it.

Elizabeth Kelly had been a Chiropractic Family Care patient since 1998, seeing Mary and Bill three times per week.

"As my condition became better, I saw them less often," Elizabeth said. In fact, during the third week of July 2015, Elizabeth was scheduled to see Mary for her one visit that month. On July 20,

Elizabeth checked in with office manager Katie Conley around 2:30 p.m.

"Good afternoon, Elizabeth. Take a seat," Katie said. "Mary will be with you shortly."

A few moments later, Elizabeth was on her way into the back office to one of the patient rooms.

Not long after Mary walked into the room, Elizabeth noticed immediately, something was wrong. "She didn't seem to be as exuberant as I would know her to be. She wasn't as bright."

Elizabeth wrote it off as Mary appearing "to have her mind focused someplace else."

Was it the potential sale of the practice nagging at Mary? Something she ate? A personal problem?

As the afternoon progressed, Mary's demeanor significantly changed. The people who knew her best, along with those patients who had seen Mary for decades, were taken aback by her behavior and temperament.

"Something is terribly amiss," Elizabeth Kelly told herself, watching Mary run in and out of the room.

As a habit, Mary and Bill "always kissed each other good-bye" before the start of their day. They had thirty-eight years of marriage behind them, and July 20, 2015, proved no different.

With split shifts at their business, Chiropractic Family Care, Monday was Bill's turn to stay at home, run errands, and have the day to himself. After a quick smooch, Bill told his wife, "I'll see you later."

Mary smiled; she had a glow about her that day, Bill recalled. "Mary was the healthiest person I know," he added.

She was the most positive, pleasant, and graceful, too. Not much got to Mary, or seemed to bother her.

This particular Monday was another beautiful summer day in upstate/central New York. It was Mary's favorite time of year. Leaving the house, Mary had one goal in mind: get to work, finish the day, and get home to garden.

"Bye, honey," Mary said.

"I'll call you later."

The Yoders were in the midst of planning a much-needed, long-awaited vacation to Europe. It was something they had discussed nearly every day throughout June and July. In the four decades of their marriage, Mary and Bill had never taken such an extended trip so far away. Generally, four, maybe five days were the most time they could get away from the practice. There were patients who needed to see them every week.

This was going to be the "first, in all of our marriage—a long vacation we never had," Bill said.

The previous Christmas, Liana Hegde, the couple's oldest child, had given her parents a cruise.

"As long as we're going to take a cruise, why don't we leave three weeks early and travel around Europe and then finish off with the cruise?" Mary suggested to Bill one day.

Bill smiled. It was going to be a "full month just with each other."

Total relaxation. Completely cut off from the Yoders' everyday, busy world of running a business, maintaining a home, taking care of family. Just the thought of getting away from the chaos of Adam and Katie's relationship, and its demise the previous year, was welcoming enough.

The trip was planned September 5 through October 5. The Yoders had arranged with a chiropractor from nearby Syracuse, New York, a man they both knew and respected, to come into the practice one day a week and handle those patients who could not miss a session.

Throughout early summer, leading up to July, Mary and Bill logged on to their computers, booked travel, made hotel reservations, and mapped out the trip. It was an exciting time. They'd worked nearly their entire lives for this moment.

Since Adam's now–ex-girlfriend, Katie Conley, had taken over as the office manager, he rarely came around the office anymore. Adam was too busy with school and other things, not to mention he and Katie were at odds. Katie seemed to have things in the office under control. Adam and Katie had been together since 2011, on and off. Every so often, a kink in the chain of their relationship presented itself and they'd break up. Contentious as those separations had been, they'd kept most of it private.

By the summer of 2015, however, Adam wanted nothing more to do with Katie romantically. They'd once talked marriage and children, buying a house together, spending the rest of their lives in love. That was all before the nasty text exchanges and rip-roaring fights between them. Each hurling spiteful and hurtful comments. Law enforcement had been involved once. Another man was involved, too. Maybe more, Adam felt. As far as he saw it, the relationship was behind him. Completely over. There was not a chance Katie was going to win him back this time.

After Mary left for work at 7:45 a.m. on July 20, 2015, Bill sat down and took a moment to collect his thoughts. Interesting thing about Mary, Bill recalled, was that she never ate breakfast. She didn't skip it, forget, or was in too much of a hurry to eat. Mary was just not a morning eater.

For Bill, according to what he said later, the day turned out to be a rather ordinary Monday. He claimed to have run errands and napped. Afterward, he did a little bit of work from home. By then, Bill suggested later, he was counting the days until he and Mary were on a plane, taking off for a month of no worries, no stress, just time together.

Throughout that day, Bill Yoder never saw anyone. Or spoke to anyone by phone. He was alone. By himself, he claimed, inside the Yoder house all day. He never left.

3

*N*EAR 6:30 P.M., ON July 20, 2015, Mary Yoder called home. She explained that she was still at the office. Bill and Mary generally spoke every night before Mary left work, if only for a brief moment. It was a daily routine: Whoever wasn't working would prepare something for dinner.

"I'm coming home," Mary said.

She didn't sound like herself, Bill noticed right away during that call.

"Mary?"

"I'm feeling really sick, Bill," Mary added.

"Mary? You okay?"

"I'm on my way home."

Mary's voice was "strained and exhausted," Bill recalled. It was unlike her. Mary was usually upbeat, plenty of energy, raring to go. Even after a full day of work.

"I don't feel well," Mary said again before hanging up.

Bill stood for a moment. He could sense something wrong. Mary hardly ever got sick. She never complained about being ill when she was.

Thinking about it, Bill decided not to prepare dinner. Mary said she did not want to eat, anyway. Whatever was ailing her, food was the last thing on her mind.

Between 6:45 and 7:00 p.m., Bill looked out through the blinds in the kitchen and watched Mary pull in. After hastily parking the vehicle, she rushed up the short walkway and entered the house through the kitchen.

Bill was sitting by the door. He heard it open. Mary's entrance sounded difficult and laborious. She was frazzled and in a hurry. Just after barging in, Mary hurried through the kitchen toward the bathroom without saying anything.

Bill got up. Followed his wife. "You okay?"

Mary was already inside the bathroom, on her knees, holding on to the toilet. She didn't say anything.

"She looked drained," Bill remarked later. "Walking dead."

Giving Mary her privacy, Bill stood outside the bathroom door. He paced, listening to his wife vomiting. "Mary! What's going on?"

"I'm feeling really bad," she said in a raspy whisper, in between sudden bursts of vomit.

In total, Mary spent the better part of thirty minutes in the bathroom. Bill knew his wife; he gave Mary the space she needed. When she came out, Mary appeared pale, exhausted. Sweaty. Barely able to walk.

Bill put an arm around his wife's waist, her arm around his shoulder, and helped her walk. Mary carried a plastic vomit bucket. They made it to the living-room couch. Mary plopped herself down, lay on her back, placed her forearm over her forehead.

She didn't say anything.

Twenty minutes passed.

Bill stood by.

At one point, Mary sprang up from the couch and dashed into the bathroom.

More vomiting.

The summer flu? A bug? Food poisoning? Bill could only guess. Mary wasn't one to get sick like this. She was careful about what she ate.

The back and forth to the bathroom and couch continued for the next two hours. Bill sat, stood, and paced, watching Mary dart in and out of the bathroom.

According to Bill, near 9:30 p.m., Mary said, "Just go upstairs to bed. I'm really sick. I'll be okay, once it passes. I need to do this by myself. I'm going to sleep here on the couch."

Bill had his reading glasses in hand. He looked around the living room. Then toward the bathroom.

"Are you sure?"

Mary shook her head yes. She wanted to be left alone.

Bill reassured his wife that if she needed anything, to yell for him. "I'll be right upstairs if you need me," Bill said before walking up the stairs into the Yoders' bedroom.

4

*I*N PRIVATE, MOST AROUND them unaware, Adam Yoder and Katie Conley had an intense passive-aggressive relationship. In several undated letters Adam wrote to Katie during the beginning of their relationship, Adam poured out his heart. Perhaps he wrote these during that euphoric high of thinking about the other person constantly, the world beyond the bubble not existing. Katie had "changed" him, Adam wrote, "for the better." He had "fallen completely in love" with her in just the "short time" they'd been dating. He had never been more "certain . . . confident . . . without any doubts" about anything in his life.

As he wrote, Adam allowed a whisper of insecurity to creep in. Based on what Katie had been telling him, during "all the times" they had expressed devotion to each other, Adam could not "understand" how she "could still say" she "wondered [about them] sometimes." It seemed as if Katie was ambivalent, holding back, afraid of falling completely. She appeared to be afraid of reciprocating Adam's willingness to share his feelings.

Adam described how they could "hit a slump" from time to time, but not a day or night ever ended without the "smile of [Katie's] face" on his mind. He was infatuated. Completely taken in. Like a young boy in love for the first time. Similarly, however, Adam understood the relationship could turn volatile within a terse text or misunderstanding, constantly teetering on the edge of breakup.

Still, he knew what he wanted. He described how, instead of being negative, he always tried to focus on those "perfect days" they'd shared. He called every twenty-four hours spent with Katie an "honor." He hoped she felt the same.

As Adam continued discussing their relationship in this early letter, he admitted that, at times, he could get "a little coo-coo-bananas." Come across as immature. Impatient. He knew his life, up to that time, had been a demanding battle he had been losing. He was in and out of school. Focused on a career, then not. He suffered from depression and anxiety.

Katie had expressed a need for stability. She wanted a man who knew exactly where his life was headed. A man working toward family and adulthood, on a path to responsibility. She was having a hard time believing Adam could fulfill those needs.

Adam considered his instability a symptom of being so much in love with her, adding how he loved her "an extraordinary amount." But then he wondered, "why . . . the evil little things come out [of you] too . . . ? Because you love *me?*"

What did Adam mean when he referenced "evil little things"? Had Katie exhibited some sort of erratic and strange behavior that he had overlooked? Or was he being flippant and generalizing? Out of the two of them, it was Katie who seemed grounded, able to set and achieve goals, stay on the path of her dreams, keep her head in the right space, fully commit to a longtime pledge of family and love.

Contrarily, Adam seemed unable to commit, regardless of all the gushing language. He had no direction. One day, he came across loving, caring, sweet. The next, a total contrast—full of anger, loathing, and verbal venom.

Adam hardly ever talked to his father about the problems he was having with Katie. His personal life was his own, he'd tell both parents. Quiet, introspective, and private, Adam did not want to burden anyone around him with his demons. He would confide in his mother. But those conversations were subject to how Adam was feeling on a particular day.

At the office, Katie was a consummate professional. Not one patient, or anyone interacting with her throughout the business day, would say different. Katie took on a task, and she did it. If she messed something up, Bill or Mary would explain how to do it properly.

"Good employee. Responsible. When we gave her a list of things to do, she'd return the list completed and we never worried that she'd *not* done it," Bill said later. "She'd do whatever it took."

One of the tasks Katie mastered was keeping records. She entered which patient paid and which patient didn't, the amount the insurance covered, co-pays, and how much a patient still owed. Mary and Bill were so dedicated to patient care, there were patients who paid with produce (vegetables). Others with pies. Money wasn't an issue; it was about making the patients feel better and putting them on a path toward their bodies healing themselves.

The accounting always balanced out, Bill explained. "Katie never made mistakes with one or the other, when it came to the books."

Neither Bill nor Mary worried about trusting Katie. It was never an afterthought or part of any discussion. Katie never gave them reason.

They'd ask Adam about Katie.

"Don't want to talk about our relationship," he'd say.

About a year after Katie starting working at the office, Adam approached Bill and Mary one night.

"Katie is not invited to any of our family events or family functions any longer. She's not going to come over and play board games anymore. Not going to go down to Liana's anymore. She's just not invited to any family stuff."

Adam said he wasn't bitter or angry. It was simply what he wanted. No details. No specific reason given.

To Bill, Adam was making a statement about his personal life. He never mentioned an event stirring the decision; he just needed it to be known.

"Everything okay?" Mary asked.

"Yes. I'm not going to say why."

Bill and Mary knew to let it go.

Playing board games became a monthly, sometimes biweekly,

event for Adam, Mary, and Bill. As they played and talked one night after Adam had explained Katie was no longer invited, Mary and Bill picked up on a different tone in Adam's comments about her. He sounded more positive and loving when he'd mention her. They felt Adam had turned a corner with Katie. They were getting along better, so Bill made a suggestion.

"Katie is still welcome to come over for our board game nights, Adam."

"We'd like that," Mary added.

"No! I told you. She's not welcome at family events any longer. She's not going to be invited to *any* family things again."

Mary and Bill looked at each other. Were Adam and Katie together or not? To Bill and Mary, the status of their relationship always felt uncertain. In limbo. They knew better than to press Adam for details.

5

MARY YODER DID NOT focus on food. On those Mondays she worked, for example, she might take a bag lunch with her, if there were leftovers. Or toss a salad together and throw it into Tupperware. Most days, however, Mary preferred those Shaklee protein shakes she mixed at work. It was easy. Healthy. Convenient. A no-fuss way to get the nutrients she needed without being bogged down all day by a heavy breakfast or lunch, bloated and groggy.

This was one reason why Bill was startled by his wife walking into the kitchen after her day and rushing by him into the bathroom. He wondered what might have brought on such a violent, sudden illness.

At six-thirty on July 21, the morning after Mary came home ill, Bill opened his eyes and jumped out of bed. Mary had not come upstairs all night. She'd stayed on the couch, close to the bathroom. Bill made it downstairs as fast as he could to check and see if she was okay.

When Bill hit the final few steps, he felt a sense of mild relief upon seeing Mary sitting up on the couch.

"Mary! My goodness. How are you?"

She was pale, sweaty. Her sitting up wasn't a sign of feeling any better.

"She was actually worse than the night before," Bill later remembered.

"I haven't slept all night," Mary uttered, her voice broken and weak. "Vomiting, diarrhea . . . abdominal pains. I've been running in and out of the bathroom. Sitting on the toilet with a bucket between my legs, nonstop throwing up and diarrhea."

Bill picked up the phone and called Liana, their daughter, a medical doctor. He explained the past twelve hours, rattling off as many of Mary's symptoms that he could recall.

"What should I do, Liana?"

Liana advised the emergency room immediately. "She needs fluids, if nothing else."

"Sit tight, Mary. We're going to the hospital."

Bill had just been through this same situation a few months before with Adam, who had come down with a seemingly similar gastrointestinal, or GI, bug.

All of the same symptoms.

"I knew what the course of this was going to be because I had been through it with Adam. You love the person. You take care of them, thinking this is going to come and go."

Bill ran back upstairs. Got dressed.

It was 9:00 a.m. by the time Bill finished dressing and went back downstairs. Mary was fading, getting worse as the morning progressed. St. Luke's Hospital was a short drive from their home on King Road in the Sauquoit section of Whitesboro, a Utica suburb.

On the way out the door, Mary grabbed her vomit bucket. A slow walk to the car, Mary's arm slung over her husband's shoulder, she and Bill struggled to get her into the passenger's seat. She was now beyond weak and rubbery.

Bill drove fast. Looking at his wife, he reassured Mary everything was going to be fine. The ER would take her right away. They'd figure it out. She'd get IV fluids. Meds. She'd be back to herself in no time.

Bill helped Mary into the ER. He explained to reception what was going on. They took Mary in without delay. Doctors and nurses pumped fluids into Mary via IV, getting her rehydrated. She got a bit of energy back, but still couldn't stand on her own feet. Bill sat by her side, watching, listening, hoping the pain his wife was suffering would soon subside. It crushed him to think Mary was hurting in any way.

Late into the day, after a CAT scan and several additional tests, Bill consulted with the doctor outside Mary's room.

"We just don't know yet what's going on," the doctor explained, adding how he'd ordered more tests. "We'll figure it out. The process will take time."

Doctors were able to control Mary's vomiting and diarrhea, giving her medications to suppress both. They also gave her "something for [the] pain," her body throbbing, every nerve seemingly pulsating.

Mary dozed in and out all day.

"She didn't look good," Bill recalled.

A patient Mary had seen on the morning she became ill described the chiropractor as "happy, enthusiastic, vibrant . . . full of life." A few hours after lunch, however, Mary became the opposite. Something between the morning and early afternoon had touched off this bout of whatever illness Mary had. She'd been fine. Smiling, laughing, being her usual jovial self. Then, after visiting her ninety-three-year-old mother at her sister's house during lunch, leaving Katie Conley to handle the calls and stay at the office, returning about 1:30 p.m., Mary was a different person.

"Can you go home and get my ADVAIR?" Mary asked Bill at about 3:00 p.m. on the day they sat in the ER. She was having trouble breathing and attributed it to allergies and not having her meds.

Bill rushed home, found the ADVAIR, then rushed back to the hospital. As he came around the corner and looked toward his wife's room, Bill saw several nurses and a doctor at Mary's bedside. They were rushing around, working on her.

Bill hurried. Walked in, placed the ADVAIR on the nightstand by her bed.

"What's going on?"

"We're giving her a nebulizer breathing treatment," the nurse said. Mary needed help clearing her bronchial tubes. She was struggling to get her breath back.

It took some time, but doctors were able to stabilize Mary's breathing and she indicated feeling slightly better, as far as her breathing. Still, she had a gaunt, pasty look. Her skin gray. Her eyes tired, heavy.

After everyone left the room, Bill sat with his wife. He couldn't help but think how the previous day they were sketching out a monthlong trip to Europe. Now, Mary was in bed, in the ER, and there had been no change from the previous night. If anything, she was worse, weaker than Bill had ever seen her.

Then some news: Based on all the tests they'd run thus far, Mary did not have the flu. Or a stomach bug.

Whatever she had picked up was far more serious.

"We want to keep her overnight," a doctor said late afternoon.

Bill looked at his wife, then back at the doctor. His first thought: *They had done that with Adam when he came down with the same bug.*

"Just to keep a check on her," the doctor added.

Being a doctor himself, Bill knew a sixty-year-old woman suffering from some type of GI illness working its way through her system was safer overnight in a hospital. Mary hadn't thrown up in quite a while. She seemed to be resting well.

Thank goodness, Bill thought early into the evening.

"But the truth is," he later recalled, "by the time we arrived at the hospital that morning, my wife was already dead. We just didn't know it."

6

ADAM YODER WAS TWENTY-FOUR years old in July 2015. One of three Yoder children, Liana and Tamaryn his older siblings, he graduated from Sauquoit High School in 2007. From there, Adam enrolled in Mohawk Valley Community College, where he studied digital animation and theater for the next two years.

After high school, Adam never found his bearings where school was concerned; he'd enroll and then drop out of college. The discipline of study was Adam's Achilles' heel, not the curriculum. In the fall of 2012, after reenrolling, Adam left for a second time.

"Transportation was rough," he recalled. "I wasn't enjoying my major, so I dropped out."

Not giving up on earning a degree, however, Adam reconsidered. He found SUNY Polytechnic in the fall of 2014 to be the best college for his needs, and recommitted himself to his studies.

Adam had met Katie at her high-school graduation party in 2011. A mutual friend knew Katie.

"Come on, man, I'll introduce you."

Adam was shy, but he liked what he saw. Katie was attractive. A shyness accentuated her natural beauty.

"Adam," he said. "Great to meet you."

Katie smiled. They looked into each other's eyes. That spark, or chemistry, was firing between them, neither able to ignore it.

Throughout that day, they flirted and talked. There seemed to be a connection.

After not hearing from Katie for four weeks after the graduation party, by August and into early September, Adam and Katie had connected and were "dating exclusively." The relationship became sexual immediately.

During that particular period, Adam was open and honest about how quickly his feelings had progressed. Katie grew up in Utica, her father a property owner and landlord, among other businesses. The family had a solid pedigree and the Conley name was popular and respected around town.

Adam kept a notebook of poetry and writings, making no secret how much he had fallen in love with Katie in the short time after they hooked up. In one entry, more of a stanza than a complete poem, Adam talked about how, when Katie wasn't around, all he could do was "sit . . . and stare" at photos of her and wonder if she felt the same about him. It was an intoxicating feeling. Adam talked about how happy he was to have found her. How much he needed Katie. Interestingly, in an obvious exaggeration, Adam explained that he would one day perhaps "kill [himself] to death [on Katie] overload," because he had an uncontrollable yearning to "OD on [her]."

As they continued dating, seeing each other every day, living arrangements came up. Adam sketched out the costs of a house, monthly bills, and what they could and could not afford. They seemed to be planning a life together.

When they disagreed and fought, according to Adam's apology letters to Katie, their fights were heated and loud. They'd hurt each other deeply. In an undated letter of explanation to Katie after one such incident, Adam pointed out how they likely acted this way because they were "crazy in love." Both guilty of "saying mean things" to each other without "realizing how much they hurt." Adam explained he and Katie had a spitefulness inside of them because "that is just how relationships work." What set them apart was an ability both had to "pull through it" and stay together. Any relationship, he went on to say, was a work in progress, with many difficulties. Adam was not about to allow it all "to fall apart" because of a blowout here and there.

After getting over one tumultuous period and reconnecting, Adam talked about a problem soiling their relationship. He described an "artificial" joy. He wasn't truly happy. It had nothing to do with Katie; it was more of an intrinsic part of himself he'd recently recognized. He asked: "Do you know the feeling of dependence?" He then mentioned a false contentment he had been experiencing, noting how "close to the real thing" it was, but then "it always fades." He blamed it on "prescription pills." How he'd "asked for it" (that dependence) because he was "curious" and "intrigued" by the prospect of the pills helping him. Concluding this thought, he admitted, "Damn me, it worked."

After another breakup, Adam realized Katie had been "unhappy for a long time in the relationship." At the office one day, after a long period of discontent and fighting, Adam expressed to Katie that his drinking was a factor. His use of Adderall, too. He'd been caught up in both and it caused multiple problems within their relationship.

"Do you want to just break up?" Adam asked Katie that afternoon. They were toxic together, or maybe they didn't match up well, after all, and needed to respect what the universe was telling them.

Katie was filing paperwork. She closed the cabinet loudly. Turned. "Yes!" she responded without saying anything more.

"And we were done," Adam recalled.

As they continued working together, staying out of each other's way, in the "close stages where there was a possibility of getting back together," something happened.

"You had sex with my friend?" Adam asked Katie.

Katie looked down. Embarrassed. Caught.

The guy was no casual acquaintance, but someone they both knew. Katie could have chosen to be with anyone, Adam considered. Yet she'd gone and slept with his gym partner, a close friend.

Such a personal demonstration of disloyalty and deception put an exclamation point on the end of the relationship. Adam couldn't believe it. He did not see himself coming back from it. She'd done the one thing to hurt him most. For a guy who'd written her poetry and dreamed of one day marrying her, Katie's decision to end the relationship in such a way was devastating to him.

Just the previous year, February 2012, Adam had written Katie a seventeen-point list of her greatest qualities. A sincere, devoted, and endearing letter: "you texted before going to sleep . . . told me you loved me"; "you still love me even when I have to blow my nose constantly"; "you ordered a buffalo chicken wrap to share with me." At the end of the list, Adam drew an engagement ring, an arrow pointing to it, a short note hinting at his feelings: "Valentine's Day is coming soon!"

Now this: Katie sleeping with one of his best friends.

Katie continued working at the office. Adam stopped working with her. He rented a room in a friend's house. The apartment did not allow cats, so sadly and reluctantly, he had to get rid of his pets. As he was finishing cleaning up the old place one afternoon, Katie stopped by unannounced.

"Can we talk?"

Adam was packing boxes. Uninterested, he shrugged. "I guess."

Katie sat down. Adam was already upset, having to bring his cats back to Spring Farm CARES, where he'd adopted them. He kept picturing Katie in bed with his friend. He couldn't get over this.

Katie broke down crying, without saying a word.

Adam didn't console her this time. In the past, he would run and tell her all would be okay. No need to worry.

"I want us to be together still," Katie pleaded. "I've been . . . I've been saving up for a long time to buy a house for the two of us to live in. Please . . ."

"*What* are you talking about?"

"That's what I've been planning."

"Wait a minute, you never talked to *me* about any of this. You cannot be working toward these goals if *we* are not working toward these goals." Adam wasn't taking the emotional carrot. He'd checked out of the relationship.

"At that point, I am already seeing someone else and I am not interested in this relationship anymore," Adam recalled. "It's been bad for years. I really didn't want to be in it for the time I was in it.

I kept getting back in for other reasons, trying to be a decent person."

"No," he told Katie. "We are *not* getting back together."

Adam liked the new woman he was dating. He was moving on, in slow increments. Katie had breached a boundary. By sleeping with a friend, Katie had made her choice. How could he ever trust her again?

WHAT ADAM DIDN'T KNOW then was that the innocent, shy, girl-next-door Katie Conley was advertising on a local social media site to participate in threesomes, while offering her "dirty panties" for sale. Katie possessed a different, more sexually charged side than Adam had really known.

"This is just so weird for me to hear and understand," Adam said later. "I have no idea what this is about. She was always relatively reserved. She grew up more conservative, more reticent. I would not say she was open-minded to a lot of things sexually. Or interested in exploring a whole lot [of] kinky stuff, or anything remotely like that. I don't know where this side of her came from."

KATIE AND ADAM SPOKE a bit more on that afternoon when he had to return his cats to the shelter, but nothing came of it. Katie walked away upset, crying. She'd made her feelings clear. She'd tried to make amends, although Adam said later she never said sorry for sleeping with his friend. And yet nothing she could have done or said would have mattered. In Adam's view, the relationship was done.

For good.

A few weeks passed. By now, Adam was spending more time at his new girlfriend's house. They'd gotten close. He was feeling somewhat better. His life was beginning to get back on track. He felt that emotional pull of Katie was gone.

Katie was undoubtedly stalking the two of them, however. Watching from afar as the relationship unfolded, realizing Adam had moved on this time for real. She understood he wasn't just talking about it anymore. Or making soft promises of never talking to or seeing her again. Seeing Adam and his new girlfriend together told Katie he *had* moved on.

With that, Katie set a new plan in place, which she would execute at the right moment. She could not allow Adam to walk away, to throw her away. Or, as she herself once put it, "kick me to the curb."

1

*D*EATH ILLUMINATES AND SURROUNDS the boundaries every human being lives within. Late into the night of July 21, 2015, Mary and Bill, along with the St. Luke's Hospital staffers, did not know that Mary's body was murdering itself—slowly shutting down from the inside. The weapon killing Mary had no antidote, its effects irreversible. There was nothing, effectively, anybody could have done, even if the doctors had known what had caused Mary to end up in the ER.

In raspy whispers, Mary said she was feeling better. Still weak as gum, yes. Dehydrated, of course, with throbbing aches and pains all over her body. But Mary was a fighter, tough. She could take all that. Her most looming complaint?

"My throat . . ."

"Your throat?" Bill asked, holding Mary's hand.

"Sore . . . dry, scratchy," Mary explained. "Raw."

At some point between 7:00 and 8:00 p.m., Mary told Bill that her throat, from nearly twenty-four hours of vomiting, hurt so bad she could not speak anymore. By then, Mary was confined to bed, checked into her own room. Additional testing was ordered.

Doctors came in at one point and explained to Bill that they had no reason to be overly concerned. She'd get through this. It would pass.

"It's likely the same GI bug going around. Another day, she'll likely be fine," one doctor told him.

"I'd love some herbal cough drops," Mary told Bill. Her favorites, "Ricola." It took everything she had to get the words out.

"Okay," Bill said.

"Can you get my glasses . . . and my . . . my . . . contact lens case. I'd like to take my contacts out."

"Yes, of course."

Mary wanted her slippers, bathrobe, and some fresh underpants, she whispered after a break from talking.

Bill called Liana. He explained what was going on, telling his daughter he was heading home to get a few things before driving back to the hospital to sit with Mary.

"Those things will make her feel comfortable."

"Yeah. Keep me updated, Dad. I'll text you some other items she'll need."

"Okay. Sure thing."

Bill drove to the drugstore and picked up Mary's lemon cough drops. Then he drove home to fetch her belongings. Not spending long inside the house, Bill raced back to the hospital, arriving just after 9:00 p.m.

Having trouble staying awake, Mary was beyond exhausted. She'd had a rough thirty-six hours. Despite the fatigue, she was feeling better. Even gaining some strength back. The vomiting appeared to be under control with medication.

"I'm so tired," Mary said.

"I'll be right here all night."

"No, no, no," Mary insisted. "I'm just tired."

According to Bill, he explained to his wife that he would cancel the next day's patients (Mary's schedule) and stay with her until she was discharged, likely the next day. Bill had written years before that "the most healing gift" we can "offer" another soul included "our own happy and peaceful state of mind." Following his own philosophy, anything he could do to alleviate any unneeded stress, anxiety, or discomfort for Mary, he was going to try.

"But I want to. I'll call in another doctor."

"No. Don't cancel any appointments. Go home. Get some rest." Mary insisted Bill cover for her. "Go. I'll be okay."

Mary did not want to be a bother. Their patients counted on one of them being in the office.

Bill did not want to upset Mary. He wasn't going to argue with her.

"If I can, before I go into the office tomorrow morning, I'll swing by and give you a good-morning kiss."

Mary smiled. Squeezed her husband's hand.

Bill said good-bye. He drove home to get some much-needed rest, followed by waking up and then, hopefully, heading straight back to the hospital to pick up his wife.

The following day, Wednesday, July 22, happened to be their split shift at the office. If Mary was going to spend the day in the hospital, Bill planned on taking Mary's patients that morning and seeing his patients that afternoon. He'd spend a full day in the white coat. He knew Mary wanted this.

"To get up very early and swing by the hospital," he said later, "see how she was doing and say hello, and then go to work. If by noon I wasn't picking her up, and she was still being kept, I'd go back and visit."

Despite how dire the situation might have seemed, Bill wasn't worried. He was sure the illness was nothing more than a flu or GI illness. The fact that doctors wanted to keep her overnight for observation and a few additional follow-up tests was a good sign. She'd likely be discharged later that day. The worst-case scenario, the following morning.

Bill once said, "As far as a practical way to learn about and understand life and forgiveness and joy and unconditional love, nothing has taught me more than my day-to-day life with my wife, Mary, and our three grown children."

After his hospital visit, Bill walked into the house. Took a moment in the kitchen to catch his breath. It had been a long day. At the time, he sported mostly gray-white hair, streaks of black, a receding hairline, a slight comb-over.

The Yoders' landline was on the first floor. They did not have a landline on the second floor, where Mary and Bill slept. Likewise, the charging station for their cell phones was located on the second floor, inside a spare bedroom.

After Bill downed a glass of water and collected himself, he spoke to Liana again. He then walked upstairs and plugged his cell phone into the spare bedroom's charging station. He washed up, got ready for bed, and fell asleep. Not putting his phone bedside was more out of habit than a conscious decision.

"Mary had moved [the charging station] into the spare bedroom about two weeks before because of phone calls we were receiving throughout the night from [a family member]," Bill said.

Someone close to both him and Mary had "psychiatric problems," as he described it. This person had recently started texting and calling "all night long." Therefore, leaving their phones in the spare bedroom became habitual. This practice freed Mary and Bill from having to wake up to buzzing and chiming in the middle of the night.

Additionally, "I was *not* really concerned at all about Mary. She was on the mend when I left the hospital," he said. He knew she'd gone to sleep the moment he walked out of the room. There was no reason to be alarmed. "Her symptoms had been good all day and she seemed okay when I left. The doctors indicated there was no problem."

8

*T*HREE MONTHS PRIOR TO his mother being hospitalized for what were "flulike symptoms," Adam Yoder was at home one day cramming for finals. Difficult stuff: calculus and other science/math-based classes. Adam knew the material, but he was having difficulty focusing.

During the previous months leading up to this day, Adam and Katie had been playing a game of push and pull. Katie knew how to rile Adam. In a series of texts on March 11, 2015, Katie mentioned something about leaving. Adam had no idea what she was talking about.

"What do you mean, 'leaving'?" he texted.

"I'm sorry," Katie darted back. "I know. It's okay, things change."

"What do you mean leaving soon, anyways?"

Katie did not respond.

"I hate when you do this. There's no reason whatsoever to be cryptic like this." Adam waited a few seconds, then texted Katie a message saying he'd be glad to meet her for tea the following day.

Katie never responded.

"Will you please just answer my questions?"

Nothing.

A month went by and there was little communication between them. Near 9:30 p.m. on April 13, Katie touched the *Notes* app on her iPhone and began writing. She titled the note, "Optimal for finals—All about that A+ life."

She wrote the note as if it were a text, or, rather, a draft of a text she would later send. "You like it? It works at its max with fat to transfer it. Take it consecutively. It's synergistic so it gets better the more you take it and lasts longer once you run out."

Katie continued writing (to herself, apparently) that if Adam experienced "vivid dreams" while taking the supplement she was going to suggest that he should take it earlier in the day. Ingesting it in the morning worked on a different part of the brain's focus. Knowing he would bite, she compared it to the drug Adderall, as far as its "cranial pathways."

"Did a lot of research on it and the brain," Katie wrote in her *Notes* app. She called the supplement a "cool nootropic." She hoped Adam would not be "offended, [it was] just . . . [that] it would be awesome for you to have going into finals." She further explained she had used it herself and could "tell the difference and it shows in accounting." Having the extra edge made her "happy . . . in my little math focus needs, so I can only imagine your crazy calc genius classes."

The next day, April 14, Adam sent Katie a text asking if she wanted to meet for lunch. He didn't seem interested in this super pill she had pushed on him in several previous texts. But after she had banged on and on about it, if only perhaps to quiet her, Adam reluctantly agreed to give the Alpha BRAIN supplement a try. Regarding meeting up, he mentioned a restaurant in Whitesboro, on Oriskany Boulevard.

"I do like Bennu. Noon?" Katie wrote back.

Based on these texts, it's clear Adam was working on being friends. The contentious divide had been stressful and draining. Adam, in particular, was exhausted from it all. Katie could rattle him with only a few texted words. But he knew how to give it back. Both were struggling to let go—perhaps Katie more than Adam. Even though Adam had started a new relationship, admittedly, he had not been able to get Katie out of his mind. He'd slept with this new woman once. It was difficult and did not feel right to him.

They met at Bennu that afternoon.

"I brought you something," Katie said. She handed Adam a bottle of Alpha BRAIN. Touting the product as "clinically studied to help [and] . . . support memory, focus, and processing speed," the company Onnit markets the product as a supplement. Katie explained how it would undoubtedly help Adam with his studies, especially his need to focus.

Adam took the bottle from her. "Thanks."

At midnight, Katie sent Adam one of those texts she had been drafting on her iPhone *Notes* app.

At 1:30 a.m., Adam responded, asking Katie how long she had been taking the supplement.

She did not respond all day.

By 4:07 p.m., Katie still had not answered, so Adam sent a simple question mark.

Two minutes later, Katie texted, "I did a month with that and daily vitamins before midterms, then I stopped, took it a couple of weeks, and started again gearing up for finals."

Katie waited a minute, but Adam failed to respond.

"All about that A+ life," Katie doubled down.

Again, no response from Adam.

"Let me know how it works for you," Katie sent near noon, after still not hearing from him.

Adam opened the bottle of thirty capsules and took one of the pills. He closed the bottle and went about his studies.

Nothing happened.

Over the course of the next few days, Adam burrowed deep into schoolwork. Yet, he was still experiencing focus issues. Throughout that time, Katie texted with no particular consistency, but she made a point to say several times how she felt Adam was ignoring her. Unlike the past, when they were dating or trying to rekindle the romance, Adam wasn't responding in Katie time: immediately. For the most part, he did not respond at all.

This infuriated her.

"Why are you ignoring me?"

Adam stood his ground. He fought his feelings. He understood the pull Katie had over him. The duplicitous, romanticized notion of her *I love you*'s and *we can start over*'s. She'd done the unthinkable, beyond all else, and he did not think he could get over her sleeping with his friend. Adam understood she was poison. Toxic. He knew they'd always fight. They'd always have issues. And Katie would always be possessive, obsessive, controlling, and domineering. He was moving on.

If Katie alone wasn't a dangerous trinity of dysfunction, disloyalty, and dishonesty, the two of them together were like positive electrical wires dangling about, a fire waiting to erupt as soon as they crossed. Adam felt his life got better every day that went by without Katie around. Less stressful. Lower anxiety. His overall attitude different. More positive.

In a text on April 22, 2015, Katie sensed Adam was struggling. She asked again about the Alpha BRAIN she'd given him, encouraging him to take it. Give the pill another chance.

Adam took a second pill.

Within an hour of taking the second pill, inside of the same week, Adam was sick to his stomach and vomiting.

"Dad, I need to go to Urgent Care," Adam texted his father.

Bill picked Adam up and drove him. Doctors prescribed medication and told Adam he likely had a stomach flu, a GI bug going around. By the time they left the pharmacy and Bill suggested Adam stay at the house, Adam was feeling better.

So Bill drove Adam home.

By noon, Adam was ferociously ill again; his symptoms had gone from settling down to full-on. Bill picked him up. Adam stayed on the couch.

The following morning, Bill walked downstairs to begin his daily routine.

"How you feeling?" Bill asked. Adam did not look good. He was pale, his skin had a green sheen to it.

"I was in the bathroom all night."

Bill called his daughter Liana.

"Adam . . . could sometimes overstate his symptoms when he was ill," Bill recalled. "So I called Liana to see what she thought."

"I don't know what to do," Bill told Liana.

"If nothing else, he's been throwing up and had diarrhea for the last twenty-four hours, so he could use IV fluids. Take him to the ER," Liana suggested.

In the car, wincing and in pain, Adam held his stomach with both arms as if he'd been kicked repeatedly in the stomach.

They spent an hour and a half waiting to be seen. Adam was on the floor most of that time, crying: "Dad, go ask them again when I'm getting in."

Bill walked up to the window.

"Look, this GI bug has been going around all spring, it's not a big deal. We'll get him in soon."

Feeling helpless, Bill returned, stared at his son, who was now in total agony, on his back, on the carpet floor, holding his stomach with both hands. Adam was 180 pounds, cut to shreds like an underwear model.

Adam's name was finally called. He was given fluids and more medication. By the end of that day, his symptoms had subsided some, but he was still ill.

The next day, April 23, Bill took Adam to see his primary care physician. He was given additional meds and told to rest.

Katie texted, asking why Adam had been ignoring her the past several days.

"Not ignoring you," he texted back. "Spent [yesterday] in ER. Very sick with stomach bug."

Katie sent a sad-face emoji. "Are you feeling better? You can text me if you need anything."

"Not really," Adam responded. "And will do. Thank you."

"Okay," Katie shot back with a heart emoji.

A day later, Adam was back at his apartment.

"How you feeling today?" Katie asked via text at 2:56 p.m.

"Really bad," Adam responded. "Honestly [I want to] give up and drop this semester." He didn't know what to do. "Constant pain." In a series of one-line texts, with no response from Katie, Adam added: "Even this late in"; "I'm so angry"; "Good talk."

"Hi," Katie texted about three minutes after Adam's text at 3:07 p.m. "What kind of pain is it?"

Nothing.

Katie encouraged Adam not to give up: "You can take it day by day . . ." She had no idea what one should do "for a stomach bug." She asked if the ER had given him anything, before suggesting that he should keep his professors apprised of the situation: "[There are] medical extensions for finals grades."

Adam discussed a new plan. He was thinking of taking an incomplete on his finals and fixing it later. He was so ill, he could not even think about studying. It took most of what little energy he had just to get up off the couch.

"It's a good plan," Katie encouraged. "Your health is important . . . it's draining to be so sick this long."

"Ha," Adam shot back.

Katie urged him to "rest up" and "take it easy." Beyond that, she did not "know what else to say."

Bill didn't hear from his son for several days. He assumed Adam's illness had run its course and he was feeling better.

"Come to find out, however," Bill explained later, "it was three to four weeks before he was fully functional again."

On April 26, Katie wondered in a text if Adam was feeling any better.

"Not really. Still."

"That's some stubborn stomach bug," Katie said.

"It's just not that," Adam said before going silent, "Nonstop pain."

9

*T*HROUGHOUT JULY 21, 2015, Liana Hegde had stayed in touch with her father, mostly by text. Liana knew Adam was close to their cousin David King, a nurse at St. Luke's. She asked Adam to text David, also called Dave, so he could recommend a surgeon, should the need arise. A doctor herself, Liana had heard from someone at the hospital that Mary's scans indicated perhaps something was going on with her gallbladder. Being prepared for any health emergency was a plus when confronting an unknown medical situation that could, at any time, go in several different directions. All indicators pointed to a full recovery and Mary leaving the hospital the following day. Being prepared for potential gallbladder surgery gave comfort to the family.

Adam had driven south on a scheduled trip to spend time with his sister and her family on Long Island. He was staying with Liana in her New York home. He'd left on July 15, six days prior to Mary becoming ill. He wanted to hang out with his niece and nephews and celebrate two of their birthdays. He'd planned on staying a week or more. Mary and Bill were scheduled to make the trip to Liana's that weekend, July 24—a trip Bill now knew was likely not going to happen.

Liana and her husband had been at their lawyer's office on the day Bill called to report Mary had taken seriously ill. They'd had a scheduled estate-planning appointment. Adam watched the kids that day, took them to the dentist and camp. That night, July 21, Adam, his sister, and brother-in-law sat in Liana's living room and ate takeout, discussing the situation back home.

"I need to head back upstate tonight," Adam said, "to be with Mom."

Liana understood.

At 10:00 p.m., after finishing eating and relaxing a bit, Adam packed and headed home to be with his mother and father. His goal was to drive through the night and be back in town before sunup.

EARLY THE MORNING OF Wednesday, July 22, Bill Yoder opened his eyes to the sound of loud banging coming from downstairs. He turned to look at the clock in the bedroom.

"Five-thirty?"

At first confused by the noise, Bill realized someone was pounding on the door.

He put on his bathrobe and walked down the stairs.

The banging continued.

"Coming . . . coming."

Bill opened the door.

Two state troopers stood in front of him.

"Mr. Yoder?"

"Yes," Bill said. "What is it? What's going on?"

Adam? Liana? Tamaryn? The grandchildren?

Instant anxiety. His heart in his throat. Had something happened to one of the kids? Two troopers this early in the morning standing on your doorstep. The knock at the door no parent ever wanted to hear.

It could not be good news.

My God, had Adam gotten into an accident on his way back from Long Island?

"The hospital has been trying to get hold of you all night long, Mr. Yoder," one of the troopers explained.

"What? The hospital?"

"You need to call them right now."

"Thank you."

Bill rushed to the phone and dialed.

Finally reaching the switchboard, he gave his name, explained the trooper visit.

"Your wife, sir . . . she's taken a turn for the worse. She's in the ICU. You should come right away."

10

*B*ILL YODER GREW UP in Phoenix, Arizona. After high school and a three-year stint overseas in the army, he returned to the States and settled in Buffalo, New York. Bill had friends in the philosophy graduate program at the University at Buffalo (UB). There was a boardinghouse near the campus with an empty room available. Beyond paying rent, Bill agreed to contribute by doing chores, cooking, and helping with the overall upkeep of the place. Bill's (uncertain) plan was to complete his doctorate and philosophy dissertation, a rather intimidating, all-consuming task. The future from that point was an open book; Bill wasn't sure which career path he wanted to pursue, although teaching was a secure fallback.

Mary Bakert was raised in Utica. The "big city" to her was Buffalo. Mary thought about continuing her education after high school, and with a taste of local community college, she was eager to finish her degree. UB seemed liked the place to accomplish both. Mary was a doer. It might have taken her a while to zero in on a goal, but once she set her sights, she would complete the assignment, whatever it had been, however difficult.

Mary had an aunt and uncle nearby, and moved into their house. The commute to UB, however, grew old as she attended classes. She wanted to live closer to campus and, as Bill later put it, "branch out and live her own life."

A room in the boardinghouse Bill and his classmates rented had opened up. They posted an ad around campus. After interviewing several prospects, with no one knocking them over with compatibility or overall character, Mary walked through the door and sat down.

When Mary entered a room, many friends and family later agreed, the atmosphere in the room changed. Mary brought with her an aura of comfort and likability. She didn't light up a room; she brought an entire grace-filled warmth into it. You met Mary once and you knew she was a person of integrity and honor—someone you would want to get to know more intimately.

"We extended an invitation to her to move in," Bill explained.

When Mary was around, you had no choice but to divert from whatever you were doing and focus on her. Not that she was saintly or narcissistic, but Mary had a way of radiating kindness without having to open her mouth.

When Bill met Mary, it wasn't a love-at-first-sight chemistry between them. "She didn't make that much of an impression on me," Bill said, laughing. "Probably because I was blind. I mean, she was kind of shy. [After] getting to know her, she explained that she had been painfully shy as a child, but was now making a concerted effort to get out and meet people."

What's more, Mary had a boyfriend. Bill was not the kind of guy to step on another man's love life. Early on, for that reason alone, he never considered Mary anything but a roommate.

"I drew a line there, mostly because at one point I had been really hurt by it—someone stepping in on me. I decided, I'm never going to hurt anybody in the same way." Bill said that he would not even "fantasize about being with Mary."

The more time Bill spent around Mary, living in such close quarters, he realized she was special. Mary had a humility and charm, not exaggerated or forced. Her kindness and depth was part of who she was, inherent in her personality.

Not long after Mary moved in, she announced one afternoon that she and her boyfriend had split. Bill and Mary had not even spent time together at that point other than bumping into each other inside the house or around campus. The breakup, Bill later said, was due to Mary and her boyfriend deciding it wasn't going to work.

Not long after, Bill asked Mary out and they started dating.

AN OPPORTUNITY SOON AROSE for Bill. Not quite the way he would have planned it, but a prospect, nonetheless. UB called Bill in and explained that after seven years in grad school, he couldn't teach, and there were no classes left for him to take. He needed to move on, or write his dissertation and finish his degree. For no other reason than procrastination, Bill had put it off.

"Look, Bill, if you do not write your dissertation, you cannot stay here any longer," a UB official told him.

After the meeting, Bill approached Mary. They had been dating for months by then. "Look, I'm going out West . . . would you like to travel with me?"

"Yes!" Mary said without thinking about it. She wanted to be with Bill. He clearly wanted to be with her. Mary, studying for her bachelor's degree, could transfer credits and pick up her studies just about anywhere in the country.

They sold all of their belongings at a garage sale, with the exception of what they could fit into Bill's "little car."

Then, without any grand bon voyage party or dramatic goodbyes, off they went, driving across country.

No plan.

No destination.

No worries.

No expectations.

Limited funds, just the two of them. What could go wrong? It was the 1970s. So many kids were in the same position. Life seemed more open to the idea of free-spirited thinking and living.

Along the way to nowhere, they decided on Arizona as a first stop. Bill wanted to see his parents and introduce Mary. After that, an open book: They could go wherever the wind blew them.

As they drove, Bill asked Mary about the future: "If we're going to choose a place to live, where should that be?"

They looked at each other and laughed.

Neither had a clue.

They discussed the subject more practically: someplace with a university, where Mary could take additional classes; a town with activities, not too big-city, but not too remote, either.

"Seattle or Portland?" Mary suggested.

They smiled.

"We liked sunshine," Bill said later. "So Washington and Oregon were out."

"New Mexico?" Bill suggested.

"Albuquerque!" Mary responded. "I just love how it is spelled. I'd *love* to write 'Albuquerque' on my return address."

"Is that so?"

"Yes!"

After an extended visit in Arizona, they bought a small, two-person, upside-down-V-shaped pup tent, loaded the car, and headed east into Albuquerque.

No plan.

No cares or concerns.

No fear.

They had each other. They could put stakes in the ground anywhere and be happy.

After finding a small camping/trailer park, Bill and Mary decided—at least for the time being—this would be home.

The first night was not a scene from a romantic Hollywood film. In fact, a storm rolled in and it rained Noah-like. They woke up in a deluge, drenched in inches of water inside the tent, everything they owned saturated to the core.

"Um, we're going to go into town today and find a place to live. And the first place we find, that's where we're going to stay," Bill said, laughing.

Mary smiled. She did not need much convincing.

They weren't upset, bitter, or disappointed in the decisions they'd made. They were beginning a life together. It was all that mattered. Their belongings would dry out. Their world would be okay.

Driving into town, Bill and Mary found this "great little adobe house." It wasn't a palace, but not a dump, either.

"We just loved it."

It was outside of town. By itself.

"And we took turns working at the local Pizza Hut," Bill explained, "to pay the small bills of living there."

Bill was also working on a book based on his studies in philosophy. He still wasn't ready to tackle the dissertation, a project that seemed so formidable, such a burdensome task. Philosophy involves lots of contemplating and thinking before committing ideas to paper, effectively locking them down. Bill wanted to be certain his concepts were fully fleshed out before being finalized into his doctorate.

Helping each other, Mary worked so Bill could write. Bill worked so Mary could take a break and focus on her studies.

"And after about a year—and I sound totally clueless when I say these things now—something like getting married, the idea in and of itself, had just *never* occurred to me as the next step," Bill explained. "We were just so happy, and busy living each moment, the topic never came up."

With Bill, his life and motivation were more about the moment than yesterday or tomorrow. Same with Mary. They weren't a couple settled inside the mainstream expectation of meet, date, marry, have children, work, white picket fence. They were creating their own path, the way they wanted, without any blueprint or predetermined belief of what their lives should be.

One afternoon, however, as Bill sat by himself in the apartment while Mary was out, a thought knocked him over: *I'm going to ask her to marry me.*

His next thought, Bill admitted later with a smile, was *Where in the hell did* that *come from?*

"It wasn't that I was against it, I had just never thought of it before that moment."

"Yes!" Mary said immediately.

They packed and drove back to Utica.

11

BILL YODER RUSHED TO the hospital and ran into the ICU. What had changed overnight? Mary seemed to be recuperating when Bill had left the hospital the previous night. She was talking, hard as it was. She was partially alert. Sick, tired, and drained, but seemingly on the mend.

Now she'd taken a turn for the worse?

Didn't make sense.

Not long after Mary was admitted to the ER the previous day, doctors took a close look at her vital signs. However sick she was upon arriving, those readings were typical and stable: temperature, 98 degrees; heart rate, 81; blood pressure, 128/62; respiratory rate, 20; oxygen saturation, 98 percent.

By those standards, Mary Yoder was in good health. Although her electrolytes were a bit low, and Mary was dehydrated, "all [of her vitals were] . . . normal," the doctor who treated her in the ER later explained.

As they looked deeper into what might be ailing her, sending Mary's blood to the lab for analysis, her doctor noticed something. "I did a complete white count . . . which was elevated to 14.6, and hemoglobin was 16.2, which was also slightly elevated."

What did this say about her condition?

"The white count elevation . . . [an] inflammation or infection can do that."

Among those treating Mary, the collective analysis was that she might need to have her gallbladder removed.

BEYOND HIS WORK AT the office, Bill—or, actually, William R. Yoder, PhD (as he went by on his website)—had an indelible passion, maybe even an obsession, with happiness.

In 2010, Bill published his second book, *The Happy Mind: Seven Principles to Clear Your Head and Lift Your Heart*, with a small independent press. Since the book's publication, Bill had turned the concepts he proposed in the book into a website, and, subsequently, a small cottage industry: a scaled-down cross between Tony Robbins and Norman Vincent Peale. Bill advertised workshops and seminars, sold CDs. He gave practical advice for changing one's life: "Happiness is a state of mind inside, and not a state of affairs in the world."

Bill's core philosophy was a rather common concept within the guru circles of self-help: A person's "ability to experience happiness [is] determined by [one's] thoughts and beliefs." Bill promoted the idea that anyone has the opportunity and power within, regardless of social or financial status, to achieve total and complete happiness.

The cover copy from Bill's book promised "an alternative way of thinking based on seven simple principles" he had developed, each leading to a "deep and lasting happiness."

According to some, however, Bill himself was unhappy—in work, life, and marriage. Mary Yoder's sister, Janine King, later said publicly, "[Bill] is a brilliant scholar, with two PhDs, and was the valedictorian in at least one of them." Janine called Bill an "avid murder-mystery buff and the quintessential detail-ist," adding how meticulous and organized Bill was in his life.

Somehow, it seemed, she viewed those characteristics as negative. Also, according to Janine, Bill had an extensive knowledge of computers, which, for whatever reason, Bill never acknowledged. More important, however, Janine talked about a deep, spreading crack in Bill and Mary's marriage. Theirs was a decades-old relationship that Bill had routinely described as happy and, not without any bumps, a soul mate–type of union.[1]

"He wanted to retire," Janine further explained. "But he and Mary had ongoing financial problems and there were no retirement savings. Just a lot of debt. Mary had told me the little bit of retirement savings they set aside had been used for advertising to promote Bill's latest book."[2]

Janine said she'd heard from one of the Yoder kids (whom she did not name) that the plan to bring the book to the masses "did not pan out."

From her point of view, and based on what Janine later wrote online, Bill Yoder was all about, well, Bill Yoder. Even with the alleged financial problems within the Yoder household, along with a side business, Bill was allegedly growing a "supercrop of marijuana." If that was not sketchy enough, according to Janine, there might have been far more serious problems: an inheritance Bill had received.

He'd admitted to one of his kids, Janine alleged, "that the inheritance . . . was not enough for two people to live on."

On the flip side of all that negativity, Bill and Mary were in the process of selling the family business, which would generate a large lump sum of money. Secondly, one could take that quote in an entirely different context. Straight up. Just as it comes across—a father telling his child: *Yeah, we received an inheritance, but it's just not enough for the two of us to live off of . . . so we have to continue to work and sell the business.*

According to Janine, a far more scandalous and alarming accusation included Bill allegedly having an extramarital affair with

1. I find this comment quite interesting. When I interviewed Bill Yoder, sitting with him for hours, I asked him to send me the pictures of Mary he had on his phone and iPad. Bill had no idea how to get those photos from his phone/iPad to my phone. "I'll have to ask Liana to do that for me," he said. "Extensive knowledge of computers," based on what I witnessed, is false. The guy could barely find his notes on his iPad without difficulty.

2. Bill emphatically denied this entire statement—and produced financial records and other documentation to corroborate his opinion.

Mary and Janine's other sibling, Kathleen. Just days before Mary became ill and wound up in the hospital, one of Kathleen's neighbors later claimed that she and one of her daughters witnessed "a passionate embrace and kiss between" Bill and Kathleen on Kathleen's front porch.

Janine also suspected that Mary had called a marriage counselor the week before she became ill. Why (and if) she called, of course, only Mary could say. Yet, one does not call a marriage counselor to sing the praises of a marriage and figure out a way to celebrate anniversaries.

The problem with the accusations was no supporting evidence to suggest Mary had called a counselor existed, nor that there were any problems within the Yoder marriage. In fact, all available evidence would lead one to believe the Yoder marriage was stronger than it had ever been.

Kathleen suffered, Janine said, "neurological disease." So the family "did not believe [she should be held] fully accountable for her actions/choices" within the alleged affair. The assumption was that Bill had taken advantage of Kathleen. The motive was not love, but rather that Kathleen was "financially well-off by most people's standards."

"That's his primary attraction to you," Janine told Kathleen the day after she found out what was allegedly going on. "I worry for your safety."

This entire narrative, law enforcement and prosecutors later said, after looking deeply into it, had been invented.

"We did a subpoena for the supposed [marriage] counselor," said a prosecutor connected to the case, "that was a no."

Likewise, Bill adamantly rejected the accusation of him and Kathleen starting an affair before Mary became ill.

BILL FOUND THE DOCTOR in charge of the ICU and asked what happened.

The state police showing up at his door.

The call to the hospital.

Intensive care.

Mary's health outlook deteriorating.

All of it gave Bill the impression of urgency. What had changed overnight?

"Mr. Yoder, your wife fell last night . . . her heart stopped . . . and we were able to resuscitate her," the doctor said. "I need you to be prepared for what you will see before you go in."

Mary had walked to the bathroom and had fallen. They weren't saying the fall had caused her condition to worsen, but it was shortly after that occurrence when things took a 180-degree turn.

Bill spent the next ten minutes with Mary's doctors discussing her condition and what Bill should prepare for.

He was obviously upset. This was not the prognosis he expected. Bill thought he'd be bringing Mary home. Now, suddenly, he was wondering if she'd make it out of the hospital alive.

While walking away from the doctor on his way toward the ICU, Bill called Liana.

As soon as she answered, Liana could tell her father was "totally devastated," Liana recalled.

They spoke briefly.

Bill handed the phone to the ICU doctor so she and Liana could discuss Mary's medical status.

Liana spoke to the ICU doctor for fifteen minutes, obtaining all the information she could. As a physician, Liana could clearly see what had changed.

For a reason no one could figure out, Mary Yoder was dying—and nobody in the hospital knew what to do about it.

12

Stay-at-home mom Liana Hegde, at thirty-eight years old (in 2015), was the Yoders' oldest daughter. A physician, Liana had been trained in family practice. Bill and Mary had Liana in 1978, the year after they married. Because Liana and her husband lived on Long Island, it was more than a quick road trip upstate if Liana felt the need to rush to her mother's bedside. With four kids and a working husband, she would have to plan accordingly. As Liana considered what was going on back home, from what her father was now saying, in addition to consulting with Mary's doctors, it appeared that her mother was fighting a stomach ailment, likely a bug or flu. However, her mother's condition had rapidly deteriorated, right after she had rebounded. After getting all of this information, Liana sensed that her mother was fighting for her life.

As dire as the circumstances seemed from a medical standpoint, the Yoder family believed Mary could recover. Optimistic, Liana could make plans to go up for the weekend and see her.

Bill stopped and took a deep breath before walking into the ICU. After he spoke with her doctors, "warning lights went off in my head," Bill recalled. One statement in particular: "Mary coded a few times, Mr. Yoder . . . she died."

Mary was now intubated. Strapped to her bed. IVs stuck into her arms. Her limbs were swollen. She couldn't move or gesture. The only parts of her body Mary could control were her eyes.

"Going into that room was the worst moment of my life," Bill said.

He stood bedside. "Mary?"

13

*A*FTER ADAM YODER COMPLETED classes that May, only partially finishing his exams, he traveled southeast to Long Island for that visit to see his sister, brother-in-law, niece, and nephews. He was feeling much better after his monthlong battle with what he assumed was the stomach flu. Two of Adam's nephews were celebrating a birthday that summer. Adam wanted to be there. Back in June, Liana's daughter had gone in for routine surgery. Adam had made the trip then, as well, looking after the other children while Liana and her husband spent as much time as they could with their daughter at the hospital.

Adam's niece, who had made it through surgery fine, was set to celebrate a birthday on July 25. Days before Mary entered the ER, Adam had made plans to travel from Oneida County to Long Island. There had been no indication, as far as Adam knew when he left, that his mother was ill. Or he would not have gone. As Liana later explained, Adam planned to "kind of hang out with us for the summer because the kids were all home from school and [he wanted to] be there for my daughter's birthday."

Furthermore, Adam welcomed the notion of getting away from Katie Conley, who was still playing games and messing with his emotions. For Adam, there was a clear disconnect. By July, he was certain he wanted nothing to do with Katie whatsoever. They had not seen each other on a regular basis since the last breakup in the fall of 2014. They might have gone back and forth, broken up and gotten back together in the past. But it was unquestionably finished now, even though Katie still worked at the family business and routinely tried to bait Adam into another chance.

Mary and Bill were scheduled to make the same trip to Long Island on July 24, after their workday. They were excited to spend the weekend enjoying the birthday party and "possibly staying until Monday as well."

Visiting Liana's family was nothing new for Adam. When they were together, he and Katie had visited. They'd made the trip "multiple times during the summers of 2012, 2013, and 2014," Liana confirmed. Sometimes Adam showed up alone, but "once or twice a year," he always brought Katie.

"I liked Katie," Liana said. In fact, since Mary had taken ill, Liana was in near-constant contact with Katie via text, trying to figure out what had happened. Katie was comforting, willing to assist Liana in whatever she needed.

BILL YODER STOOD AND stared at his wife. Mary was conscious.

"Lying on the bed, strapped down, a tube down her throat, needles and IVs everywhere."

It was a sobering scene, giving Bill an immediate feeling of how serious the situation had turned overnight.

Confined, only able to move her eyes, Mary woke up and looked terrified. She had no idea what was happening. She couldn't speak, of course. As Bill began to say something, Mary's eyes darted back and forth, giving Bill a message: *What is happening to me?*

"It was torture," Bill explained. "Not just for me, but for her, too."

Bill spoke briefly. He stood by her side, held her hand. "I love you so very much . . ."

By then, Adam, Liana, and her husband were well aware that the situation had a ticking clock attached to it. Bill had been texting and chatting with Liana.

At some point in the ICU, Bill called his other daughter, Tamaryn (Tammy), who lived in Cooperstown, New York, less than an hour's drive south of Utica. On his way back from Long Island,

Adam had also called Tamaryn, filling her in as best he could with what little he knew.

At some point, Adam called his dad. Bill assumed Adam was still on Long Island.

"I drove all night," Adam clarified. "Just getting back into town now."

Bill texted Adam and Tammy: "Come right away, your mother is really, *really* sick."

Liana called Tammy near 6:00 a.m. Liana had tossed some clothes in a bag and was on her way upstate—a six-hour drive with traffic at that time of day.

Throughout the morning, into early afternoon, Bill sat with Mary as doctors shuffled in and out.

"Because nobody," Bill said, "had an idea what was going on."

Mary died "six or seven times" throughout that day. As each death occurred, the monitors made a loud, piercing noise. Teams of nurses and doctors would rush in, loudly barking orders. They would ask Bill, Adam, and Tammy to leave the room (which meant standing on the opposite side of a curtain extended around Mary's bed). After each death and resurrection, doctors emerged exhausted, as if having run a short marathon, saying: "We revived her again. You can go back in."

"This happened again and again," Bill noted.

Earlier that morning, as Adam drove up from Long Island to Utica, he texted Katie: "I'm sorry to put this pressure on you. You don't owe me anything. But I need you."

Near 2:00 p.m., Adam and Tammy were at the hospital, and Liana was close by, but still driving. The monitors screeched once again and the entire Code Blue action plan went into effect.

Emerging this time, after saving Mary's life, the doctor looked sullen. He approached Bill, Adam, and Tammy. "She came back, but her eyes are fixed and dilated." A respectful pause so that Bill could take it in. Then: "She is probably brain-dead. I am so sorry to have to say."

The doctor disappeared behind the curtain after hearing a mild commotion, adding, "Give me a moment."

Bill, Adam, and Tammy stood astonished. Speechless. Holding on to one another. Crying.

"I don't know how this happened," the doctor said, emerging from inside the curtain moments later. "But she's responsive again. You can all go in and see her."

14

*A*FTER A PERIOD OF time back home, now married, Bill and Mary Yoder took off for an extended honeymoon to Kauai, Hawaii. Bill later described this place as "the littlest island." They were "scraping by at that point." They had just enough money to live on. Without fear, the young, happy couple tossed two backpacks filled with essentials into a plane, landed, and hit the ground hiking. Once again, no particular plan. Just the two of them living life on their own terms.

They stayed overnight in several public campgrounds. Then they found their way to a remote area around the north side of the island along the coast: Kalalau Valley.

"You can only get there by a ten- to fifteen-mile hike, along these narrow paths," Bill recalled. "Or by taking a boat ride. Or flying in by helicopter. But we walked."

The views and countryside were breathtaking.

Kalalau is essentially a valley leading to the ocean. People are scarce. Think of the backdrop during the opening sequence of *Magnum, P.I.* as Magnum and pilot T.C. peruse the island from the belly of T.C.'s helicopter. Kalalau Valley was once a destination to Hawaii's swathes of *loi kalo* acreage, described by natives as "irrigated wetland taro fields." An isolated sect of land farmed by early Hawaiians.

Bill and Mary hiked in. They found a small spot under a mango tree close to the beach, overlooking a waterfall.

"It was, quite literally, paradise," Bill said.

They stayed about a month.

Both were focused on a "spiritual path." They were not searching for a purpose, but rather a deeper, more meaningful way to understand one another. They believed that the grace and joy of life were within the journey, not the destination.

"Our marriage vows said we were committed to each other, but we were also committed to 'love' itself—to service. Contribution. We had no idea what form this would take, but we were committed to loving people, ourselves, and each other," Bill said.

Bill sunned himself on the beach one afternoon. Beauty and wonder surrounded him. Soft and silky sand, tall waves crashed at the shore in a rhythmic, constant pulse, relaxing and comforting. They could have stayed there the rest of their lives. Time had no meaning. They did not answer to anyone. In a world without much social distraction, life moved at the pace of nature. Perhaps how it was meant to be.

As he took in the sunshine, another thought "came through," as Bill put it: *Finish your dissertation.*

"I was sure, at the time, that God had the wrong number," Bill said, laughing at the memory emanating from nostalgia and longing.

They were living in nirvana, Bill remembered. "Buffalo, New York, well, not so much paradise—once you experience a winter there."

Yet, this particular inclination to complete his dissertation was so powerful and profound, it became a thought Bill could not escape or let go.

When Bill arrived back at camp, he approached Mary.

"I need to go back and write the dissertation."

"Let's go do it," Mary said without argument.

When they made it to Buffalo, and eventually Utica, Mary had a surprise. "I'm pregnant."

"I had *never* thought about having kids. Just never entered my consciousness. But I was delighted at the news and we looked forward to our new adventure—*together.*"

As Mary's belly grew month after month, Bill focused. He rode three different bus lines, transferring twice daily, to the library. He was there when they opened, and walking out when they closed. He was on a first-name basis with all the librarians. He planned to finish his doctorate a month before the baby was due.

Bill met that goal—and their daughter Liana was soon born.

15

*L*IANA WALKED INTO THE ICU at 2:20 p.m. Like her mother, Liana sported a petite frame, long blond hair, and, during happier moments, a smile that spoke of a woman filled with the joy of life.

"If there was anyone in the family like Mary," a source close to the Yoders said, "it was Liana. She and Mary were so much alike in many ways."

Bill filled his daughter in as best he could under his emotional turmoil. All of Mary's children and Bill were now standing by her side. It was a somber time. Unsure what should be said, they stared at the family matriarch. Mary was the one person the Yoder family had looked to for guidance, empowerment, love, empathy, and sincerity.

Mary always had an affirmation to offer, no matter how negative things might have seemed. Mary didn't look at life as either a glass half-full or half-empty; she was grateful for just having something in the glass at all. She could find the good in almost any situation. She believed in people. She honored family and love. After the most recent Code Blue, and her reemergence from her brain-dead diagnosis, the family was impressed by her tenacity and will to live.

"I've never seen it," the doctor said, regarding losing Mary completely and then bringing her back. It wasn't as though Mary's eyes opened and she blankly stared into space. She was looking around, gesturing with her eyes. This occurred after the machines had declared the woman dead. "I cannot believe she keeps coming back," the doctor said after the seventh Code Blue.

"I know what it was," Bill recalled, torn up and crying. "Mary was not going to die before Liana arrived."

At 2:23 p.m., the monitors sounded for an eighth time. Mary was in full cardiac arrest. The team flooded in, while Bill and the kids waited beyond the curtain.

"They were in there just forever," Bill said.

After about a half hour, the doctor stepped out.

"We're trying and trying, but we cannot revive her."

Looking on, Liana understood the situation. The others were in shock.

"Can we call time of death?" the doctor asked, looking more at Liana than her family.

"Yes," Liana said. "It really is the right thing to do."

"It was so hard to say, 'Let her die,'" Bill remembered.

At 2:54 p.m., July 22, 2015, Mary Yoder was pronounced dead.

Bill asked for a moment alone with his wife. He stepped beyond the curtain, tears streaming down both sides of his face. He turned his head slightly to one side; his body shook. What in the hell had happened? They were planning retirement and vacation days ago. Mary was at work. She'd walked into the house with a stomach bug.

Now she was dead?

Bill held his wife's hand and "said good-bye," spending fifteen minutes alone with Mary.

Stumbling out of the hospital sometime later "into the sunlight," Bill next remembered that he sat "alone" on his bed, "in the dark, sobbing and hurting so badly." He had "no memory of the six or so hours" he'd spent at the hospital as Mary fought for her life. It was there, inside him, he just could not access it.

What would Bill do now? His entire life, which he'd known with Mary for forty years, was gone. She was walking around the house, gardening, laughing, exercising, making plans, talking to family, and doing pottery two days ago. Here she was now, sixty years old and seemingly healthy, dead.

And nobody could tell the family what had happened.

PART II

BLOOD CHOKE

16

AN OTHERWISE HEALTHY, VIVACIOUS woman, Mary Yoder was at work—having treated forty patients—and in great spirits on the day she became ill. Within twenty-four hours, she was uncontrollably vomiting. After a brief recovery, she had been admitted to the ICU, where doctors told the family she was fighting for her life. A day later, Mary Yoder was dead.

To family members, such a sudden turn of events was beyond surreal. The Yoders had been blindsided by tragedy, outside what any one of them could have imagined possible the moment before Mary became sick. Mary's doctors wanted to know *why*. Not *how*, necessarily, but *what* had made her so ill to begin with? What had caused Mary to go from bouncing back from a stomach flu, or gallbladder issue, to eight cardiac arrests, before finally succumbing to whatever sickened her?

"This is an extremely tough time," the doctor said before Bill left the ICU. "I understand completely. But I was wondering if you would release your wife's body for autopsy?"

"Yes, of course," Bill said without hesitating. "Absolutely."

Though that day was a blur later when he thought back on it, Bill made it clear to Mary's doctors that he wanted to know what happened. The entire family did.

After agreeing to have Mary's body brought to the medical examiner's office in Onondaga County, Bill walked out of the hospital. He'd been inside the hospital so long, in an area without windows, the sunlight blinded him as he stood outside the doors. He took a moment. One hand against the building, the other draped across his eyes.

Mary.

17

*I*N EARLY JUNE, ONE month before Mary died, Katie sent Adam a pithy text. All numbers: "$22,839.99."

Such an exact amount, Adam thought.

With no immediate response, she texted again: "ASAP."

"?" Adam texted back. "Are you telling me to come up with 23K *this* month?"

Still recovering from what doctors had claimed was a stomach bug that past April, Adam was feeling ill into early June. As he thought back on it, he became sick only after taking the Alpha BRAIN supplement Katie had given him. *Coincidence?* Adam wondered. It was hard to believe Katie might have put something in the pills to make him ill. But at this point in their contentious relationship, Adam wasn't ruling anything out.

Katie said no in response to Adam's text. She was only reminding him of the "current balance."

Adam was confused. "That figure . . . is comically high. I wonder how many things were added in there that you had said you didn't want to be paid back for. You're amazing."

"Compound interest," Katie texted.

Adam pushed back, mentioning how bad an arrangement the loan had been. Katie had offered this favor long ago, and it now felt like a shakedown. She'd lent him money to buy a Jeep Wrangler, along with cash for credit card debts Adam had accumulated and student loans.

"One of the things I hate myself for was taking this money," Adam said later. "I didn't need it. I wasn't in a great position financially, but I did not need it. Sure, did it really suck making minimum payments on credit cards and student loans? Yes. But I didn't go to her and ask for anything. She offered."

Now Katie was demanding the money by the end of June.

"She was desperate for a way to get back into my life. She had been nearly totally cut out."

Adam suggested a meeting at their favorite restaurant, Bennu, adding, "It will be the last time you *ever* see and talk with me in person . . . So take it or leave it."

Katie said she was busy.

Adam asked for "five minutes," even if they could meet on the side of the road or at a commuter lot somewhere in town.

"If you want to be paid back anything at all, you will make it work today. Otherwise, feel free to attempt to sue me, Katie . . . I have *nothing* to lose anymore."

Katie was concerned Adam was "trying to renegotiate" a deal they had made.

"Nope. I'm trying to meet and have a brief discussion," Adam responded. "After that, I will be trying to get you paid so I can get you out of my life forever."

Katie said she did not see the need for a meeting—at least now. If all Adam wanted was to be rid of her for good, she wasn't interested in being berated by him in person.

"Have a meeting. Get paid. That simple."

Katie did not respond.

"Oh, all the sweet, sweet lies about how much you want to still see me regularly and me [be] in your life. Yet five minutes is just too difficult to get from you."

Katie sent back a simple reply, quoting one of Adam's texts: "'After that, I will be trying to get you paid so I can get you out of my life forever.'"

"Because you're despicable," Adam said.

Katie sensed Adam's anger and said she'd "feel more comfortable meeting" when he felt "more relaxed."

They squabbled a bit more. Adam said he was about as relaxed as life allowed. Clearly bitter, he seethed about how Katie was forever trying to manipulate a situation into her favor and evade blame. He wasn't buying it any longer.

"Good-bye," Adam texted.

Katie said, "You can't expect me to be available for five minutes in half an hour or you refuse to [repay] your debts."

"You have your chance to pick a time. I'm not interested in discussing anything further with you. You're a liar, Katie. Through and through. And I can't make any progress with a purely dishonest person."

After arguing for a few more minutes, by the end of the afternoon, Katie agreed to meet another day.

Adam said one more day—"[at] the latest"—or forget it.

Katie didn't respond.

Two days later, Adam texted, "Hello?"

Nothing.

The following morning, Katie texted and said she was at work, but would text "tomorrow, promise."

Over the next two weeks, they intermittently texted each other. It was not as combative as the previous go-round, but there was hostility in Adam's texts, and remorselessness and sarcasm in Katie's responses. She wasn't interested in any sort of discussion about the loan amount. She claimed the loan was $20,000, the rest compounded interest. By July 1, 2015, Adam was having an issue with a wisdom tooth and it sidelined him. The pain had steered him away from lashing out at Katie.

By the Fourth of July weekend, they were communicating civilly. Katie was always too busy to meet, but had no problem texting, and Adam pointed that out. After approaching him with a text on July 6, Adam explained he "really didn't have [his] thoughts organized now" and didn't want to text. Then, after a second thought, he replied, "I was just going through a box of old memories, and it was very difficult. I still don't know what happened. There was a time when things were happy. Or so it seemed from old letters."

"I can imagine. I cleaned through my room last week. It was happy, Adam."

They reminisced for a few minutes. Adam picked up on something Katie said about tossing out gifts and love letters and other items he'd given her, adding, "It doesn't really matter. I was still right about the big picture . . ."

"We make things what we want," Katie responded.

"That's a poor excuse. Katie, we spent a final miserable year together. You pushed hard to be with me, from around December to August [2013 into 2014], if I remember correctly."

"That's not an excuse."

Adam reassured Katie "during that time I always assumed you had sex with [my friend]. I never bought the lie [that you never slept with him]. You had countless opportunities to come out with the truth." If only, Adam continued, she would have gone to him with "the truth," there might have been a "chance things [turned out] different—but instead I had to find out on my own."

The bottom line, Adam reiterated, the relationship was finished. But he still wanted an apology from Katie for all he believed she'd done to him.

Katie said she wanted one, too.

"I didn't fuck [your friend]," Adam shot back. "But if in the future I do, I will call you right away and apologize."

Katie kept pushing to meet. "Is the tea for company or for business?"

"Business." A pause. Then: "With a side of company."

"The only way she can keep me is to leverage this money as a way to get me to meet with her," Adam recalled. "Otherwise, there is no reason for us to ever communicate."

It was, Adam surmised, the sole reason why she'd offered the loan in the first place. She wanted to forge a direct connection between them she could always fall back on in the event he cut her out of his life.

They made plans to meet for tea at some point that week.

Teatime had been one of those cozy, cute things that people in relationships did together.

"You wound me," Adam texted.

No response.

So it was: Wednesday, July 8, tea for two at their old hangout was in the books.

18

*L*ooking into her eyes, placing her palm on Sharon Groah's hand, Dr. Yoder said, "Hi, I'm Mary." It was the first time Mary and Sharon met. It was such a gentle, comforting gesture from a woman who could espouse grace and ease to a patient simply by introducing herself. That's who Mary was, many of her former patients agreed: kind, calm, reassuring, friendly, warm. Mary had an aura about her of serenity and peace.

"It was almost like everything was good in the world because of Mary," Sharon commented later. Because of issues with her knees, Sharon had been dragged into Mary and Bill's practice. She did not want to go to a chiropractor because she never thought treatment would help. She sucked it up, however, and made the trip into Utica to appease her friends' strident insistence.

"Mary became part of your family," Sharon added. "She accepted you as part of *her* family."

There came a time when Sharon's insurance no longer wanted to pay for three sessions per week. Sharon decided that until the insurance company could figure out how much they were going to pay, she'd stop going.

Mary found out.

"We don't worry about money," Mary explained to Sharon, exemplifying her overall character. "We worry about the patient." She told Sharon to keep coming and they'd sort out the insurance issue later.

Mary was one of six girls. Growing up with so many sisters gave her a strong incentive to take care of people, but not in a codependent way. It derived more out of love and service.

Echoing this point, Liana mentioned her mother's joy in life was the utter enjoyment she took from "playing with her four small grandkids." Mary was a ball of energy, a woman who took care of herself physically, mentally, and spiritually.

"She was probably the happiest she'd been in years [during those days leading up to her sudden death]. She loved life, everything about life," Liana concluded.

WITH HIS PHD IN Philosophy, Bill Yoder attended a job fair convention with over two thousand people. There were fewer than two hundred jobs available. Not a great ratio. But Bill was someone who did not sweat hurdles. Nor did he worry about where his path in life took him. Rather, Bill stayed grounded in a sense that opportunity would present itself when he was ready for it. He and Mary believed that everything would work out the way the universe had intended it to be.

"This convention," Bill explained, "was a cattle drive—a hopeless one at that. So Mary and I are sitting around thinking, 'Okay, we'll figure something out.' I think our entire marriage we were that couple, clichéd as it sounds, who believed as long as we had each other, life will be good and everything else will work out."

They lived at Mary's parents' house. Mary had an undeniable talent and passion for arts and crafts. Friends, family, and customers said later that her pottery was the most unique and soulful they had ever seen. Mary put her entire being into each piece. Bill helped Mary where he could. They attended craft fairs and festivals, selling her pieces to make ends meet.

As they settled into parenthood and considered the future during the summer of 1979, Bill took a call from an old friend.

"Hey, Bill. You finished your doctorate. Well, I'm up at Vassar and we just had a position on the faculty unexpectedly open up. It's not in your field at all. But I can allow you to have it, if you want to cram over the summer and be prepared."

"Sure," Bill said. He understood he didn't need to know everything about the subject. "Just on any given day, I need to know more than the students." Bill likened it to being chased by a bear: You didn't have to be an Olympic sprinter to outrun the bear; you just had to run faster.

As he taught, the job became unfulfilling. Bill didn't feel he was doing what he was meant to do. Or what he had envisioned for himself at that stage of life. The gig was bankrupting him spiritually, which he knew would affect his overall demeanor and attitude in the long term. How many people clock in and out of life every day not satisfying their wants or dreams, their needs? Bill and Mary were not those people.

Another job fair came through the area.

Bill met three men from Furman University, in Greenville, South Carolina. They talked. Hit it off.

"We'd like you to come down and visit us, Bill. Can you do that?"

Bill was taken right away by how well he and the Furman people got along. It felt right. Like he was going with the grain this time. After heading South for a visit, the "country club atmosphere" of the place struck Bill immediately. "It was even on a golf course."

They offered Bill the job. Back home, he approached Mary and asked her what she thought.

"We both hooted and hollered, and jumped up and down together."

They bought a little farmhouse in the country close to home, and then moved South so Bill could start teaching.

For three years, Bill fed his soul and earned great money. Mary had Tamaryn in 1980.

Life was good.

The next summer, Bill had a conversation with another old friend.

"Chiropractic school," the friend mentioned. "I'm going now."

Bill was intrigued.

They talked about how the field was heading in a more mainstream direction within the medical field. Even the mystical aspects of it were being more clearly understood and accepted. Bill and Mary had conversations about it. A chiropractic practice was a field offering the opportunity for Bill to put his core beliefs and passions together with a vocation.

Becoming a chiropractor felt like a natural fit to how the Yoders lived their lives. In some respects, the goal of the chiropractor was to relieve a person of pain. Take away a bothersome backache, achy hip or joint, and restore some modicum of comfort. For Bill, it seemed to be the ideal balance: mind, body, spirit. These were the three most driving forces of his and Mary's lives.

By then, Bill was in his midthirties. He needed to make a move toward a career. As he thought about chiropractic work, he opened the newspaper and turned to the "Dear Abby" section, which he habitually read every morning. The question of the day was based on the notion that the writer was thirty-five and had "always wanted to attend medical school," but it would take eight years to complete. The writer worried about being forty-three years old after completing his medical degree. This was a growing concern on Bill's mind as well.

In her response, Abby had solid, practical advice: How old will you be in eight years if you *don't* attend medical school?

"The idea I took away from that answer was that you'd be a lot older if you were not doing what you loved in life."

That was all Bill needed to hear.

"Mary?"

"Yes, Bill?"

He explained.

After considering her husband's ideas, Mary decided she wanted to study chiropractic medicine, too.

"I'm totally on board."

Bill finished a year before Mary because he'd had more science classes under his belt. So he taught at the South Carolina college while Mary completed her studies. The school even worked it out so their schedules would not overlap. One or the other could always be home with the children. With degrees, they went back home and set up shop in Utica.

"We lived on student loans."

What interested Bill about settling in Utica was that he'd not grown up in an extended, close-knit family.

"I was rumored to have one cousin back East."

He wanted to give his children that traditional family life. The large and loving gatherings. Cousins and uncles and aunts. Holiday get-togethers. Sunday dinners. Grandchildren and birthday parties and BBQs.

As they wrote a business plan, Bill and Mary noticed that all of the chiropractic centers in town were clustered in one specific area of Utica. With that information, they placed a pin on a map of the town and chose a location away from the other businesses. As luck (or the universe) would have it, exactly where they'd placed the pin was an office building available for rent. The owner was willing to build it up to Mary and Bill's specs.

After they opened their practice, philosophy became a major part of what Bill and Mary wanted to pass on to their patients. Bill clarified that chiropractor work did not involve taking patients' pain away. That was a contradiction within the popular conception of the field, a way for most to look at how the practice works.

"It's about wellness," Bill insisted. "It's not about fixing something. It's about opening the channels of the body to allow life to extend outward into the body so the body can heal *itself*. Mary and I believed the wisdom of the body knew how to fix itself."

Over the years, Bill said, "we witnessed what I can only describe as miracles. We didn't take credit for any of it. All we did was remove the blockage. It was all tremendously satisfying."

They shared a dream, Bill concluded.

"We did it together. The two of us and our children."

19

BILL YODER DUG DEEP for a bit of strength, pulled himself together as best he could, and drove home from the hospital early on the evening of July 22, 2015.

The entire day had been somewhat of a tragic blur; yet, at the same time, it was so perfectly clear. It was as if someone else had experienced it all and Bill watched from afar.

Bill and Mary were healers who had spent their professional lives helping patients overcome chronic pain. That dedication to wellness, Bill contended, started on the inside. Bill claimed on his website, echoed in the book's author bio, that he'd "studied Eastern and Western philosophy and religion for over forty years." He'd also written a doctoral dissertation on comparative mysticism. Bill had taught philosophy courses for ten years at three different universities.

As time passed, he "left the academic world to pursue a career in holistic healing." He had also "given presentations and taught workshops in both private and corporate sectors on the topics of health and healing, human potential, self-actualization and spirituality."

Bill and Mary Yoder were intelligent, highly educated people who cared deeply about the world, how people moved within it, and dealt with the emotional and physical pain they experienced. Mary wanted nothing more than to give her patients a fighting chance at the best life they could create for themselves. She preached herbal remedies and suggested organic foods and the healing properties of herbs and holistic medicines.

Mary and Bill encouraged not only their patients but those they knew, and family, to live the lives they dreamed of having. Don't think of the dream as a dream—but rather as a place you will land someday. A major contributor to ultimate happiness began with family: "We've welcomed seven fantastic grandchildren who are marvelous teachers in their own right (and a boatload of fun)."

All of that seemed to disappear in one afternoon. Bill's best friend, the mother of his children, and his business partner was gone two days after entering the ER with a supposed stomach bug. In those hours after Mary passed, Bill was overwhelmed as he sat in bed, staring at the ceiling, uncontrollably crying.

His wife of decades was suddenly gone. Her belongings were still where she'd left them: a sweater, gardening gloves, tools, watering pot, and her favorite mug. Bill could still smell his wife in their bedroom. He could see the smile on Mary's face whenever she walked through the door. Somehow, inside of forty-eight hours, the healthiest person Bill Yoder had even known had left without warning.

The pain, Bill added, "was so bad . . . I have absolutely no memory of the other six hours or so there [at home that night]."

Beyond family, once it became clear Mary was not going to make it, the one person who had gone to the hospital was Katie Conley. Bill recalled seeing Katie on his way out of the hospital. He knew she had not been part of Adam's life romantically for nearly a year, but Katie still worked for the Yoders. Showing up to support the family showed Katie's concern and compassion. Whatever had happened between Katie and Adam was their business, Bill felt. The immense void they'd all experienced in losing Mary wasn't about that. Having Katie's support was incredibly important.

"I think [Katie] may have come into the hospital," Bill said later, referring to the hectic afternoon when Mary coded eight times. "I think at the very end of the day, I might have seen her briefly."

Katie and Adam had been in touch all that day. Katie had responded to Adam's texts early in the day and drove straight to the hospital.

"She's important to me, too, you know," Katie had texted that morning when Adam reached out and sounded emotionally lost, and in a terrible state of mourning.

"How you holding up, Kate?" Katie's sister asked in a text after hearing Mary had passed.

"It's really, really hard," Katie responded. "I've been crying literally all day. Thanks for calling."

Katie's sister was empathetic, explaining how she would tell everyone on their side. Katie shouldn't have to "go through it, over and over," and make those calls.

Katie's sister let her know she was just a call away if Katie needed to "vent or just cry." She would always be there. "I cannot pretend to know what you are going through . . ."

"[Mary] was so really great," Katie texted back.

THE LOAN KATIE HAD extended to Adam, which they had been texting about into early July, a few weeks before Mary's death, was Katie's way of keeping Adam within her grasp. This became obvious as Adam and Katie continued to text.

Katie dangled the money in order to wield control over communicating with her former boyfriend. The money gave Katie a reason to call and text Adam, after he had made it clear he wanted nothing to do with her.

Conversely, Katie had been a vital part of Mary and Bill Yoder's lives, along with Adam's extended family. She had been with Adam and his sister Liana when two of Liana's children were born. She'd taken care of Liana's children while Liana was in the hospital. She visited Long Island frequently after the children came. For Katie to offer Adam a loan when he obviously needed it was a kind and generous gesture two people in love did for each other.

After they met for teatime on July 8, 2015, Katie texted Adam, stating once again how nice it was to see him.

"I know life is hard and I don't know the best way to work through it," she said. "Guess we're just supposed to experiment and see what works."

Katie waited a minute.

No response from Adam.

So she texted how "important" he was to her: "You always have been and I imagine always will be."

Adam responded fifteen minutes later. He explained the struggle he was experiencing managing his life, adding, "You're important to me, too, Katie."

He then sent Katie a link to a song by Vanic x Aquilo, "Losing You." The lyrics depict a man wrestling with the idea of letting go as he stares back at "what we were." There's a dark finality to the song, with its slow tempo and deliberate, pulsating-drone rhythm.

Adam called the song "saddening," if "somewhat healing at the same time."

Within this same text exchange, Katie and Adam called a truce. Perhaps they realized life was better—with far less anxiety—when they acted out of empathy instead of scorn. Their texts during this time frame leave an impression of two people trying to work on remaining friends while understanding the romance was dead. The tone for the remainder of that day suggested they were miserable knowing the relationship had run its course, and they couldn't do anything to rekindle it.

"We must've been pretty entwined for [the relationship] to feel like this still," Katie texted.

"I'll text you tomorrow after the dentist," Adam said, leaving the door open for further communication.

The intensity of Adam and Katie's relationship spoke to how codependent they were on each other's affection, participation, and reaction to what the other said and did. Adam was a guy unafraid of expressing his deepest emotions and feelings for Katie. A part of him needed to save Katie. Rescue her.

During one breakup early into dating, in a letter, Adam asked Katie if she knew "how much" he loved her, before explaining how all he could do when she was not around was "stare" at pictures of them together. He wondered if she felt the same, adding, "I'd rather be dead than live without you." In his notebook, describing his most earnest feelings about the relationship, Adam wrote "kill myself to death" on a page, before admitting a desire to "OD" on

Katie. Then he drew a heart monitor chart with the spikes and dips that a needle on paper makes as it records a beating heart.

On the next page, still in the midst of dealing with the dissolution of the relationship, Adam spoke of how he had recently started "breaking down." "Love" was nowhere "to be found." He was clearly lost without hearing from Katie, "starin' at the phone . . . wishing, hoping, praying" she would call or text.

According to Adam, he and Katie were together two years before their first serious breakup. Katie had said she was "unhappy" in the relationship "for a long time . . . [and] told me . . . many times."

So they agreed to end it.

Those who knew Katie claimed she was a "loving sister, aunt, daughter, cousin, niece, and friend . . ." One of seven daughters, Katie was part of what friends labeled a "devoted family." Her father had been an army major. Those closest to Katie believed the time her father spent in the military instilled "certain values and morals" in Katie as she grew. Her most admirable trait was "loving others," claimed one friend.

Katie's passion was tennis, which she excelled in, having played competitively in high school and later in college. At Sauquoit High School, records indicate Katie finished in the top 10 percent of her class. Several former classmates remembered her only by a nickname: "Crazy Katie." There were stories of her keying an ex-boyfriend's car after a breakup and acting bizarrely when she didn't get her way.

She earned an associate degree in liberal arts from Mohawk Valley Community College. Later, Katie enrolled in Utica College and State of New York Polytechnic Institute, receiving a bachelor's in business, with what has been said is a perfect 4.0 final semester grade point average. So tenacious and studious, in fact, Katie earned honor society status in high school and college.

This was the one area where Katie and Adam diverged: Although highly intelligent, Adam struggled academically—or, rather, he lacked the discipline, structure, and hours required for study, which seemed effortless for Katie.

One of their biggest challenges as a couple occurred in October and November 2013—and threw Adam into a spiral of negative emotion, depression, and anger. Perhaps this incident recon-firmed for him in 2015 why he wasn't with her anymore. At the time, Adam was seeing someone. He'd texted Katie, saying, "I can't remember what it was like being happy with you and I have finally moved on."

Katie suggested that "living alone" had made Adam unhappy, not the demise of their relationship.

On October 30, 2013, Adam had called Katie. "Moving out to-day," he said. "You can come see the cats tonight and say good-bye if you'd like."

She responded by saying she might.

He never saw her.

The next morning, while staying over his new girlfriend's house, Adam woke up and looked at his cell phone. A call had come in after midnight. Adam had been asleep.

Katie?

She hadn't been phoning. She'd texted occasionally. Mostly, however, she gave the impression she was leaving Adam alone. Yet, at five o'clock in the morning, as Adam stared at the screen, some-thing felt urgent about this call.

"I was like, 'Is she okay?' Believe it or not, I am a decent person. I was trying to maintain some sort of respect for her, hard as it was."

Adam checked on his new girlfriend, who was still asleep. Then he stepped outside for privacy so he could call Katie.

No answer.

The day went by and Adam had not heard from her. Just as well. He was finished. In a good place. Not great, but he was getting over Katie, moving on with his life. Katie still worked for Mary and Bill. She was a reliable employee, as far as anyone could tell. No complaints from patients. Everyone seemed to like her. Bill and Mary did not have a problem with Katie's work ethic or ability to do her job.

Later that night, Adam's cell phone buzzed.

"I get this long, detailed text from her," he recalled.

In that text, Katie explained how she'd driven herself to the hos-pital the previous night—that was the reason for the late-night call.

"According to Katie in that text, I had gotten her pregnant. I could have had a baby. It was a weird moment for me. *Oh, my god, I could have gotten someone pregnant and had a child. I had never really thought about that before.*"

Adam texted back, saying he was rushing to come see her. Being at his girlfriend's house, he told Katie to meet him where he rented a room, which was a two-minute drive from Katie's.

He understood that what Katie had gone through the night before was traumatic in so many different ways. She was going to need support. He needed to be there for her.

He texted Katie on the way over: "God, Katie. Life isn't fair."

"I know. That's why we have to make the best of it. Do what we want."

"I'm sorry," Adam responded.

"We would have come to the same conclusion, anyway," Katie suggested, referring to her medically induced miscarriage.

This text conversation, according to Katie, was in reference to her losing their child, the reason for the emergency hospital visit that night. If she'd not lost the child, Katie implied, they would have likely agreed to abort it, anyway.

"If we talked about it before or not," Katie continued in her text, "you were going through your own things. You expressly told me you did not want a child. I respected that. Damn it, Adam, if you had said otherwise."

As Adam thought about it, he considered what Katie was saying: *If only we were still a couple, we could have made this decision together.* Adam had once told Katie how scared he was to have children at that stage of his life.

Texting her back, Adam ranted: "The things I say don't just give you the right to make decisions that involve me by yourself! I'm so torn up and hurt and confused now." Adam told Katie the day was the "fucking worst" of his "entire life."

He was referring to Katie saying she would have had an abortion if she hadn't lost the child.

As Adam drove toward his home, rushing to be by Katie's side, he was livid, fearful, and concerned. After all, this was the first he'd heard of her being pregnant with his child.

He stopped to pick up a twelve-pack of beer on the way. He needed it, Adam said later, to cope with the unfolding events.

When he arrived, he rushed into the house, sat on the couch upstairs with Katie and talked.

She was crying, upset over having lost their child.

Adam comforted her. "It's going to be okay, Katie."

"I . . . cannot . . . believe this has happened."

"We'll get through this, Katie. Don't worry. We'll get through it together."

Katie tore into Adam via text throughout the next few days, describing how "explicit" he had been about their not having kids. "I didn't want to do that alone and you didn't want to be there . . . Two weeks later, you're *ready* to have kids?"

In all caps, Adam texted, "YOU WOULDN'T HAVE BEEN FUCKING ALONE. IM NOT A PIECE OF SHIT." He continued, saying how the decision she'd made at the hospital without him should have been made "BY 2 PEOPLE EITHER WAY."

Adam wondered why she'd called him only once, near midnight. Why hadn't she kept calling so he could meet her at the hospital and they could decide together what to do.

"You were quite clear. I was very alone," Katie shot back. "What does it change . . . you don't want to [be] tied to me. That was my life. You left me alone!"

"Fuck you!" Adam shot back. "That officially cuts us. I want *nothing* with you. You're fucking selfish."

Katie repeated how he hadn't been there for her, so she was forced to make such a tough decision on her own.

They bickered back and forth for a few moments.

"I hate you," Adam said. He insisted he would have supported her at the hospital. If the baby had survived, he said, he would have taken care of them both.

"You'd've gone to doctor [appointments] with me? Just like that? Why'd you leave! You aren't even here!"

The conversation became even more combative as the days passed. Even vicious at times. Hostile and accusatory on both sides. Katie warned Adam about "her head" and how he'd messed with her emotions in the past.

"FUUUUUUUUCK," Adam texted back.

What actually happened at the hospital that night?

Katie claimed to have gone home by the time she called him. In a text on November 3, 2013, Katie explained how, after that midnight call, she'd rushed out of the house, leaving her phone at home. She had pains in her stomach and severe bleeding. She went directly to the ER. It turned out to be an ectopic pregnancy. "Internal bleeding. Positive yours. Ironically I got to go to the birth floor! Given cancer med to fix it. Told them you were coming. Missed you. Left by myself. All better, right. So fucked up. They kept telling me how lucky I am."[3]

"Please tell me [what] this means?" Adam responded. "I called you right back."

"It means I was pregnant. But the baby wasn't where it was supposed to be and they had to inject me and they killed it like it was some kind of tumor, Adam . . . The bleeding should've killed me but they stopped it."

"You called me once and just fucking left your phone?"

"I was sick and apparently in shock."

"Fuck."

They argued for the next few moments, Katie pouring it on heavily, letting Adam know she'd wanted him there. Needed him there. Because they'd broken up, she implied that she was now "used to doing things by" herself.

After calming down, feeling Katie "was [still] going to need some help emotionally," Adam texted at six thirty-five that night: "You want me to come over?"

Katie went into self-loathing mode, trying to make Adam feel guiltier than he already was: "I don't feel lucky . . . I can't do anything right, Adam. Not even what I am supposed to do unconsciously." Regarding his question, "Yes," she concluded.

Adam drove over to her house immediately.

Leaving the next morning, after having sex with Katie that night, Adam decided they needed to be together. He drove back to his

---

3. There is no documentation I could find proving Katie ever went to the hospital that night, or had an ectopic pregnancy.

new girlfriend's and explained that he'd made a decision to rekindle his relationship with Katie.

On November 5, Adam texted Katie: "I'm no longer seeing anyone. Like I told you, we weren't dating, and there was no sex. And now there is nothing."

Katie and Adam were back on.

20

ADAM YODER HAD AN unpredictable side to him, as far as college and career goals. He kept his personal business to himself, mostly, but would open up to Mary. He dabbled in many different career choices, never settling on a major while in his early days of undergrad. None of it had to do with Adam having trouble with the curriculum, or his intelligence. He had taken Chinese for a while and wound up being president of the Chinese club, speaking the language nearly fluently. He was the only non-Asian in the club. He'd master something, or as close as he could get, then take a year off and head in a different direction. Mathematics became a passion for a time, then computer science.

"Why don't you finish?" Bill asked his son one day.

Adam shrugged. "Thinking about it."

Katie toying with his emotions had a lot to do with Adam's uncertainty where school and life were concerned. She was routinely confusing him about what he could and could not accomplish.

Adam became interested in pursuing many different aspects of life, but Katie somehow managed to spoil these—without Adam knowing what was happening. He was so focused on her needs, he ignored his own.

In primary school, Adam decided to dance. Near his middle-school years, Adam immersed himself. He took an entire banquet of classes, hoping to get into competition. During one event, Adam and his family received the surprise of the year. After the competition, the judges announced they'd chosen one boy and girl for a trip to Caesars Palace in Las Vegas to participate in a weeklong study program. It was seven days of professional instruction, concluding with a recital.

Adam was chosen.

"We just promptly fell out of our chairs," Bill recalled, speaking about the moment Adam's name was called. As Bill remembered this day, the memory was so profound, it brought tears to his eyes.

Mary accompanied Adam for the week. Bill flew out for the recital. It was a special trip for Mary.

"I've never seen a more loving mother than Mary," Bill said.

Even as the kids grew, started families of their own, managing their way through adulthood, Mary was intimately involved. Liana and Mary spoke every day on the phone, right up until the moment Mary died.

"Her top three priorities in life were mother, grandmother, and wife," Bill said.

This close relationship provided an open channel for Mary's children to confide in her with issues and problems, as well as accomplishments and happier moments.

Especially Adam.

"He would not come to me," Bill said. "But he'd go to her with anything that was bothering him."

Even when he was in a bad place, Bill concluded, Adam would go to his mother and unload. Some would later claim Adam was mean to his mother at times. He'd say untoward things to her—leaving an impression that Adam bullied his mother. This was completely untrue. Adam would get agitated and "spout off," his sister and father recalled. But the next day, Adam would hug his mother, and say he was sorry if he'd hurt her in any way or had yelled. Mary never feared her son, and Adam never gave her a reason to be afraid.

21

As Liana Hegde collected her thoughts after saying good-bye to her mother in the hospital, it occurred to Mary Yoder's oldest child just how helpless she felt. Mary was suffering—dying—and no one could do anything for her. Liana drove directly to her parents' house from the hospital. It was near 4:00 p.m. when she arrived.

Bill was on the back porch, sitting, "sobbing," Liana later recalled. She put a hand on her father's shoulder, squeezed lovingly. What could she say? There were no words. She walked inside the house—the first time she'd been there since her mother was gone.

Every detail of the house reminded Liana of her mother: the plants, the rug Mary had picked out, a piano just beyond the short breezeway. Mary Yoder was everywhere. But *she* was missing.

Bill walked in behind his daughter.

Like the rest of the family, Liana was functioning more on autopilot, even though she had been trained to deal with trauma and loss. During a time such as this, your brain switches to reflex mode. It finds a temporary way of coping with unexpected, overwhelming grief and loss. Essentially, our brains produce a defense mechanism, protecting us from more psychological pain and damage than we can handle. We function on adrenaline, one of the reasons why Bill later said he could hardly recall what time it was or much of what he did when he returned from the hospital.

With her dad at home, others arriving, Liana took a moment and thought about how, when she'd gone in to see her mother, "you wouldn't have recognized her." As a physician, Liana knew to look for symptoms that others did not. Mary's legs were "very swollen . . . edematous." Twice their normal size, Mary's legs had turned colors, mostly a "dusky pale," while the rest of her body remained yellow as an egg yolk.

Liana had noticed a Foley bag, which drains urine from the body, so she'd walked over for a closer look. She saw "dark-colored sediment at the bottom [of the empty bag]." When that occurs and the person is cold to the touch—which Mary was by then—it means the body is overloaded with fluid and the kidneys have stopped functioning. By then, Mary had been put on the maximum dosage of medications, but doctors were unable to raise her blood pressure. Blood was not moving throughout Mary's body any longer.

Her organs had shut down.

The obvious question for Liana was how had her mother gone from healthy one day, exhibiting flulike symptoms and stomach issues, to her body shutting down twenty hours later? What had been introduced into the situation to cause such a sudden turn of events?

The one consistent factor was that Bill had been with Mary that morning and when she returned home ill. Additionally, he was present throughout that day and the following day when she died.

Outside the immediate area around Mary's hospital bed, just beyond the curtain, the family had sat on chairs and waited. Her three children, of course, were sullen, crying, and equally as stunned. They were unable to process such an abrupt, tragic turn in their mother's life. After Katie arrived, Adam had taken off during the day. As far as Liana knew, he had left to retrieve a couple of items he wanted to give to his mother. At the time, despite the circumstances, they were all under the impression Mary would pull through.

Liana viewed Katie as a family friend. She "had spent a lot of time with us . . . My kids loved her and they were with her all the time."

During what turned out to be her final code, before it was decided to call Mary's death, Liana texted Adam. She told him to get back to the ICU immediately. As the alarm rang and doctors and nurses filed in around Mary's bed, Bill did not move from the chair on the outer side of the curtain.

"He had tears and was in shock," Liana said later.

Bill looked at his daughter as Liana stepped behind the curtain a final time. "Why?" he asked. How had this happened?

"I don't know, Dad."

Adam came running back. In his hand was a picture he'd painted for Mother's Day that past May. He wanted it near his mother. As Liana stepped in to watch medical personnel work to resuscitate Mary, Adam knelt on the tile floor by his father, clutching the picture to his chest, sobbing.

Then it was over.

From her medical training, Liana understood that when an unexplained death occurred, or a patient had been admitted to the hospital and died within twenty-four hours, it was automatic, standard practice for the body to be autopsied. After Mary's death, Liana stayed behind in the ICU to confirm the hospital followed that protocol. She and her family wanted answers. They needed some sort of understanding.

After being told by a physician that Mary's body would be forwarded to the ME, Liana left. By then, Bill, Adam, and Katie were gone, too.

STANDING INSIDE HER PARENTS' house, Liana did not know how to help anyone, including herself. After Bill got up and had walked in, Liana grew concerned as she heard her father speak.

"I don't want to be here," Bill said. "Without her, I don't want to be here anymore."

"Talk to somebody who lost a spouse, Dad, because I don't know what to tell you."

Liana suggested her father speak with her aunt—Mary's sister, Kathleen Richmond—who had lost her husband the previous year.

"I felt . . . he might be suicidal," Liana recalled.

As Bill retired upstairs, Liana did what she could to stay busy. So she called the local funeral home and explained that after the medical examiner's office performed Mary's autopsy, her mother's body would be ready for cremation. It would be a day or two at the most.

Speaking with the ME's office next, Liana was told her mother's autopsy was scheduled for the following morning, July 23.

"Good, we can get some answers," she told herself.

22

*T*HE SPRING OF 2014 brought a cold snap in through the hills and valleys of Oneida County. Meanwhile, Adam and Katie's relationship was held together by a cobweb. They'd reunited on the basis that Katie had endured a traumatic ectopic pregnancy. Still, an underlying hostility existed between them they could not seem to move past. Were they together because (according to Katie) she'd lost their child and nearly died? Was it love? Did they have a future, especially after such a tumultuous history?

Adam felt he was back to where he'd started, emotionally speaking. He'd only reunited with Katie because of the pregnancy. He was worried about her. Now, though, he found himself drinking more. Being with Katie was not what he wanted. They were toxic together. There was no "happily ever after"—and he knew this.

Katie sensed Adam slipping away. One night, she mentioned how he was paying far too much money in interest on his student loans and credit cards. There was no need to do this, Katie suggested. "I can help you."

Katie explained her idea. She had money in the bank. It was just sitting there: "I'll loan you the money at a lower rate."

Adam was reluctant. "I don't know, Katie." This would tie him to her, until the debt was paid off.

"We can sign a contract," Katie suggested. "I'll set up a bank account for you. You can deposit money into it so we can keep track of how much you pay me back."

It didn't feel right. Adam was hesitant. It would put him in an awkward position of having Katie exert control over part of his life. "I'm not sure, Katie." He thought more about it.

Katie was adamant: She needed to do this. Couples helped each other.

"Okay," Adam agreed.

Katie paid off Adam's bills, totaling about $12,000. They never signed a contract. She never opened a bank account.

A few weeks later, Adam was grumbling about a new vehicle he'd found, but he did not have enough money to buy it.

"Let me help you," Katie said. She offered another $3,000.

Adam already owed her $12,000. Why not another $3,000? He took the money and bought a used Jeep Wrangler he'd found on Craigslist.

As he considered the loan, Adam viewed it two ways: They were building the relationship and trying to work through past issues. Partners were there for each other. Still, that little voice on his shoulder told him he was now indebted to Katie more than having his heart on the line. She held something over his head—not that Katie strutted around with an attitude, talking about how much money Adam owed her. But to Adam, the loan was always there at the center of their relationship.

Festering.

Percolating.

Just one argument away from becoming an issue she would use to yield power and control over him.

23

*B*ASED ON THE INFORMATION the ME's office was given regarding the day and night of July 22, 2015, Mary Yoder entered the hospital an otherwise healthy sixty-year-old female. She was diagnosed in the ER with "gastrointestinal symptoms," which became the official medical analysis leading up to Mary's death. This seemed ambiguous in a sense of ruling cause of death. After looking through the history of Mary's hospital admittance and sudden death, the ME sought more information in order to pinpoint an exact cause—and manner—of death.

One early thought included the possibility of an infection in Mary's colon leaking into her bloodstream, effectively poisoning her to death from the inside.

"We really didn't have a good explanation for why [she died]," Chief Medical Examiner Robert Stoppacher, of the Onondaga ME's Office, said later. Stoppacher had held the position since 2009, after spending five years as deputy chief.

With no particular explanation of Mary's death, a routine death investigation was opened by the ME's office.

Stoppacher did not need consent from the Yoder family to perform the autopsy under the circumstances of Mary's death. All of the Yoders demanded it, however, and remained resolute that an autopsy be performed as soon as possible.

Dr. Stoppacher assigned Dr. Kenneth Clark to conduct the autopsy. In the real world of forensic death investigation, an autopsy into cause/manner of death is not about cutting the body open, sending blood and tissues samples to the lab, sitting back and waiting for an "aha!" moment. That is television's version of the autopsy. The actual world of autopsy investigation includes a multipronged approach: full toxicology screen, complete forensic investigation done by the medical examiner's forensic investigators (not law enforcement), and, of course, the autopsy.

Investigating the cause and manner of a death is a cumbersome responsibility. All of Mary's medical records were requested for a thorough evaluation. Every report and note from her time in the hospital was subjected to scrutiny and discussion. Blood work. Each organ cut open and studied, tested, weighed. The chain of custody at the hospital would need to be looked into. Consultation with Mary's doctors. Interviews with family members and nurses.

If any questions arose from those inquiries, a consult with law enforcement could be in order. If the situation appeared the slightest bit questionable, law enforcement would then be asked to join the investigation.

An otherwise healthy woman does not show up to the ER one day with a stomach bug and die. It's possible, of course, but Mary Yoder was a health-conscious female. She respected and took care of her body. And, perhaps most important to the ME's office, before taking that turn for the worse, Mary rebounded and seemed to be on the mend.

The ME's office determined immediately that over a twenty-four-hour period Mary suffered "multi-organ failure," which the ME and pathologist considered peculiar. Mary went into the ER under the presumed parameters of the flu, before all of her organs showed signs of malfunction, including her lungs.

That is not supposed to happen.

"In other words," Stoppacher said later, "a relatively quick presentation and death in the setting of someone who had abdominal pain, nausea, and vomiting."

None of it made practical, medical sense.

24

ADAM AND KATIE ENDED their relationship as the summer of 2014 wound down. So much had happened between the time Katie gave Adam the $15,000 loan and the breakup. That August, after Adam could not take any more of Katie's obsessive need to patronize him and muddle his emotions, he explained to her that it was over. He couldn't do it anymore. The relationship, where he forever tried to "save" Katie and heeded to her demands, had all at once become soul-sucking and emotionally exhausting. Adam had become a shell of himself, belittled by Katie, yet existing to please her.

"We continued some sort of friendship," Adam recalled. He made a conscious effort to meet Katie once a week for conversation at their favorite teahouse in Utica. He did not want the relationship to end on aggressive terms. They'd been best friends, and had dated since 2011. Katie still worked for his parents. Adam needed to maintain a healthy friendship with her, if possible.

Katie's duties as office manager at Chiropractic Family Care included billing and scheduling. She maintained the front desk. Answered phones. Checked patients in and out. Managed the secretarial and business needs arising throughout the day as Bill and Mary treated patients.

Despite working all day, one source explained, Katie, a lifelong practicing Catholic, spent hours per week caring for "an elderly shut-in . . . cleaning, cooking, shopping, and running errands for her." This was Katie's way of service. She wanted to help her community and responded in the Christian way of "loving thy neighbor." The woman she cared for, however, served another purpose for Katie.

ONE NIGHT, THE TWO were texting. Adam was in a bad place. Feeling down. Grappling with depression and anxiety. Life felt overwhelming: school, bills, no serious job, the drinking, the passive-aggressive relationship with Katie, in addition to her intense and overbearing emotional needs.

As they texted, Katie sensed Adam was planning to end his life. As they conversed, and Adam shared his desire to end the relationship, Katie sent an ambiguous text. This was a frequent ploy on her part. She implied that she was also severely depressed. The text indicated to Adam that Katie was preparing to do something about her depressed state.

"It was cryptic," Adam recalled. "But I knew what she meant. She was clear in conveying that she was going to hurt herself."

Suicide. A card Katie had played before. It seemed so typical that as he opened up and talked about suicide, she stole the moment.

For Katie, this was a setup—and Adam fell for it every time.

"After she said several scary things to me, I texted back, trying to console her."

The trap.

"But she stopped responding."

The bait.

Adam rushed over to Katie's house. Not having a vehicle at the time—this was before he purchased the Jeep Wrangler—he took his roommate's car. The guy had told him previously if it was available, and he ever needed to borrow it, just go. No need to ask.

Driving over to Katie's, Adam was "screaming and panicking," he recalled. "I was just hoping and praying she would be okay."

Pulling up, Adam rushed into the house. Katie's sisters were having a little get-together. Hanging out in the basement with a few guys, playing a game of beer pong.

"Where's Katie?" Adam said, out of breath.

"We have no idea," one of her sisters responded.

Adam rushed upstairs, looked around.

No Katie.

He got back into his roommate's car and drove home. Minutes after leaving, his cell phone rang.

"Katie! You okay?"

"No, I am not . . ." She sounded distressed and reserved. Not herself. She wouldn't tell Adam where she was.

Adam calmed her down. "Listen, drive to my place. Can you do that for me?"

Adam pulled up to his house. He waited, nervously. Pacing. Twirling the keys in his hand. Smoking cigarettes.

Then he saw Katie, coming from the opposite direction of her house, where she had claimed to be earlier in the text exchange.

He ran up to her vehicle.

Katie was crying. She had a bottle of pills in her hand.

"Katie, turn off the car and come inside. Please. Now."

"No . . . no!" she screamed.

"Katie, come on. Just come inside."

In a flurry, she hid the bottle of pills. Jumped out of the car. Ran inside.

After making sure she was okay, Adam went back outside and searched the car. He needed to be certain the pills were not in her possession.

He found the pills under the front seat. Looking at the label, he realized she had stolen them from the elderly shut-in she allegedly cared for. Adam could not recall specifically if they were Valium or Vicodin.

"It was one of those two starting with a *V*. I know it was a five hundred count. I saw the woman's name on the prescription."

Adam took the pills inside. He found an old lunch tray his roommate had, poured the pills out on it. Counted the entire lot. He had made the decision beforehand that if one pill was missing, he was taking Katie to the ER.

"It was the main reason why I stayed with her—to make sure she wouldn't kill herself. That is how she made me feel. Like if I broke up with her, she would commit suicide."

They were back together again.

* * *

KATIE RAN HER OWN painting business, according to family and friends. From an early age, she maintained a passion for free enterprise and small business. The image she projected was that of a small-town country girl making it on her own.

"[She also] has always had a soft spot in her heart for animals," claimed a source on a website devoted to Katie. She'd rescued "many animals and [gave] them a loving home." Not just dogs and cats, but horses, chickens, goats, even a donkey.

Adam Yoder agreed with this. He also added that Katie had a sheltered childhood: "Really restricted. 'Old-fashioned' is how I would put it." In the house where she grew up, for example, the kids were not introduced to technology. "Katie did not have any understanding of technology when I met her. She did not grow up with that stuff. When it came to electronics, they never had it. No wireless. No Internet. An old bubble-screen television in the living room. When I started dating her, she did not even have a smart phone . . . She grew up strangely simple and low-tech."

"My dad said the Internet was a fad, when it came out," Katie had told Adam one day.

"What!"

The fact was, Adam noted, when he met her, Katie had no idea how a smart phone or computer technology worked. She had only a vague understanding of the basics behind how information and data were stored, the mechanics of software foreign to her.

"On the flip side, she was extremely manipulative," Adam continued. "She was also extremely private. She did not let anyone in. We did talk. But I understood later that from a very early point in the relationship, I was being controlled. So whatever she told me, it was all bullshit and lies."

Looking back, Adam realized that within the first few weeks of knowing Katie, she worked at setting up a foundation for future sympathy. She laid the groundwork to apply her manipulative techniques later. This was by design, Adam insisted, so he would later run after whatever she threw at him—especially when she thought he might end the relationship.

"I was twenty years old. Young. She was pretty. I was stupid. When things went wrong, she set out to take control and get me back."

The ectopic pregnancy was a good example. Adam had left her. He was seeing another woman. She came back with this supposed pregnancy she'd been medically forced to lose. And it worked. He wound up back with her.

Within a few weeks of knowing her, Katie told Adam a story about having been raped in high school. It sounded unbelievable to him, but one does not question a woman claiming to have been raped.

"She told me this ex-boyfriend . . . pushed her down on a bed and said, 'Do you love me?' When she said yes, he spun her around, bent her over the bed, and brutally raped her. Then, after it was over, he supposedly made her have dinner with his family."

Adam needed to keep peace, he said, describing the ebb and flow of the relationship during the summer and fall of 2014. Those teatime meetings had started out once a week whenever they first broke up. As time passed, even that became too difficult to maintain.

"I still had feelings for her, so emotionally it was hard for me to continue that friendship."

Both were students at SUNYIT, so they'd run into each other on campus at times. Adam stayed away from the family business as much as possible. He felt as though he were trapped, the relationship constantly on a tightrope and emotional seesaw for three years. Then, for the sake of his own sanity, he forced himself to be done with it. The pain and anxiety of being with Katie proved too much.

For Katie, as the summer of 2014 ended, she felt crushed by Adam once again. He was there and then gone. It was over. She knew Adam was serious this time. She sensed a finality to it.

25

ON AUGUST 25, 2014, a Monday, just before getting out of work, Katie took out her cell phone and opened up her *Notes* app. It was 4:48 p.m. She began writing, titling the note: "Hi. I don't know about this. Haven't told . . ." before ending the title abruptly. In the body of the note a few minutes later, she clarified her early thought, again writing out the title, concluding it with ". . . anyone and no."

What was Katie referring to? What hadn't she "told anyone"? What did "no" mean as part of the title?

The note was long. It took her fifteen minutes to write. After getting out of work, at 5:05 p.m., she went back into the app and modified the same note.

The story she told in this note, obviously addressed to Adam, was violent. The memory she spoke of—if true—would put Adam in a precarious position. If Katie decided to press charges, law enforcement would become involved.

Weeks went by after Katie crafted the note. They did not communicate often. A gulf had developed between them. Adam had made it clear he was finished. Katie surely understood this, for their breakup, compared to the others before it, had a serious finality. Adam wasn't going to be rehashing the past and working things out any longer. He'd made a choice. He wasn't going back on it.

Weeks later, on September 15, and again on September 17, near the noon hour, someone sitting at Katie's desk at Chiropractic Family Care created a Gmail account: Mr. Adam Yoder 1990 at Gmail.com (mradamyoder1990@gmail.com).

Most everyone involved later agreed Katie was the only person who could have done this. She had opportunity, access, and was in the office at those times.

Adam was not even in the area.

A month went by. On October 18, after not hearing from Adam, Katie texted him. Within her cryptic and sarcastic first few texts, she dangled a dark secret she held and was planning to expose.

"I'm still angry about things, as you are," Adam texted back. "I'm sorry."

"You don't know?" Katie shot back.

"I don't know what?" Adam mentioned he was at the movies with a mutual friend and would contact her in a few hours.

"You text me," Katie said.

"I will. But what do I *not* know?" Adam asked.

"Don't worry about it now . . ."

Three hours later, Adam texted, saying he'd just gotten home. "You want to tell me what I *don't* know now?"

Katie ignored the request, instead texting that she hoped he'd had fun at the movies.

Then a jab: "You sleeping soon or celebratory drinking?"

Adam ignored it. Instead, he went back to the earlier topic: "Please answer my question."

"Not so much."

"Not so much"? Adam thought. "'You don't know.' That was your text to me. That's what I'm asking about," he stressed.

They exchanged a few more inconsequential texts. Adam inferred she was once again messing with him, trying to wield that control she knew for certain was slipping away from her.

Frustrated, Adam played it off as if he didn't care.

"July 26," Katie texted after not hearing from him. "After we went swimming, I brought you home."

"I know." He gave it a beat. Then: "Katie, if you have something to say, then *say* it. FUCKING SAY IT OR DON'T BRING IT UP AGAIN."

Nothing.

Another beat.

"KATIE!"

"I don't know what you remember," she finally responded. "You were really quite drunk."

"You're either sending a massive message or you deleted what you were typing. If I don't get something soon, I'm going to bed."

Katie began typing. Adam watched on his end as the three dots blinked as she typed.

He waited.

But no text came.

"I saw you typing. I've received nothing. Did you actually send it? Are you still typing?"

"It's a lot," Katie explained. "It can wait. You go to sleep. It's pretty late. Time for sleeping really."

"Don't you fucking dare!" Adam said. "This is your last chance to send it. Finish typing and send it."

It took Katie another ten minutes. It was now 1:20 a.m. on October 19, 2014. She had not been typing out a long text. She was sitting, waiting, preparing to send that long note she'd written long ago.

After a moment of not texting anything, she copied the note, waited another moment, then pasted it into a text and sent it.

Adam sat in bed, waiting, staring at his iPhone, as the text finally came through.

26

DR. KENNETH CLARK TOOK tremendous pride in his work. Clark was board certified in 2014. Forensic pathology, Clark later explained, included tissue analysis, bodily fluid analysis, toxicological analysis, microbiology, and, on occasion, genetics.

Clark had a short conversation with Liana, who became the liaison between the ME's office and the Yoder family. She began with her mother's symptoms, those of which her father, brother, and others present during Mary's short stay at the hospital had observed. In addition, Liana talked about what she noticed near the end, just before Mary was pronounced dead.

As Dr. Clark listened, he realized just how eager the entire Yoder family was to get the autopsy results. They wanted an answer: What had killed the Yoder family matriarch? She was a woman without any apparent health problems—or enemies.

"They thought [early on] that it was something called ascending cholangitis," Liana explained. "It's a condition where an infection can get from the small bowel and travel up into the liver and the bowel duct around the gallbladder."

Ascending cholangitis can be deadly. If the condition killed Mary, an autopsy would easily prove that was the cause and, effectually, the manner of death. It was a practical theory heading into autopsy, Clark told Liana, considering Mary Yoder's risk factors and symptoms: female, over fifty; hypotension and low blood pressure; multi-organ failure; mental status changes; jaundice; fever; pain. Additionally, a preliminary study of Mary's hospital reports indicated she had "acute renal failure and failed to respond to medications and treatments."

By 9:30 a.m., July 23, 2015, Dr. Clark was dressed in his scrubs, rubber gloves snapped over each hand. Carefully inspecting Mary from head to toe, Clark went through every square inch of the body, looking for outward signs of trauma. He quickly assessed that the bruising, scrapes, and minor cuts on Mary's body, which were visible to the naked eye, had been caused by the intensity of treatment she endured while in the ICU. Each Code Blue and the chaos of trying to revive her had left injuries all over Mary's body.

Clark then took a large scalpel and made a deep incision in the shape of a Y, starting at Mary's shoulders, slicing down her upper abdomen (chest region), before concluding vertically just above her pubis. "And then we simply open the body cavity, take off the rib cage, and we just look at everything as it is, before we do anything."

With Mary's innards exposed, Clark noticed several anomalies, which he noted aloud into a recording device. "Most striking abnormality is the color of her intestinal tract."

Clark had conducted over one thousand autopsies by the time Mary's body was on a slab, filleted open in front of him. In a large number of those autopsies, he added, "organs tend to be certain colors and consistencies."

Not Mary's, however.

"I'd never seen this mottled red, green, purple."

Clark found it to be "very bizarre." At first glance, he didn't know what to make of it. "I had never seen anything like it."

He focused on Mary's liver. "Some discoloration. Also a mottled appearance." By "mottled," Clark meant a homogenous brown, which is a normal conditional change that takes place after death. Mary's liver, though, also exhibited patches of staining, large spots—all were a marked, different, darker color.

The heart was also an odd color, unlike what Clark had been

used to seeing. Those organs were mild, however, when compared to the gastrointestinal tract, which Clark looked at next. Taking Mary's colon and digestive tract in hand, staring at it under the bright spotlight above, Clark was astonished by what he saw.

Taking a moment, he wanted to make sure he was actually seeing what was in front of him.

27

*F*OR MARY YODER, PLANTS and pottery were, in many ways, her life. Mary maintained a large garden in the back of the home, with beds and flowers spread all about the yard, front and back. Everything was laid out in perfect rows, green beans and squash over there, corn and flowers here, tomatoes and peppers lined up like soldiers. Mary's garden was spread throughout the yard in clusters to beautify, as well as a means of growing organic produce.

One of her favorite things to do every fall was purchase a bucket of bulbs and plant them all around the yard. The joy came when spring hit and she'd forgotten where she'd planted each one. Mary and Bill would marvel some mornings in spring at where the blooms had poked up through the soil: explosions of colors, like fireworks, then tall and healthy plants. Her front-yard displays of flowers actually drew people from town to drive by the house for a glimpse.

"Even now," Bill said, "I see those bulbs pop out of the ground. With Mary gone, there she is. There is her work, her passion." Mary left her mark on the world as her plants rose up through the earth to beautify the community she'd lived in all her life.

Important to Mary, all of her plants and their plant products had to be organic: the fertilizer, the soil, the bug sprays. She did not want any toxicity anywhere near her plants, family, or herself. Not even the slight chance of it.

Since the Yoders were doctors who ran a practice, medical and medicinal salespeople would visit the office, peddling various health products to display and sell. Bill passed it all on to Mary, who took the time to check out the products. Nothing seemed to impress Mary much, or meet her specifications of organic, healthy living. Then a Shaklee rep walked in one day. Everything about Shaklee met Mary's needs and, more important, her standards. She believed Shaklee products were healthy and organic. Moreover, the quality control of the company was something Mary had looked into and perceived as top-notch.

Heading into the summer of 2014, Mary suggested split shifts, which she and Bill ended up agreeing to. Because of Mary's maternity leaves and other life interruptions, Bill had worked more hours in the thirty-year practice. Mary put in lots of time, but Bill helmed the practice for the most part as they raised a family.

"You've worked so long, Bill. You're moving toward retirement," Mary said. "I'll pick up the extra time."

Bill considered it to be just one more of Mary's delightful, loving gestures. He was nearly ten years older. Tired. A chiropractic practice is demanding work, physically. Bill and Mary could never shut down for more than five or six days because their patients depended on them always being there. After Katie came on board in 2011, Bill had mainly dealt with insurance companies and the bookwork, along with seeing a certain number of patients every week. It was a natural progression for Mary to take over most of the chiropractic work as Bill moved toward retirement.

"Mary had a rocket on her back," Bill recalled.

Nothing stopped the woman. She woke in the morning and began her day, buzzing around from one task to the next like a thirty-year-old, right up until the day she became ill. Mary Yoder was full of life and energy, never sitting down for more than a few minutes. She had a lust for life, and for the wellness of others. This made her sudden death especially confusing for all those who were close to her.

BILL YODER WAS NOT functioning normally during those immediate days after his wife died. Having his family around was not only important, but a blessing, Bill later shared. It was specifically true as he began to mourn and accept Mary's death.

July 25, 2015, was Liana's daughter's second birthday. It was also the day the Yoder family had chosen to honor Mary with a Celebration of Life. Her body had not yet been released by the ME, but Mary had requested cremation, so the celebration was planned for Mary's friends and family to pay their respects and remember this great woman. Liana, Tammy, and Adam took over most of the planning. Katie stepped up and said she'd help any way they needed.

They were not about to call this "a wake" or "a funeral." The focus would be on the wonderful human being Mary was, the goodness and humility she'd brought to life and those around her.

"Always very welcoming—she treated you really like one of her family," Deborah Weiss, a ten-year patient, later said.

Since Mary's garden was in full bloom, the family decided to have the gathering at the house.

"I'm just going to stay upstairs," Bill told Liana and several other family members before the celebration. Katie was on hand all day. She'd stuck close by Adam's side since Mary's death. She'd even gone out and picked up hundreds of dollars' worth of food and beverages for the celebration.

"I just can't face seeing people and talking to them," Bill continued. "I don't want a receiving line or anything."

The guy was devastated. The woman he saw himself spending his retirement with had disappeared. It had all happened so fast. Bill did not know what to do with all the pain.

Mary and Bill's former secretary, who had heard about Mary's death from the family, called Sharon Groah the day before the celebration. Sharon was a longtime client and Mary's good friend.

"Are you sitting down?" Mary's former secretary asked Sharon.

"What's wrong?"

"I want you to know that Mary is gone."

"Gone where?" Sharon wondered.

"No, she passed away."

"I was just at the office! I just saw her. What do you mean? How?"

The former secretary explained all the details she knew at the time.

Sharon broke down. She could not fathom a world in which

Mary was not present. They had shared so much. As she took it in, trying to accept the loss, three hours later, she received a call from Katie.

"Mary passed, Sharon. I'm so sorry."

Katie could be extremely introverted, Sharon recalled. From Sharon's point of view, the dynamic between Katie and Mary was much more than employee/boss. Many times throughout the day, Mary would walk by Katie, place her hand on Katie's arm, and say, "You look nice today. How are you? What's going on that I can help you with?"

They loved each other, Sharon said. "No doubt about it."

"I heard, Katie," Sharon responded. "I cannot believe it. Just so shocked and in pain. Thank you for calling."

"There will be a Celebration of Life tomorrow. I am putting it together now with the family. I'll let you know."

"I want to bring food," Sharon said. She and her family were going to a wedding and were not going to make the celebration. But Sharon told Katie she would stop by and drop off the food and pay her respects.

"Aqua Vino is catering the celebration," Katie said. A staple on Harbor Lock Road in Utica, Mary was friends with just about everyone in the restaurant, many of whom had been patients.

The day of the celebration, Sharon drove over and knocked on the door. She had a plate of food in her hands. Sharon was a mess. Crying. Confused. In mourning. Disbelief. She could not believe Mary Yoder, a bastion of health and good living, was dead. It was as if the soul of the community Sharon was a part of had been stolen.

"Hi," Sharon said.

Katie answered the door.

Sharon walked into the foyer. Katie hugged her. They looked at each other and cried.

As for Adam, Sharon said, "I know Katie loved Adam and wanted him back whenever they broke up. I think there was a bit of both there in Katie where it pertained to Adam—love *and* obsession. I do believe she loved him, but I think it *became* an obsession."

Sharon found Bill. Hugged him. Said how sorry she was. Bill was "doing what he had to do," Sharon explained. Obviously devastated and in pain, Bill introduced Sharon to Mary's sisters, a few others. Sharon apologized for having to run, but she and her husband had a long trip ahead.

Some were looking at Bill with one eyebrow raised, the community itself talking, rumors swirling about. Not necessarily accusing him of anything, but the husband, in such a strange, questionable, untimely death, is always the first to be viewed as someone who might have been involved. If a wife dies and law enforcement blindly arrested the husband, they'd have a five hundred batting average.

"Mary took care of everything," Sharon explained. "Bill depended on her for *everything*. God's angel on Earth—that was my Mary." Recalling the first time she walked into the office after Mary had passed, Sharon said, "It felt cold. Something was missing, and you could *instantly* feel it."

Katie saw Sharon out.

Sharon hugged Katie. "We're going to be all right. We'll make it through this."

"We will," Katie said in tears.

DURING THE CELEBRATION, LIANA again suggested to Bill that he should approach her widowed aunt, Kathleen Richmond. Liana knew it would be good for him. Understanding has a way of emerging among people who share common pain.

"You're not alone, Dad."

There were "over two hundred people" at the Yoder house celebrating Mary's life. A table displayed a photo of Mary, a beaming smile across her face. Alongside the photo were pieces of Mary's favorite art and pottery. Groups of friends and patients and family milled about the house, inside and out. Just about everyone at the celebration approached Bill and wished him well. He appreciated the support. However, as each person came up and offered condolences, he thought, *You don't know what this is like for me.*

After talking to Liana about it, Bill felt he could trust Kathleen. She knew what he was feeling. They could relate. Over the past year, Mary and Bill, together, had reconnected with Kathleen. She did not live far away from the Yoder house.

"Can we get together sometime and talk about this?" Bill asked.

"Sure," Kathleen responded. "Call me, Bill."

The day after Mary died, Kathleen wrote Bill a lengthy letter. Seeing how distraught he was at the celebration, Kathleen knew Bill was "feeling the grief I remembered so well," she later explained. Kathleen reached into her purse and took the letter out. "Read it when you have a chance."

A few days later, Bill called his sister-in-law. They made plans to meet and talk. Before those conversations, Kathleen and Bill had little interaction. Back in May, Bill had sent Kathleen a few links to some grilling gear she'd asked about during a barbeque Mary and Bill hosted at the house. Save for a few e-mails and texts, they had not communicated much.

On July 29, 2015, Bill texted Kathleen. He was thinking about visiting her the following day. "I'm really glad we'll get a chance to do this. Thank you."

Kathleen told Bill to send a text when he left the house.

On July 30, at 7:53 a.m., Bill followed up and explained he was heading out soon as he could. They had talked on the phone, and Bill felt a slight touch of hope. He identified with someone who was suffering the same pain.

As he drove down Kathleen's street, near 10:15 a.m. on July 30, Bill had a hard time figuring out which house she lived in. Mary had always driven. He never paid much attention. He didn't know exactly which house was Kathleen's.

He pulled over and sent a text: "I think I passed your house . . . Stand on your porch and wave me down." Bill included a heart emoji in the text.

Driving again, Bill inched slowly down the street, saw Kathleen, and pulled into her driveway.

Kathleen had a large family reunion to attend in another state, so they had limited time, but Bill stayed for about an hour. It helped. They understood each other. They made plans to get together again soon.

28

*F*IVE DAYS AFTER THE celebration, Liana left for Long Island. She invited everyone down, including her father. Adam expressed interest in going along. He had nothing happening in town and needed to get away, to be with family. The past week had been a dark and gloomy blur. New surroundings would help.

Adam invited Katie—for company, nothing more. He made himself clear. Liana and Adam, along with Katie, left for Long Island on July 31; Bill departed a day later, August 1. Bill and Adam decided to take off on a trip to the Southwest, and maybe the West Coast, to visit family after staying a few weeks at Liana's. Bill stressed that being home in Utica was not something he could deal with.

On July 31, Kathleen sent Bill a text: "I'm always here if you want to talk. And it helps me, too. I love you. You're closer to me than some of my siblings."

By August 4, 2015, Liana had not heard anything new from the ME's office. She called and left Dr. Clark a message to call her with an update.

"What's puzzling is the culture results," Clark explained when he called back. "We're not finding *any* evidence of bacteria."

The ME's office had swabbed samples of Mary's intestinal tract and had tried growing out bacteria in petri dishes, with no results.

Liana was interested in this.

"What's more," Clark added, "we received the microslides and it was showing apoptosis, cell death, as you know . . . It is present, moreover, in a picture that goes along with toxic exposure or a toxin versus infectious cause."

Dr. Liana Hegde now knew that her mother had not died from an infection. Test results proved it.

Clark asked Liana to find out what she could about Mary's eating and lifestyle habits prior to her death. Had she come in contact with a toxin without realizing it?

Bill, Adam, Tammy, Liana's husband, and Katie were all present at Liana's house when this new update came in. Liana hung up and filled everyone in on the news. Mary was poisoned by some type of toxin. She'd regularly taken a large course of supplements. They all talked about it and agreed to have a look at the ingredients of the supplements, to get an idea of the food Mary ate in the days before her death.

Liana also told Dr. Clark she would speak with one of her mother's closest friends. Mary and her BFF alternated gardening duties: One week, they'd work in her BFF's garden; the next week, it was Mary's garden.

"They had been doing this for years," Liana said.

It was also agreed that they'd look into Mary's gardening habits and what type of pesticides and fertilizer she used.

Clark told the family that the ME's office was going to run additional tests. Could Mary have mistakenly poisoned herself? Had Adam's bout with "the flu" and his trip to the ER a few months before Mary's death been a clue that the family was ingesting a toxin without knowing it?

As KATIE AND ADAM headed to Long Island in Adam's vehicle, they talked, but their conversation had a passive air about it. Adam was in a bad place. Katie did not know how much to pry into his feelings. The one thing she didn't doubt anymore, however, was their relationship. In her view, it was back on. And the texts they exchanged during this period suggested as much.

As they traveled, Katie asked if she could listen to an audiobook she'd once downloaded onto Adam's computer.

"Go ahead."

Katie plugged her iPhone into Adam's laptop.

Later that week, after Adam left for California with his father, Katie drove Adam's car back to Utica so she could hold down the office. One of the Yoders' doctor friends was filling in.

As they split up and went their own ways, Katie texted Adam: "Can you please delete my phone backup?"

When she'd plugged her iPhone into Adam's laptop, his computer downloaded Katie's iPhone contents, including the metadata. Adam's computer now had Katie's entire phone on his laptop. Not that he could access all of it, but it was there.

"I love you and I trust you like no other," Katie added. She reiterated her request by explaining how she wanted Adam to one day help her back up her phone contents and manage the phone's storage. "But I have some things on there [that] other people have trusted with me."

Adam didn't respond—and never deleted the backup.

29

*A*FTER DEATH, THE BODY goes through a series of scientific changes. Those vicissitudes, especially in the organs, occur relatively the same way in every natural death. That is, it's similar if no external factors or intrinsic characteristics accelerate or retard the decomposition process.

Pathologist Dr. Stephen Clark was struck by the discoloration of Mary Yoder's intestinal tract. He wondered if such an obvious irregularity was indicative of an external condition or foreign substance being introduced into Mary's system. What was the reason why Mary's organs presented so abnormally discolored? It was a reaction, Clark knew, that never occurs on its own.

"It's a nonspecific finding, to be honest," Clark said later, explaining how the discrepancy did not mean anything beyond requiring additional investigation. Such a noticeable discoloration meant a toxin had likely killed Mary, but which toxin and how she ingested it were open-ended questions. After all, people died every day from accidental poisoning by toxins found in every household.

First thing Clark made note of was that Mary Yoder had not died under "traumatic" circumstances. He did not find any evidence of bullet or stab wounds, indicators of strangulation, suffocation, or any other violent manner.

Considering the extent of the discoloration he'd uncovered, however, Clark took the next step. "I collected lots of tissue samples for microscopic examination."

Toxicology is a comprehensive science, which can explain the scientific facts behind a death. So Clark extracted samples from every organ, along with a collection of bodily fluids.

As Clark began taking samples, he discovered a condition called apoptosis, or cell death.

Another anomaly.

Regarding cell death, Clark thought about the two ways in which cells died inside the body. One is necrosis, a blood clot found in a vessel. You have a blood clot in your brain, for example; then all of the tissue downstream from the clot is choked off and eventually dies, leaving behind evidence of the blood clot.

The second is apoptosis. A cell, fundamentally, sustains an injury and doesn't die, but ends up dysfunctional and crippled, thus creating a reaction (or signal) to kill itself. In the medical community, it's known as "preprogrammed cell suicide."

Clark walked several samples over to his microscope. He placed them on slides, dialed in the focus, and began to carefully examine.

"Under the microscope," Clark explained, "apoptosis has a very distinct look."

The samples that made him step back and scratch his head were from Mary Yoder's gastrointestinal tract (the most severe), lungs, spleen, liver, and gallbladder (not as severe). He also found "scattered apoptosis" in the heart as well.

"Almost every organ I looked at."

Clark thought about how unusual this was within the day-to-day findings of his work: "I can say that between my residency and my fellowships and *all* of my autopsies, I had *never* seen this before."

Clark called the chief medical examiner, Robert Stoppacher. Over the next few days, they talked about and studied Clark's findings and decided what to do.

"It could be a virus or a toxin," Clark suggested.

The chief agreed.

"These cells were definitely injured and they were all undergoing programmed suicide."

It was obvious an outside source had entered Mary's system, thus injuring the cells, facilitating the process of cell suicide, which ultimately caused her death. Was this the reason for that slight rebound Mary had experienced before her sudden relapse leading to all those codes?

Both doctors believed there had been a toxin introduced into Mary's system—and that toxin killed her.

Toxicology was sent out.

All of it came back negative.

This was even more disconcerting and baffling.

The results were another abnormality, telling both doctors they must now begin a process of pinpointing which toxin might have made Mary sick and killed her.

"Essentially," Clark said, "what we do is we start looking for more exotic things we don't commonly see, but every now and then, we *do* see." Cyanide. Arsenic. Barium (an alkaline earth metal). Antimony (a metalloid).

Samples were sent to an outside lab, specifically focused on those four toxins. The lab in the ME's office did not routinely test for specific metals or poisons. A general panel was conducted. Each of those results also came back negative.

Quite puzzled by the results, Clark felt there had to be a rare toxin they were missing. As they began talking about next steps, a major problem arose. The lab said they had almost no blood left to send out for additional testing. By then, Mary's body had been released and cremated.

One of the toxicologists involved called Clark: "Listen, we still don't have an answer, but we have a very limited sample left. So whatever you want to test for next, you should choose it carefully, because I do not know how much we can get out of the [final sample]."

Clark met with Stoppacher.

"Let's take a walk across the street," Stoppacher suggested, standing, beckoning Clark to follow him.

It was a suggestion that would change everything.

Across the street from the office was the Poison Control Center (PCC) building.

Stoppacher introduced Clark to two PCC doctors.

The advantage of utilizing the PCC was its vast library of medical data collected on poisoning cases. That data correlated consistencies, dynamics, and anomalies in death-by-poison cases. But more important, similarities. The data can, in effect, point a pathologist in a direction by simply linking a finding to a previous death by toxin. The database searches through symptoms, pairs them with the ME's findings, thus looking for cases matching one another.

Parallels.

As Clark dealt with the PCC, additional medical records from Mary Yoder's time at the hospital came in. Clark now had Mary's full chart. He could provide that information—symptoms, reactions, medications—to the PCC as part of her history.

More data, better results.

"She had multiple cardiac arrests before death," Clark explained to his contact at the PCC.

The PCC doctor made a recommendation after studying all the documentation and PCC data, reviewing the autopsy, and comparing it to other PCC database cases.

"What do you think?" Clark asked.

One toxin kept coming up.

"Colchicine."

Colchicine is an anti-inflammatory generally prescribed to treat Mediterranean fever and gout. Inflammatory arthritis (gout, basically) was one reason why people went to a chiropractor.

Could Mary have been poisoned by error?

Stoppacher and Clark agreed to send that last sample of Mary's blood to the lab and request a colchicine comparison test.

30

ON OCTOBER 19, 2014, at 1:20 a.m., after Katie had sent Adam that long, detailed text she'd teased him with for several hours, Adam was sitting up in bed. He could not believe what Katie was accusing him of.

The text described what Adam had allegedly done to Katie on the night of July 26, 2014. According to her, she'd hesitated to send it because she believed he was too drunk on that summer night to remember what happened. Yet, after Adam warned Katie—"This is your last chance to send it"—she texted him the narrative.

His heart racing, Adam read through it several times.

Three minutes after receiving it, he responded: "Well, I don't know what I'll do at this point."

He waited a minute.

"Are you there? That is infinitely worse than I thought it could be."

"Yeah. I don't know. You really don't remember anything of it. I really don't think you do."

"I had a slight memory of the slap, but I couldn't remember the context or if you hit me too or what. I don't think we should ever see each other again. One slap, but not *that*."

"I didn't slap you. You did. More than once. Pretty hard. Really?" she added, responding to never seeing each other again. "You think that will help?"

Katie waited a beat before texting, "?!"

"I don't know what's wrong with you in your head to not hate me. Apparently, I'm an attempted murderer, Katie. This is not good news. Please talk to me. Just for a little bit. I'm sorry I upset you. I was hoping we could continue this conversation. Let me know. The choice is yours, Katie. Might check myself into suicide watch, too, if it gets bad enough. Going to AA tomorrow. If you still want to see me, you can see me. Please text me back so I know you're okay."

Katie waited three hours, responding at 4:07 a.m.: "I don't know what I'm going to do, Adam."

"Will you talk to me on the phone, please? I really believe you love me. Or you did. I don't understand how [the incident] could've happened."

"Just to talk," Katie said. "I'm going out to the porch to call you."

During the phone call, they discussed Adam's use of Adderall. After they hung up, Adam texted, "I had a 4.0 before that. I don't need to be a pill popper. I'll go dump the Adderall in the toilet . . ."

Katie responded by explaining how Adam could "swing from one way to another extreme . . ." She "supported" him finding a new apartment, which they'd discussed on the phone. Then, randomly, completely out of context, she said: "Maybe it's time for me to put some money into a house?"

In the text Katie had sent, she detailed what Adam had allegedly done to her on July 26, nearly three months before. Katie described a sexually violent rape. Yet, she was now talking about being open to Adam living somewhere else, but leaving his belongings at a new house she'd buy?

If that's what he "needed," she added, "I think that's a good balance. So there's still time for us to be ourselves separately, too. So you don't feel like I'm pressuring you and vice versa. It can get better. No, you don't need that medication. I really believe that."

Adam failed to respond. What could he say? Katie was talking about his emotional pendulum swings and how unstable he was. She was summarizing a rape he'd committed in one text, and now saying she was buying them a house to live in?

"I did not know what to say," Adam recalled later. "I just knew at that moment I needed to keep her close. I was so scared. Even an accusation like that could ruin my life."

ACCORDING TO KATIE, THE incident started at 11:15 p.m. on July 26, 2014. She and Adam were swimming at her house. One of Katie's sisters and a friend were there, too. They'd all come from a graduation party. Adam and the other guy were "drinking heavily," while Katie and her sister were not.

Katie became "upset and disappointed" as the night progressed because Adam had promised he was going to stop drinking. Yet, here he was living it up excessively in front of her. At one point, Katie became so distressed, she excused herself from the pool, walked inside the house, and locked herself in the bathroom.

Her sister's friend followed and waited by the bathroom door. When Katie came out, he said, "Hey, calm down, would you."

They were having fun. A night out together. Lighten up.

Still upset, Katie emerged. Then walked outside.

"Where's Adam?" she asked, looking around.

"Gone," her sister said.

Knowing Adam had probably left on foot, Katie grabbed a towel, wrapped it around herself, picked up her car keys, and took off.

After driving a short distance, she saw Adam walking down the street.

"Get in," Katie said, pulling up alongside him. "I'm taking you home."

She pulled into Adam's driveway a few minutes later and shut off the car.

Adam looked over, reached toward the steering column, and pulled the keys from the ignition. Without saying anything, he then ran inside his house.

Katie collected his belongings, which she'd brought with her from the house, and ran into the house.

"Once I got inside," Katie insisted later, "I went to the bathroom."

Katie later explained that she was on her "period . . . and I was bleeding through a little, so I wanted to go home and change."

Walking out of the bathroom, Katie went into Adam's room.

Adam was on his bed. The lanyard with her house keys and key fob attached was on the floor—except the fob and keys were gone.

"Where are my keys?" Katie asked, according to a law enforcement report of the incident. In her descriptive text to Adam (the one that she'd drafted on her iPhone *Notes* app long after the incident), she said: "You wouldn't tell me where they were, so I looked around. I only found my car starter. You were furious I was going to leave."

After demanding to know where Adam hid her keys, Katie claimed Adam refused to speak.

So she walked into the living room and began searching.

No keys.

After making it back into Adam's bedroom, she asked, "My keys, Adam?"

"Turn off the lights."

"I'm looking for my keys. I can't. And I want to go home, Adam. Come on."

Katie then spotted her key fob on the floor and grabbed it.

"Where are my other keys? I. Want. To. Go. Home."

"You cannot drive," Adam said.

In her October 19, 2014, text, Katie described this moment differently from what she would later tell law enforcement: "I told you I could come right back, but you told me I was a liar and couldn't leave." She claimed Adam then picked up the key fob and told her he'd call someone so she wouldn't have to drive herself.

In Katie's recollection that she detailed in a report to a county sheriff (three and a half months *after* the alleged incident), she claimed Adam jumped from his bed at that point. Took her key fob. Then stood in between her and the door leading out of his room. Blocking the door, he grabbed Katie.

"I am going to break your wrist and snap all your fingers."

Then, according to Katie, Adam tossed her on his bed without warning. "Nobody will believe you! Nobody is going to help you, and nobody is going to find you. I am going to kill you," he threatened.

"He had me pinned down, with both hands around my throat," Katie explained to the sheriff.

"Say 'good-bye,' Katie. I am going to kill you. I am going to kill you."
By this point, Katie added, Adam had a death grip on her throat.
He said it again: "I'm going to kill you . . ."

The way she described the same scene in her lengthy text was
different: Katie told Adam that he wouldn't let go of her, so she
"tried to drop" her weight, hoping he'd let go, fall to his bed, and
pass out.

"You picked me up. 'I'm going to kill you. I'm going to kill you,
Katie.' The way you said it. The way you looked at me. And then I
was afraid. 'You lying cunt. No one cares about you. No one wants
to help you. You are a cunt. Slut. Liar. You lied to me. You aren't
even bleeding. No one will miss you.'"

Katie told the sheriff she blacked out because Adam had put his
hands around her throat. When she came to, Adam was kneeling
on her shoulders and "pulling her hair with one hand and . . .
using the other to put his penis inside [her] mouth . . ."

In that same law enforcement statement, Katie described how
Adam then flipped her over on her stomach. Adam "inserted his
penis in her vagina" without Katie's "permission to do so," the sheriff reported. While this happened, according to the sheriff's re-
counting, Katie was crying and told Adam to stop "multiple times."

In her text, she said: "You threw me on your bed, so I was looking up at you. 'Say "good-bye," Kay-tee. "Good-bye." You were smiling a little. My towel was twisted around my thighs and legs. Your
hands were around my neck, your arms locked, your full weight on
me. I couldn't break. I thought, *This is what choking is . . . I am going
to die.* Then I was awake. My bottoms were off, my top hanging. You
said, 'I'm going to choke you,' kneeling on my chest, fingers scraping the roof of my mouth, you in my mouth. I gagged. Couldn't
gag. Then couldn't breathe. Flipped me around by my hair. You.
Fingers. Flipped back over. Yanked my hair, twisting my neck. Bit
my lip. Hard. Blood. Bit my body. Biting. Pulling. You went down.
Pulled me on top of you. You slapped my face. My ear rang. You
slapped me again."

Continuing, Katie claimed in her text that Adam "slapped and
slapped," before twisting her around as he "kept going and going."
Then, immediately after an allegedly brutal, violent, and control-

ling rape scene, Katie claimed, Adam suddenly "rolled over next to" her and "fell asleep—a light sleep." So she reached "around the bed softly," in hopes of not moving and waking him, found her keys and bathing suit, got dressed, and ran into the bathroom.

In that October 19 text, months after the incident, she sent a detailed list of her injuries: "Bruise on my upper lip. Above my eyebrow. Two mirrored on each jawline. A small raised lump on my left cheek. Bruises on my forearms. Just slight ones on my thighs. Bruises and red bites on my collarbone. Brown bruising and cuts on my breasts. Two large purple-black bruises on my neck. A larger one on the left side. A darker one on the right. Thumb. Four fingers. Different-size bruises."

Cuts, bites, and bruises.

It was as though she was looking at photos she'd taken that night inside the bathroom, dictating what she observed into a text message. It had been three months, however, and not a mention of that incident, or any of the injuries, to Adam or law enforcement until the October 19 text and subsequent trip to the Oneida County Sheriff's Office (OCSO).

"And that's when I knew," Katie ended the text. "I was alone. I had to reach up inside me once, twice, to grab the tampon pushed so far in. I didn't know who to call. I didn't want people to worry about me. You really didn't remember it. So I was quiet. And that's how things end."

In a text two minutes after outlining the alleged rape, Katie said she'd gone home after assessing her injuries. She needed to take a shower. Oddly, however, she admitted: "I sat in my car. I looked for your inhaler. And then I sat next to you. Because I still thought maybe you might need help. And still you were important."

The way Katie wrote it in her text, she left Adam's, took a shower at home, found his inhaler, and then drove *back* to his house and sat next to him on the bed as he lay passed out.

Weeks later, close to November, Katie sent Adam a series of photographs, once again detailing the injuries she'd claimed to have sustained that night inside his bedroom. The photos showed an injury on her finger, a rather prominent bruise. The next was a large bruise on her left shoulder, about the size of an apple. The photos also showed a smaller bruise on her ankle, one on her wrist, and another on her foot.

No cuts or bites.

Adam texted back right away: "If you hang up on me during our conversations"—he was about to call her after seeing the photos— "I will not continue to meet with you and attempt to continue this friendship."

Adam called.

Katie didn't answer. She texted back.

"I didn't think even after it happened, that bruises show up so dark and soon. I would never want to live in fear of you. I guess you really did want to kill me then. You knew it was me. You said my name . . . Those are from you," Katie said, making sure Adam knew the photos were from the night of the alleged incident. "It sucks."

"Done speaking . . . ," Adam said. He'd called her twice in between the texts and she'd hung up on him both times.

As serious as the injuries appeared in those photographs (all bruises, Katie's face not visible in any of the photos), none matched up to the injuries she'd described in her text to Adam. Had she not photographed herself just after the alleged incident? Where were all the bite marks and neck bruises and facial injuries and cuts on her breasts? What about Adam biting her lip, causing it to bleed?

As Adam looked at the photos she'd texted, he had one thought: *She's downloaded random photos from the Internet.*

NOT HEARING FROM ADAM much after they'd discussed the text detailing the alleged rape, Katie called the sheriff's office on November 1, 2014, to file a rape report. The impetus surrounding filing this report, however, was rather telling.

"Katie was dating someone new," two law enforcement sources explained. "For whatever reason (probably sympathy or some other control thing), she told the new boyfriend [that] Adam had raped her." It was almost exactly what she'd done not long after meeting Adam: claim an ex-boyfriend had raped her. "But she was unprepared for the new boyfriend's reaction, which was to put her in his car and drive her to the sheriff's department and force her to report it."

Near 1:00 p.m. on November 1, OCSO investigator Fredrick Peck took a statement from Katie.

At one point during the "deposition," as Peck referred to the document, Katie broke down. She said she could not continue to talk about what had happened.

Peck understood.

Then, after a deep breath, collecting her thoughts, Katie said, "I do wish to pursue criminal charges."

Katie never went to the hospital after the incident, and the bathing suit she wore that night had been washed, Peck included in his report.

What's more, Katie never showed any of the photos of her injuries or bruises she'd sent to Adam to the sheriff's office. Plus, she never told the OCSO investigators that the house where the alleged rape had occurred was full of people—Adam's roommate and his friends—on the night of the assault.

31

*D*R. STEPHEN CLARK RECEIVED results from the initial testing after consulting with the PCC and confirmed Mary Yoder had died from colchicine poisoning. There was no question. The task was now to determine how the poison had entered her system.

Meanwhile, Bill and Adam took a trip to Arizona to see Bill's sister in the weeks after visiting Liana. Then they flew to California. Adam had played a part in a small independent film and flew back home on August 20 to attend the premiere. Bill stayed behind.

When Adam landed in Syracuse, Katie picked him up at the airport and drove him back into town. Adam moved in with his cousin Dave King, a registered nurse, Mary's sister's son. Dave and Adam had been "close since third, fourth grade," Dave later said. They'd lived together back in 2008 before having a "falling-out," as Dave put it, and didn't speak to each other for several years before reconnecting.

Throughout September 2015, Adam continued a relationship with Katie. Now living at his cousin's, Adam was communicating with—and seeing—Katie regularly. When he found out colchicine was the source of his mother's death, Adam was determined to help locate the source. One day after school, Adam picked Katie up on campus and explained that he needed to do something.

"We have to stop at the office." Adam was wound up, anxious. Determined to get to the bottom of the colchicine source.

"Okay . . ."

After parking, "Look, I just need to run in and gather up anything that has . . . that *had* the potential to have been ingested by my mother."

"Oh?" Katie said.

"Something was found in my mother's system."

Adam insisted later that he never told Katie what specific toxin had been found in Mary's system.

They both got out of the Jeep. Adam's key to the office was at home.

"I have mine," Katie said.

Entering the building, Adam said, "I'm going to gather up every single box, unopened or not, and then bring all of it over to the medical examiner's office." Adam was referring to Mary's Shaklee products and anything else he deemed a possible carrier for the toxin.

Adam pointed to different items he wanted collected and brought to the ME. As he watched Katie, he thought, *Why is she being so unhelpful gathering things?*

As Adam searched the office, he felt Katie hovering around him, almost keeping tabs on what he was doing.

"Don't look there," Katie said.

"Why not?"

"There's no chance," Katie said.

"So what." Adam's point was to leave no stone unturned; allow the ME to make that call.

"Don't grab that," Katie said, referring to items in the immediate space around her desk. "Your mother would never go over there," she said as Adam searched Katie's desk.

At one point, Adam became angry. "Look! I cannot tell you what's going on yet. I just need help gathering the stuff. I do not care how much of a long shot it is. I want to bring it *all* over."

The conversation became so contentious, Adam stopped what he was doing. "Let's go."

"What?"

"Come on."

They left the office.

Adam drove Katie back to SUNY and dropped her off. While he was in the office with her earlier, Adam had taken the key on the front desk. So he drove back to the office by himself.

Before doing anything else, Adam called Liana from inside the office. He explained what was going on.

"No," Liana said. "There are HIPAA violations involved. Don't touch anything." She was concerned about Adam being around patient records. "Don't do this now. Let Dad do it."

Adam left. Later that day, he was able to secure permission to go back. One of the items he grabbed was an opened carton of almond milk, a product Mary used in mixing her Shaklee powder. Adam brought it, along with everything else, down to the ME's office.

BILL YODER FLEW TO Long Island from California on August 25, 2015. He'd left his car at Liana's.

"Hi, Kathleen," Bill texted his sister-in-law. "Got into Liana's late last night." He mentioned how happy he was to see she had texted him. "I've missed you over the last couple of weeks and am looking forward to some time together soon . . ."

In between the celebration and Bill returning to Long Island, Kathleen and Bill texted periodically. Most of it was innocent conversation, cheering each other up, wishing each other well, talking about getting together to talk.

On that same day, August 25, Katie and Adam exchanged texts regarding the state of their relationship, which was once again cracking. Katie had a rough time getting past the anger Adam displayed while they were in the office. She sensed things were off, pressuring Adam about the lack of time they had been spending together.

Dealing with a lot of raw emotion after his mother's death, Adam mentioned he could never seem to get hold of Katie when he needed her most. He'd just learned that day about the incident involving his mother falling the night before she died and how hospital staff had called his father with the news. Bill, however, had not answered the phone. This upset him, Adam told Katie.

"So nobody got to the hospital until seven a.m."

It was more than painful for Adam to think his mother had fallen, needed someone, and yet no family member was available to console her. She was all alone.

Then Adam brought up the new guy that Katie had been seeing. "I think about you constantly, Katie, and I only get pain back. I'm done. You only make excuses and give dishonest answers. You truly tricked me into believing you wanted to be an honest couple with me again."

"You think it happens instantly?" Katie asked. She then explained how she had been thinking about Adam for "days and weeks and months and years."

Adam said he needed someone "right now more than ever."

"You break me," Katie said.

"And you hopped back around with other guys while I stayed lonely . . . I've loved you for years, and I'll love you for years more."

Katie mentioned how the current state of their relationship was not her choice. "You wanted me gone. You pushed me out. Forcefully. Do you remember this? You said it should be an open relationship. That I should go out because I couldn't possibly know what I wanted."

"And I was right."

Katie called Adam "broken." Then: "I love you, Adam."

"And I love you."

Adam further outlined how she could have had him back entirely if only she could find "the first stride in honesty."

Katie described the past month as "heaven and hell." She added how Adam had taken "a swing" at her while bringing her home one night recently. She alleged that he'd thrown things at her. "Told me I was worthless . . . [and] that you didn't love me. That you could not."

"Katie, I do not need any of your embellished stories from my drinking."

They bickered angrily for ten minutes, combing through the remnants of the relationship, bringing up the past. They blamed each other. Adam explained he needed someone there emotionally for him now. "No sex." He wasn't interested. And he was concerned that the Katie he knew was *not* the Katie he'd fallen in love with.

Katie pleaded with him to help her be that person he needed.

Adam said, "Be the person you *want* to be. Not the person I want you to be."

After another few rounds of shaming each other, Katie said, "Do you want to make plans to see me? Because I look forward to every teatime?"

The love-hate, passive-aggressiveness continued: "I would love nothing more than plans with you."

That comment drew a cease-fire, as though they might be getting somewhere. But talking it through, they decided teatime was probably not a good idea.

The next morning, Adam awoke to a text from Katie. He was now feeling like he didn't want her in his life anymore. She asked Adam why he'd left her in the first place.

"You have quite some balls," Adam said. "Don't send that shit to me like I'm an asshole that could have just gone to you."

"You couldn't have?" Katie shot back.

"Don't put your bullshit on me!" Adam seethed. Then he yelled: "YOU *HAD* TO FUCK [my best friend]?!"

Katie tried talking her way out of it, mentioning how Adam had shown "no interest" in her at the time. What was she supposed to do? Wait forever?

Adam wouldn't bite.

"Your timeline is fucked. And you are a liar in general. Your brain is filled with bullshit."

She tried to justify her behavior, saying Adam had explicitly said he didn't want her sexually—how *she* was "enough" for him, but also how she "couldn't do anything right . . . and I still loved you?!!!"

Adam had a simple reply: "You're a cunt."

"You fucked some bitch and I never asked," Katie wrote back.

Adam accused Katie of not being able to "keep her legs closed" while he was away for two weeks with his dad. Nor was he certain how many guys she'd slept with.

"I miss the *you* that wasn't a slut," he said, before mentioning how, out of all the people in the world that Katie could have slept with, she'd chosen not *one* of his "buddies," but *two*.

"Now it's my turn to laugh," Katie said. "They aren't your buddies. Maybe once were. But they weren't and aren't."

She waited a beat. Then: "That number is true . . ."

"You're a mighty fucking bitch."

"So are you."

"You stay far away from me outside family matters," Adam ordered.

The conversation—and any type of relationship, even friendship—was over.

Again.

32

AFTER BILL RETURNED TO Utica during the week of August 25, 2015, he still could not go back to work. He needed more time. The past month had been agonizing. He was lost. Part of the post-trauma was due to how Mary had died. Heading into September, after a discussion with Liana, Bill googled colchicine. The family had been told the rare toxin had been responsible for Mary's death.

"I'd never heard the word," Bill said. He had actually spelled the word incorrectly the first time he tried to search for it. "It seemed like the symptoms I read about exactly matched Mary's and it was always fatal." The family was left with more questions, however.

In September, the relationship between Kathleen and Bill took a turn. They had been leaning on each other rather innocently. On September 8, Kathleen texted she was just getting back from the orthodontist's office. She wanted to say hello. Bill was on her "mind and heart" a lot these days, she admitted. She'd first typed the word "heart" without the *r* and realized it said "'heat,' which is true, too." Their texting began to sound like two people who were dating, flirtatiously bantering with one another.

Over the next several days, they gave each other gifts. Spent hours on the phone. Referred to each other as "sweetheart." Still, within this new direction, Bill maintained a sense of loss and mourning for his wife. He was distraught and full of tears on certain days. Kathleen, it was obvious, was helping him cope.

"I completely understand the waves of different emotions that are part of the experience of loss and change and healing," Kathleen texted on September 17. "Have a peace-filled night."

Later, Kathleen explained: "Experiencing such profound grief intensifies all our other emotions." She felt fully alive now, just over a year after her spouse had passed. She was going to a jazz concert that night. Socializing again. Looking forward to things.

ONE OF BILL'S GRANDCHILDREN has Down syndrome. On September 18, 2015, a Down syndrome celebration was held in New York City. Liana and her family were going. Adam and Bill drove in from Utica to meet everyone.

"Colchicine," Bill told Adam as they drove. "They're certain now."

Details were trickling in. The ME's office was keeping Liana updated. She relayed the information to the rest of the family. Dr. Clark had sent out samples of Mary's gastric tract to test for colchicine. The result was positive. Since it was present there, it meant she had likely ingested the poison orally.

Clark then did something clever. He had the ME's office subpoena the hospital for a sample of Mary's blood from when she was admitted. Those results were also positive for the toxin.

This result proved that when she walked into the ER with Bill by her side, Mary's fate had been sealed. There is no antidote for an overdose of colchicine. Once a certain amount of the poison enters your system, you might be walking and talking, but you're dead.

33

*T*HROUGHOUT NOVEMBER 2014, DURING those days after Katie filed the rape allegation against him, Adam stopped communicating with her. He was terrified of what might happen, and he could not comprehend how he could have done what she'd claimed. The day after hearing this from Katie, Adam sat and went over the night. More important to him was what happened the day after the alleged incident.

When Adam woke up the morning after Katie alleged he had raped her, Katie was next to him in bed. They talked. Adam was hungover and upset with himself for getting so drunk the previous night. A flush of depression washed over him.

"I drank so much," he explained later. "I needed to get out of the house. I felt horrible."

On the night in question, the house Adam rented a room in was loud and busy with people. Katie lived with her parents down the street.

"Can I come over and get some sleep there?" Adam asked Katie, knowing her parents were out of town. Katie lay next to him in bed.

"Yes, of course," she said. "I'll drive."

Adam slept a bit in Katie's bed. When he woke up, he realized he had lost his inhaler.

"I need my inhaler. I don't have any money."

"I can go to the pharmacy and pick up a new one for you," Katie suggested.

"I'd so much appreciate that."

When she returned, Katie not only had the new inhaler, but she'd stopped and picked up food. They then got into her car and went back to his place. After arriving at Adam's, they ate and had sex.

"It was a shitty morning mentally because I had gotten so drunk the night before, I was pissed at myself," Adam recalled. "Katie had gotten me a new inhaler and food. She spent the entire day and into the night with me."

As he thought about the night before and the day after, Adam considered: *If I had done what Katie later alleged, seeing her naked that morning and later that day, I would have noticed all the injuries and bruises she'd described.*

On top of that, Adam was certain she would have said something about what had happened. Instead, she had sex with him twice and took care of him.

"I can confirm," Adam said later, "that Katie did not have any bruises and no injuries on her."

True, they had a tumultuous, sometimes confrontational, relationship. However, there was not a chance he'd turned into some kind of violent predator who'd brutally raped and beat her.

Was it even possible to recall roughing Katie up and choking her, then raping her orally and vaginally, as she'd claimed, if Adam was in a blackout? Could he have committed such a crime without having any recollection of it?

"Look, if she was raped, she would not have had sex with me in the morning. If what she says [is true], that I attempted to murder her, actively kill her, she would not have woken up next to me. She would not have spent the day with me."

Furthermore, why had she waited three months to mention anything about the alleged incident? Why had she left and driven back to the house where Adam lived and had sex with him the next morning? Why had she continued to see him after July 26? It was not until Adam ended the relationship—and Katie found a new boyfriend—that she made the allegations.

On that November 1 afternoon, while Katie was at the sheriff's office reporting the rape, the investigator made a suggestion.

"Controlled call."

"What's that?" Katie asked.

The deputy explained that Katie would call Adam from the sheriff's office. They'd record it. She would try to lure Adam into talking about the incident to see if he'd admit anything.

What Katie didn't know as she placed the controlled call was that Adam had discovered something on his laptop. He had gone over the night in question several times. The house where the supposed rape had occurred was filled with people. Adam lived in the basement. Just beyond the walls of his room was a large group of people hanging out. Any roughhousing or screams, or Katie darting in and out of Adam's room, would have startled the group. They would have heard it. One guy in particular was a staunch defender of women. He was also a mixed martial arts (MMA) fighter.

"And if he felt, or heard, anything like this going on, he would have checked in on us and beat my ass," Adam said later. "On top of that, anybody who knows me can tell you that when I would get really drunk, every time, I always retreated off by myself quietly and went to sleep."

Once Katie had made the allegations, Adam tried to find anything he could to prove or disprove what had happened. No one had ever before alleged that Adam had ever been violent in any way. He needed to know.

"The thing about this type of allegation is that once you're accused, you're a rapist. It will follow you around the rest of your life. How much damage could that have done to my entire life. You're looking at jail time, a record, employment problems. That [screws] up my whole life when someone lies about it, whether I'm convicted or not. I was so scared. I could not see myself doing this."

That fear had sent Adam in search of anything he could find relating to the incident. Between the time she'd sent the long text about the incident and this controlled call, Adam had discovered the backup of Katie's iPhone on his laptop.

"Which worked out really well for me in terms of protecting myself."

Searching through it, he'd uncovered a number of revealing items. The narrative of the rape was the biggest find at the time, along with various drafts of the long text she'd sent, and other information proving to Adam she had fabricated the entire rape story.

"And here is what I learned about Katie then. Whenever she sends a long text, you can bet that it is all bullshit lies. That's her giveaway."

During the search through her backup, Adam found (and confirmed) that she had cheated on him with his workout partner. And the affair wasn't the way Katie had been trying to sell it to him: that Katie and this guy had innocently met at the gym one day and starting talking. She'd spent a year convincing Adam through manipulation that the affair was all in his head. Nothing had happened.

"I spent that year inside my head, thinking, 'Am I trashing a good relationship and giving up happiness because I'm a paranoid idiot?'"

The truth was found in her iPhone backup.

"She fucked my friend, all right. That long text I got from her about meeting him at the gym, going over to his place for dinner, and nothing happened, it was a lie. They wanted to hook up. They planned it. They met at hotels. Yes, I looked in her phone and violated that space of hers, but it was all there inside her phone, the texts prove it."

She had saved the guy's name as a contact inside her phone as "Jen," a close friend of hers at the time.

"So, if I ever saw her texting, she would be texting 'Jen,' not my friend."

As that controlled call came in and Katie started talking, a thought struck Adam. Every time he had received a long text message from Katie, so detailed and pointed, like the rape allegation, "It's a fucking lie. There was a pattern. I saw the pattern on her phone. Only she did not know I knew this, or had her iPhone backup, when the controlled call came in."

Katie began her spiel as the sheriff's office listened and recorded. She went right into that night.

"Katie, I have a reason to believe you are fabricating this," Adam said.

Because Adam had the contents of her iPhone, he began asking her questions about his gym partner friend, being vague, trying to get her to give him details.

"I wanted to check her honesty before moving on to the rape story."

Katie wasn't having it. She kept bringing up the rape.

"Look, Katie, I have reason to believe you're lying about this!" Adam said that a number of times.

Katie, frustrated and caught up in the middle of her own story-telling, hung up on him.

BY NOVEMBER 18, 2014, after not hearing from Adam, Katie turned to desperation.

"Can I call you quick? I'm in a bad spot. I need this. Rather talk to you about July than the police."

"Would have called you right away, but I didn't feel the text," Adam said. "You can always call me. I just tried to call you again. It made a beep like you were on the other line." Further, Adam explained in his text, the call went straight to voice mail. He believed Katie had turned off her phone.

Puzzled by the circumstance, Adam asked, "Are you trying to call me at the same time?"

"I'll call you in a few minutes," Katie texted back nine minutes later.

By the end of that phone call between them, Katie had made a decision. Shortly thereafter, she called the sheriff's office and retracted her rape allegation report.

She'd decided not to press charges.

34

BILL MET UP FOR lunch with a friend and colleague, Stephen Wechsler, near the end of September 2015. Stephen had been friends with Mary and Bill for thirty years. Bill had called him back in June. "Can you cover our practice in the fall? We're taking, like, a second honeymoon to Europe, a long holiday."

"I hope Steve can cover," Mary said aloud as Bill held the phone in the air.

Steve agreed.

When Mary died, Stephen Wechsler stepped in to cover. He worked one day a week at the Yoders' Whitesboro office. By late September, he later recalled, patients were asking questions, wondering what was going on. Was he taking over the practice? Did Bill plan on ever coming back?

They didn't chat long over lunch, as Steve had to get back to the office. But he wanted to know how long it was going to be before Bill was back at work.

Bill said he was going to transition into his daily office routine beginning in October.

"Colchicine," Bill told him as the short lunch came to an end. "That's what killed her."

Bill was still as mystified as anyone else close to the family regarding how his wife had died. Colchicine wasn't a substance one went down to the local pharmacy or farm store (it is also used for plant growth) and purchased. It required a medical license or a medical practice routinely ordering the toxin, proving with documents you were an authorized buyer.

This was the first that Stephen Wechsler had heard the cause of Mary's death. When he returned to Chiropractic Family Care after his lunch with Bill, Katie was sitting at the front desk. He stopped and faced her, his elbows on the counter. He googled colchicine because, like most everyone else who had heard, he was curious about how Mary might have ingested it. He told Katie what he was looking up.

She seemed interested.

Standing, he read aloud from the Wikipedia page he landed on. After the first paragraph, which spoke of colchicine's connection to gout and Mediterranean fever, "'It is a toxic alkaloid and secondary metabolite, originally extracted from plants of the genus Colchicum (autumn crocus . . . also known as meadow saffron).'"

Katie didn't say much, as patients were trekking in for afternoon appointments.

For a number of days afterward, the autumn crocus/meadow saffron connection gnawed at Stephen. He knew Mary was such an avid gardener, and the possible plant link was on everyone's mind. Mary had a green thumb all her life. So it was hard to conceive that she could make such a deadly mistake, overlook this, and kill herself—on top of endangering her family—without realizing it.

To add to the anxiety surrounding the connection to the autumn crocus, the ME's office was calling Mary's death a possible "accidental contamination." A forensic investigator working for the ME's office called those family members closest to Mary and asked questions of them.

Bill and additional family had collected all of Mary's supplements, personal food, and drink items from the office and home, and turned them over to the ME's office.

Then Bill got an idea. He texted Katie: "Do you remember if any patient brought Mary anything to eat or drink on her last day of work? If there is any old food in fridge . . . just leave it. Trying to track down how Mary might have ingested the toxin they found in her system. I know all of this is hard to keep revisiting. It is for me, too."

Katie responded: "I don't remember anyone bringing something in. I know she went to Grammy's on lunch break to eat . . . came back here, and had her shake fresh and brought the vitamins from home. Nothing different/new for lunch and she didn't eat at Grammy's."

By "Grammy's" Katie meant Mary's ninety-three-year-old mother.

Later that day, Katie texted back, adding, "I didn't know there was a toxin. Before Mary started feeling unwell, it was a normal happy Monday . . ."

35

*I*F THERE WAS A routine that Mary Yoder appreciated, it had to be the simple pleasure of pulling into her driveway during warmer months and passing her plants as she made her way into the house. She adored this gift of taking in the beauty of what she had created.

As Mary slipped away while hospitalized, the garden at home was bursting into life. It was the last week of July, arguably the pinnacle of summer in New York and the Northeast. Temps in the eighties. The sun low, bright, hot. The air warm and comforting, with August's heavy humidity not quite moved in yet. Beaches and campgrounds were packed with vacationers. People were home on vacation from work. Local produce was showing up at farm stands and farmers' markets.

Bill Yoder had trouble recalling most of that day Mary passed. Liana had told her father they sat and talked. But Bill could not recollect much, other than sitting on the edge of his bed upstairs. He remembered weeping, wondering how his life could have changed so drastically overnight.

Mary left behind five sisters, two brothers. She had been closest to her oldest sibling, Kathleen Richmond, with whom Bill was now talking to and seeing regularly. Kathleen's husband had died unexpectedly in 2014. According to Bill (and Kathleen later on), he and Mary had not seen Kathleen much during those immediate days after she'd lost her husband.

"We knew she was in a lot of pain and grief."

It was back on Mother's Day, May 10, 2015, while Bill and Mary were visiting Mary's mother, that they ran into her. Kathleen happened to be at her mother's house. Mary and Kathleen got to talking. Mary mentioned a barbeque in the backyard with Adam later that day and Kathleen asked if she was welcome.

"We were delighted to have her," Bill said.

During the barbeque, Mary, Bill, and Adam talked about their latest obsession with board games. Kathleen sat and listened, interested. They agreed that they'd plan a board game night at Kathleen's house soon. On June 20, Bill and Mary went over and had a nice night out. Kathleen was emerging from her fog of grief by then. She even laughed that night. Life seemed to have a purpose once again—however small—for the widow. Bill and Mary could not have been happier for her.

A week after board game night, Bill and Mary saw Kathleen at a pottery workshop in Cazenovia, about an hour's drive west of Utica. It turned out to be a beautiful day of art and sunshine, friends and family.

As Mary slipped away a month later, Kathleen and Mary's sister Greta (pseudonym), whom Bill later described as having "some psychological problems," showed up at the hospital to console everyone clustered outside Mary's room. Greta was not there long "before she started wailing," Bill recalled.

"Excuse me," a nurse said to Kathleen, pulling her aside, "can you please take your sister somewhere else? She is kind of distracting."

Kathleen agreed.

Bill looked on. He had his own grief to contend with. Later, he said, "Liana was on one side of me, crying and crying, and Adam was just kind of huddled up in the corner, kneeling beside the wall and crying. Tammy was sitting next to me, her entire body shaking. I wanted to help them, but I was falling apart, too."

As Bill sat, he watched Kathleen walk out of Mary's room, go to each family member, put her arm around them, and say, "It'll be okay."

"I was just very grateful," Bill said of that moment, "because I couldn't do anything."

Adam was as devastated as his father and the rest of the family, later recalling a moment during the same afternoon while standing by his mother's side: "She couldn't speak. She couldn't write anything down. She wanted to communicate. Her hands were swollen. Her arms were swollen."

It was dreadful to see this woman they all loved so much, a bastion of health, dying in such an awful way, and nobody could do anything. Even worse, nobody knew why.

As Adam rushed to the hospital earlier that day after hearing from his father, he hesitated, but decided to text Katie. He realized in the days after, however, contacting Katie—knowing they were broken up—was a "panic" move on his part. He didn't know where to turn. The person he would have gone to first was in the hospital, fighting for her life.

"Katie knew my mother and was one of the only females, I would say, I was close to, somewhat, at the time. I just reached out for somebody, anybody," Adam said later.

"I need you right now. I'm sorry to put pressure on you. You don't owe me anything. But I need you." It was 7:45 a.m. on July 23, 2015. Adam had just gotten back into town after driving through the night from Long island. "I want my mom to hold me like she does when I'm sick."

Katie texted back two minutes later: "Okay. Give me five minutes and I'll leave the office. I'll be right there."

At 8:12 a.m., Adam texted Katie again. He was going to wait outside the hospital for her.

"I'm in the lobby. It'll be a while. It's up to you if you want to stay. She coded. She's back now but we all fell apart."

"They have no idea what brought this whole thing on?" Katie asked. "I was with her Monday. She was her happy self. She only started to feel poorly at the end of the day. She's important to me, too, you know."

"I'm not telling you to go. Stay. You can come up even. I'm sorry. I'm not trying to be insensitive. I can't think straight."

Katie arrived. She and Adam met downstairs in the lobby. Then they walked together up to the ICU to be with the others and Mary.

As they sat, consoled, and comforted one another, Adam asked Katie, "Would you take me to the Barnes and Noble?" He wanted to get his mother a few gardening magazines. "I don't know what to do."

That long history between Katie and Adam as they drove toward Barnes & Noble was like a rotten smell in the car. It was a negative energy they could not ignore. Adam had poured out his heart and soul to this same woman who was now someone he felt he did not know anymore. With his mother fighting for her life, the only other person he'd confided in, he didn't know what to say or how to deal with it all. He'd trusted Katie with his deepest feelings before, only to be struck down by her insensitivity.

"I will never be with anyone else," Adam had once written to Katie.

Admittedly, in the same letter, Adam talked about battling self-esteem issues. He said how sorry he was for "not loving" himself, knowing it had an effect on their relationship.

In another letter, in a large font, Adam wrote: "I love you. I want kids."

At the time, Adam kept a list of "morning reminders." For one, he believed he needed to do more for Katie. Treat her better. He talked about how he would begin to buy "one present for Katie every day" and "take notes" of those places Katie wanted to visit and things she wanted to do. Near the end of the list, Adam promised "never [to] raise his voice," because Katie didn't "deserve that." He added bullet points, two of which included: "No breaking things" and "No hitting things." At the end of the page, he wrote a final reminder: "Do what Katie says—always . . ." On the next page, Adam wrote, "I love Katie"—eighty-eight times.

Adam had Katie take him to Michael's after leaving Barnes & Noble. "My mother had her sixtieth birthday that March," Adam explained. "I had planned to do an art project . . . So again, in a panic, not thinking clearly, I tried to do it for her back there at the hospital."

Adam and Katie also stopped at his place to pick up a painting he'd made for his mother. "I just want to heal my mother," he said.

Katie spent most of the day Mary had died with the Yoder family in the hallway outside Mary's room. Adam texted her many times. He also stepped out of the room to update her.

Adam approached Katie that afternoon. "I don't know how long this is all going to be, or what is happening, but you don't have to wait here all day."

Katie agreed, and left. "Text me . . . please?"

"I will."

Not long after Katie left, from her car, she sent Adam a text. She was sitting in the parking lot, crying. She'd gone out to her car and broke down, she claimed.

"Your mother is not just important to you," she concluded, telling Adam how upset she was not being allowed into Mary's room.

Trying as best he could under the circumstances to be responsive and sensitive to her needs, Adam walked down into the parking lot.

"You can come up for a quick visit. They'll allow you in her room."

36

On December 2, 2015, Bill Yoder called Lorraine Kreimeyer, Mary's final patient on the day she became ill. Bill wanted answers. He wasn't getting much out of the ME's office other than colchicine had killed his wife. In addition, Bill felt as though he was being viewed as a suspect, rather than the grieving husband.

Bill needed to know how the toxin had found its way into Mary's system. He felt people were looking at him strangely. Making matters worse, Bill and Kathleen, Mary's sister, were now seeing each other regularly.

"Sitting here with a glass of wine and your photo," Bill texted Kathleen on October 7. "Telling you about my amazing day. Your smile melts my heart and I keep falling in love all over again . . ."

Bill's sister-in-law Greta had a problem with the relationship. She saw it as Bill taking advantage of Kathleen—and perhaps something more disturbing, which she was now focused on looking into more closely.

A self-employed artist, Lorraine Kreimeyer had been a Yoder patient for twenty years. On the day Mary left work ill, July 22, Lorraine was at the local library up the street from the practice. A fierce migraine came on, Lorraine nearly unable to stand or think. Looking at her watch, Lorraine "realized if I left right away, I might be able to get in and see Mary." A visit to the chiropractor "usually helped" Lorraine cope with her headaches. Wasn't a cure-all, but it lessened the degree of pain.

Leaving the library, Lorraine headed toward Chiropractic Family Care, calling the office on her way.

"Can you get me in?" she asked Katie.

"I can."

Lorraine was five minutes away. At about 4:00 p.m., she walked in. Dr. Mary—the name every long-term patient called Mary—had Lorraine go into the back treatment room with the three blue tables. Another patient was in the room at the time.

Lorraine struggled. A migraine can affect vision. Mary did a few manipulation techniques on Lorraine and told her to sit quietly and relax.

"Why don't you go into the other room," Mary suggested after a short time. It was private. Lorraine could be alone.

The migraine pain increased as Lorraine got comfortable in the private room.

Mary popped in. "How are you?"

Lorraine indicated she was not doing well. In fact, Lorraine felt she could not drive herself home.

"Dr. Mary, you think you could give me a ride?"

Mary had driven Lorraine home in the past under similar circumstances.

"No, not today," Mary said, failing to elaborate. She sounded matter-of-fact, which surprised Lorraine. She also thought it odd Mary had said no. So she called home and asked her mother if she could find someone to come to the office and drive her home.

Mary went back into the other room, where she had one other patient, the last one of the day. It was just after 5:00 p.m. by then. Luciann Gold had been going to see Mary and Bill for two decades, at times three visits per week.

"Typically, Mary was very engaged with me and the other patients. You know, very conversational and smiling."

As soon as Mary entered the room on July 20, however, Luciann saw a marked, obvious change in Mary's demeanor.

"She either didn't feel well, or something not good was going on." The word Luciann used, which others later agreed with, was "disconnected." An otherwise fully present, completely involved, sociable, interactive doctor (even earlier that same day) was now quiet, introverted, and just not herself.

A second unusual behavior Mary exhibited was darting in and out of the manipulation room. Mary never did this. She generally entered the treatment room, focused on and treated her patients, talked procedure and health, socialized, then hugged each patient before leaving the room.

As Luciann thought about how differently Mary was acting, she could hear the bathroom door nearby open and close several times. In twenty years of going to see Mary, Luciann recalled, Mary had never done this.

Luciann walked out of the treatment room and stood at the reception desk. Katie checked her out. Scheduled her next appointment. The office was closing.

While Luciann dug in her pocketbook, Mary rushed out the door without saying a word or making eye contact with anyone.

Outside, sitting in the passenger seat of her car, waiting for someone to drive her home, Lorraine Kreimeyer was upset. That pulsating migraine was back in full. She could not understand why Mary had not agreed to drive her home. It had never been an issue. Had she done something to offend Mary?

Looking up, Lorraine saw Mary drive around the side of the building toward her. Lorraine had no ill feelings and wanted to let Mary know she would be okay. As Mary drove by, Lorraine looked Mary in the eyes and gave her a thumbs-up.

Mary didn't respond.

Lorraine got a good look at Dr. Mary as she sped past.

"She looked at me and she didn't smile, like normal. Her face looked really gaunt and long. And her skin looked green."

37

AFTER KATIE DROPPED THE rape charges in November 2014, she tore into Adam about the incident. Katie was now using the alleged rape and her decision not to press charges as leverage to manipulate and control him. At 2:00 a.m. on November 28, she texted, referring to what she called a "blood choke."

A blood choke is a stranglehold. You come up from behind someone, place one arm over their shoulder and around their neck (the inside of your elbow under their chin), grab that hand with your other hand, the back of the victim's head below your chin, lock it in place. Then you apply as much pressure (like a nutcracker) as possible. It's a common judo maneuver, used in ground fighting/grappling and Brazilian jujitsu. The move immediately stops blood flow between both carotid arteries and the jugular vein, blocking blood to the brain. When done properly, the maneuver causes the victim to black out in a matter of moments.

"I didn't know 'blood choke,' but it makes sense," Katie continued. "I know it takes a few minutes to lose consciousness without airflow. July, it didn't take that long at all. I think it was an accidental blood choke. It's crazy that works."

Katie was now implying Adam had accidentally choked her out?

Adam responded, saying he wanted to "avoid" any "painful conversations. A lot of lying that hurts me deep . . . I'm doing my best to let it go and maintain a friendship with you now. Let me know if you want to do the same."

"Lying from who?" Katie popped back.

"From you! Please don't make this harder. Please don't."

Katie became incensed. She warned Adam. If he thought she was lying about what happened: "You know better." Her dropping the charges, she continued, was indicative of her "trying to be okay with what happened. To not have PTSD over it. What would be the point of lying about YOU doing THIS to Me??"

A moment later, she mentioned how she could have told everyone about it: his parents, hers, their friends. But she chose not to. "I would never lie that that would happen to me, especially by you. If it were to try and keep a friendship going"—something Adam never mentioned—"why would I say you did this to me?"

Next, Katie said how little she had to gain by lying, explaining how "painful" it was to her for Adam to suggest as much. "I never asked what you remembered. I told *you*."

Strangely, she concluded with: "I'm trying to keep you human. I want to be okay. I don't need this to haunt me, you to haunt me."

Perhaps in an attempt to win him back, Katie then brought up the notion of Adam drawing a false conclusion regarding her sleeping with his friend.

"Your friend lied to you to hurt you and I'm sorry."

She described what happened. It was late summer, she remembered. "It'd be less embarrassing to say I had sex with someone vs. I thought about it . . ." She added how she had planned to sleep with him. But as she undressed, she "started completely freaking out over it." So she never went through with it. "This is not being strong or in control. I have already lost."

"Stop," Adam said. He wasn't interested in hearing some concocted narrative. Though he never mentioned it, Adam had the proof in front of him via her iPhone backup. He could see the planning and corresponding between them.

After failing to bait him with the idea she'd chickened out of sleeping with his friend, Katie opted for a guilt trip, reminding Adam of what he had allegedly done to her.

Adam said he would not be discussing any of it via text anymore. "If you need to speak to me, you can call me."

Katie made up an excuse that her phone died and she lost the connection. Three minutes later, however, she texted: "It's pretty specific, what I'm telling you. I think assault would be bad enough. Not to include sexual and choking and death threat. It could be worse, but it could be better." She added how humiliating and revealing it had all been. "I'm a private person and you think I want that kind of attention?" She then threatened Adam, saying she had texts from him admitting he'd committed another crime.

Adam ended the conversation, disturbed and confused by all he had seen and heard.

PART III

AFFECTIVE BLINDNESS

38

Mark VanNamee began his law enforcement career with the Oneida County Sheriff's Office in June 2001. VanNamee (pronounced Van-Name-ee) had worked his way up to investigator in the OCSO's Criminal Investigation Division (CID) by 2010. The guy struck the classic detective look: short-cropped dark hair, military buzz cut; average height; an earnest, confident, charming, likable demeanor; some beef on his bones. He had a tenacious, maybe even obsessive, attitude toward the cases he was assigned. He wore dark suits, white shirts, simple-patterned ties, a gold badge clipped to his belt, his 9mm Glock strapped on his right hip. VanNamee had investigated all types of felonious crimes throughout his career, including complex murder cases.

On the brisk afternoon of October 15, 2015, VanNamee settled into his shift, two o'clock to 10:00 p.m. While sitting at his desk checking e-mail, close to 4:30 p.m., a call from a woman came in. The caller asked to speak with someone in the CID. She identified herself as Sharon Mills.

"I was wondering if the sheriff's office is investigating the death of my sister Mary Yoder?" Sharon asked.

Sharon Mills had met Bill Yoder when she was thirteen. Mary had brought Bill home and introduced him to the family. To Sharon, Bill was gregarious and pleasant, but he also could appear quiet and a bit intense. Living in Naples, Florida, now, Sharon had not been able to make the trip to Utica quick enough to be by Mary's side when she passed. Their sister Janine had called Sharon throughout that stressful period with regular updates, and Sharon was able to fly in for the Celebration of Life on July 25.

It was the first time VanNamee had heard the name Yoder. He asked Sharon for a bit of detail.

As she spoke, VanNamee jotted down the information Sharon shared: Mary's date of death, the name of the hospital, the circumstances.

"The medical examiner had determined Mary died from colchicine toxicity," Sharon said, explaining later how she had supposedly "sat on" the information "for probably . . . a week and a half, two weeks, trying to figure out what to do." When she hadn't heard much else from Liana or Bill after the colchicine revelation, Sharon decided to call the OCSO to see if they knew anything.

As VanNamee thought about it, he concluded that colchicine poisoning was a very rare cause of death. Most detectives had not heard of colchicine, let alone as a potential murder weapon. An unfamiliar poison, colchicine is unlike arsenic and cyanide, which are, by investigative standards, easy to come by. Colchicine, in contrast, is difficult to purchase—which, VanNamee knew, would leave a paper/digital trail.

"I'll contact the medical examiner's office and find out if another police agency is actively investigating the death," VanNamee told Sharon. "I have to see if there is an open investigation."

"I had heard from my niece [Liana] that she passed away from ascending colitis, but later found out that wasn't true," Sharon said. "She died of a lethal dose of colchicine."

VanNamee ended the brief call by assuring Sharon he would look into it and let her know when he had any information to share.

VanNamee called the ME's office. They confirmed an ongoing death investigation with regard to Mary Yoder's untimely death was happening. However, no law enforcement agency had been assigned the case. From that initial call, VanNamee sensed that the ME's office had been exploring all possibilities since conducting Mary's autopsy. They were not going at it from the point of view of nefarious criminal activity. It was an odd death, certainly, but there were so many variables at play. Finding out how the toxin had entered Mary's system was akin to locating the source of a hazardous liquid found inside a sewer drain.

They agreed to stay in touch.

Next, VanNamee knocked on his lieutenant's door. "Got a sec?"

"Sure," Lieutenant Robert Nelson said. "Come in, Mark."

They talked. Agreed on several preliminary, tactical curiosities they both wanted to satisfy before letting go of the case.

Lieutenant Nelson then had a conversation with Sharon. She presented several theories regarding how Mary could have ingested the colchicine, along with those whom she suspected could have been involved.

Listening, the lieutenant grew concerned.

"They were only interested in hearing about Bill," Sharon later said about that call with Nelson.

"Bill Yoder, Mary's husband?" the lieutenant asked.

"Yes. And if he did it, you're never going to catch him."

Nelson was curious about the comment. He asked why.

"Because I believe him to be brilliant," Sharon added.

After the call, Nelson found VanNamee. "You know what, Mark, open an investigation as the lead. See where it goes. Keep me updated."

If nothing else, OCSO investigators would sleep better knowing what, exactly, happened to Mary Yoder. If the public was at risk, because, say, Mary's death was brought on by something in the water supply, or Mary had been poisoned by food or another silent killer, they'd done their jobs. If it was nothing more than accidental, again, this was one reason cops like VanNamee and Nelson went to work every day. And if Bill Yoder had murdered his wife, they would eventually place metal bracelets on the guy and charge him with felony murder.

VanNamee sent "preservation letters" to Verizon regarding Mary and Bill Yoder's telephone numbers. He needed to make sure those records were not deleted. Then he did a database search for any potential insurance claims filed under the Yoder name. Generally, when someone is poisoned to death, a motive presented itself.

Follow the money and the lovers. As an investigator, you begin at the most obvious first. Money, love, revenge—the three main motivations for murder. Which one—if any—could be applied to Mary Yoder's death?

As far as VanNamee could tell from his insurance claim search, no one had made an inquiry at this point to collect life insurance on Mary Yoder.

ON OR ABOUT THE same day Sharon Mills called the OCSO, Bill Yoder texted Kathleen. She had just returned from a short trip.

"Good morning. I love you. XXO."

"I love you, too."

Kathleen was suffering from the aches and pains of aging. Bill wished her well. Said she'd be okay and perhaps just needed to relax.

Kathleen described a particular condition she believed she had. She encouraged Bill to "look it up."

"Sure sounds like what you've described," he said. "And all the articles I read recommended sexual activity as part of long-term treatment and prevention . . ."

"Yeah," Kathleen replied. "I read that, too." She included a winking icon.

39

MARK VANNAMEE WAS RAISED in Holland Patent, a small village of about five hundred people, a twenty-minute ride north of Utica. "I grew up as a country boy. My parents owned a dairy farm."

As Mark entered the fourth grade, his parents sold the farm. His mother went back to teaching, her first love. Mark's father landed a job working for Oneida County, becoming the first director of the 911 call system. With one older brother (just over a year), Mark listened as his dad talked about how effective the 911 calling system became for Oneida County. They did not have one in place until then.

"As we grew older, my brother moved to Hartford, New York. He actually passed away from cancer [in 2007]."

Out of high school, Mark enrolled at Mohawk Valley Community College in Utica, criminal justice his focus.

"Two years out of Mohawk, I go to SUNY with my major being what I love, business and accounting," Mark explained. He was twenty. A year later, "on a whim," not thinking about it too much, "I took the sheriff's exam."

"The academy starts in two weeks," the OCSO said, calling Mark weeks later. He was twenty-one, between his junior and senior years of college. It was August.

Mark went home that night and spoke to his father.

"I think I'm going to become a cop. If that doesn't work out, I'll go back to college and finish."

It was a solid plan.

Four days after his twenty-second birthday, Mark VanNamee graduated from the academy. He started on patrol with OCSO. Soon he was assigned to a station four minutes from his house. Things seemed to be working out for VanNamee careerwise. He'd found his calling. Loved what he was doing.

CONTINUING HIS INVESTIGATION INTO the unexplained death of Mary Yoder after Sharon Mills called, Detective VanNamee's interest grew. That little investigator on his shoulder was beckoning. More questions than answers arose—always a red flag in policework. Early days of a poisoning investigation can be like walking into a cave without a flashlight. You're not sure where you're going, but you have a sense there's something inside that you need to see. You don't speculate what you'll find. You follow the path and see where you end up—most important, *accepting* the answers you arrive at, regardless if they fit into theories or thoughts.

After speaking to Sharon Mills, VanNamee took away that Mary's sister had drawn her own conclusions. Namely, they were centered around Bill Yoder. These concerns needed to be explored, but so would every other possibility.

By the end of November, VanNamee, Lieutenant Nelson, pathologists Stoppacher and Clark, along with Oneida County District Attorney's Office assistant district attorney (ADA) Laurie Lisi, met at the ME's office to discuss Mary Yoder's death. VanNamee had uncovered several perplexing facts requiring deeper investigation. The main purpose of what turned into a three-hour meeting was to get everyone on the same page. Flesh out all the facts in the case they knew then, especially cause and manner of death.

After that meeting, VanNamee sent preservation letters to UPS and FedEx regarding any shipments to the Yoders' office. Had anyone ordered colchicine? Had Mary ordered the product for some reason that no one knew? Was it a chemical the office used? Since colchicine was a treatment for gout, one could argue that gout, a common, however complex, form of arthritis, can affect anyone at any time. Mary was a chiropractor. It wasn't a stretch to think she could have prescribed colchicine to patients.

Additionally, Mary had a pop-up supplement store in the office. Perhaps she stocked colchicine for some reason? She might have been poisoning herself, without knowing it.

How was the relationship between Mary and her husband? VanNamee kept thinking. In these types of cases, the husband has to be suspect number one.

Contemplating all of this, VanNamee felt the same way the ME's office did: Mary Yoder's autopsy was incomplete. Both Clark and Stoppacher were unsatisfied with the answers they'd uncovered.

Three days after the meeting, on November 23, VanNamee took a call from the ME's office.

"We have some additional information."

"What's up?"

"We received an anonymous letter this morning regarding Mary Yoder's death."

"Letter?"

"Yes. Typed. Two pages."

VanNamee drove to the ME's office to collect the letter, making sure the integrity of any potential DNA evidence on the letter was secured. He also ordered buccal swabs from anyone at the ME's office who might have come in contact with the letter.

When he got back to the OCSO, Lieutenant Nelson called him into his office. "Mark, look at this." Nelson had a piece of typed paper, inside a plastic evidence bag.

"What's that?" VanNamee asked.

The OCSO had received the same anonymous letter—a letter making it perfectly clear who was responsible for Mary Yoder's murder.

40

*T*HOSE AFFECTIONATE, OUTWARD DISPLAYS of emotion found in the letters and journal entries Adam Yoder had written while dating Katie Conley in the early days of their relationship disappeared after he broke up with her in late 2014. Adam was still suffering from the effects of the relationship. Specifically, it stemmed from his conscious, consistent contact with Katie and the extreme pull of resentment he was feeling.

She'd damaged part of his soul. This became obvious when one compared Adam's early writings about Katie with the person he realized she was after that traumatic period during the fall of 2014, when she accused him of violent rape. Adam's individuality had taken a crushing blow since the day he met Katie. The tacit aggression between the two of them had, effectually, fueled a volatile codependency. Yet, even while in the depths of desolation, Adam fought for the relationship. He'd put himself out there repeatedly, admitting to Katie how transfixed by her he'd become.

In turn, from those letters, Katie absorbed the infatuated and enslaved nature of Adam's love. Additionally, she filed away that whatever she did, he always came back. Katie consciously shaped, molded, and later weaponized Adam's weaknesses against him. Adam never schemed to punish Katie in any severe, preplanned way. His negative interactions with Katie were verbal put-downs or depriving her of attention—bad behavior toward her that was primarily reactive. In reality, he was more comfortable punishing him-

Mary and Bill Yoder met in college and began a storybook romance, traveling to Arizona, living in New Mexico and Hawaii, before getting married and settling down in Sauquoit, New York.

Mary was described
as a woman full of life,
who put all of herself
into everything she did.

Mary's talents included gardening, painting, and making pottery.

In the four decades that
Mary and Bill Yoder were married,
their happiness deepened.

Mary and Bill Yoder started Chiropractic Family Care near Utica, New York,
to help people heal "from the inside out."
(Photos courtesy of the author.)

A loving mother and a doting grandmother, Mary adored her family.

Mary's son Adam and his girlfriend, Katie Conley, met at a high school graduation party in 2011. Adam soon got Katie a job as office manager of Chiropractic Family Care.

Mary took a sixtieth-birthday selfie on March 18, 2015. It was the last birthday she celebrated.

After Mary's death, some of her art and favorite pottery were displayed at a celebration-of-life ceremony in her and Bill's home.

An anonymous letter informed the medical examiner and the Oneida County sheriff that a bottle of colchicine could be found inside Adam Yoder's Jeep. *(Photos courtesy of Oneida County District Attorney's Office.)*

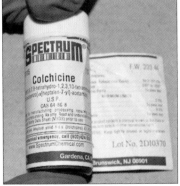

Under the passenger's seat, investigators discovered a bottle of colchicine. *(Photos courtesy of Oneida County District Attorney's Office.)*

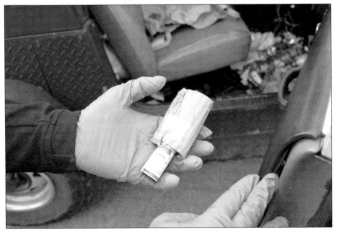

This plastic bag shows the miniscule amount of colchicine—0.6 milligrams,
about 100 granules equal in size to one sugar granule—it took to kill Mary Yoder.
(Photo courtesy of the author.)

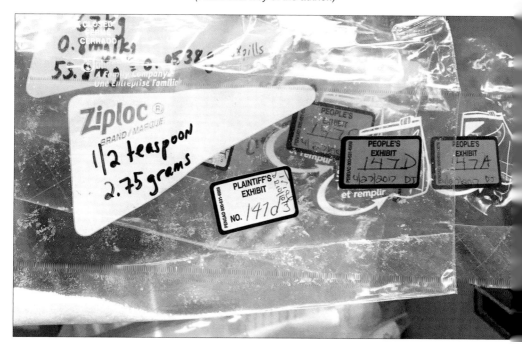

As a comparison, this bag contains just a half-teaspoon of colchicine.
(Photo courtesy of the author.)

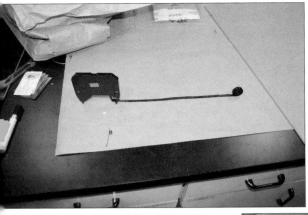

A typewriter ribbon, taken out of an old-school typewriter inside Chiropractic Family Care, was imprinted with words and phrases from the envelope containing the anonymous letter, pointing to Adam Yoder as his mother's killer.
(Photos courtesy of Oneida County District Attorney's Office.)

Oneida County Prosecutor Stacey Scotti points to portions of the typewriter ribbon where those phrases and information were uncovered. The ribbon also contained information used in the false documentation created to support the purchase of colchicine.
(Photo courtesy of the author.)

In November 2015, Oneida County Sheriff's Office Investigator Mark VanNamee took a call from Mary Yoder's sister, who asked him to look into her sister's death. *(Photo courtesy of the author.)*

After exploring the possibility that Adam Yoder or his father, Bill Yoder, could have killed Mary, Investigator VanNamee interviewed Katie Conley. *(Screenshot from the police interview courtesy of Oneida County District Attorney's Office.)*

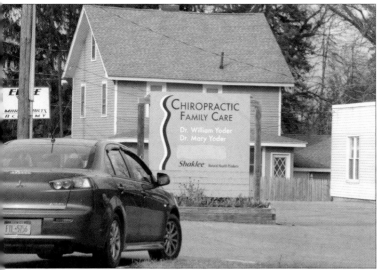

The Oneida County Sheriff's Office began surveillance of Katie Conley— pictured here inside her car as she drove into the parking lot of Chiropractic Family Care. *(Photo courtesy of Oneida County District Attorney's Office.)*

Katie Conley's iPhone became a major source of evidence. *(Photo courtesy of the author.)*

Investigators believe this bottle of Alpha BRAIN (a supplement), given to Adam Yoder by Katie Conley, also contained traces of colchicine— which caused him to go to the emergency room on April 2015. His symptoms were the same as those his mother experienced three months later. *(Photo courtesy of the author.)*

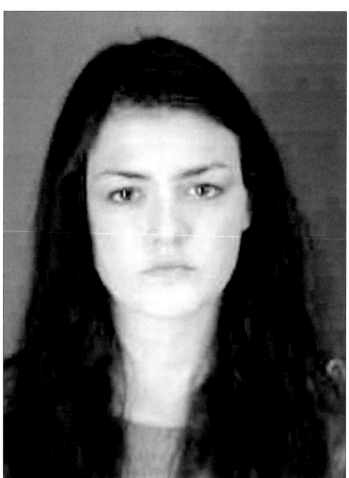

In January 2018, after Katie Conley's first trial ended in a hung jury, she was convicted of first-degree manslaughter in the death of Mary Yoder. *(Photo and screenshot courtesy of Oneida County District Attorney's Office.)*

Despite the evidence against her, many in the community showed their belief in Conley's innocence. *(Photo courtesy of the author.)*

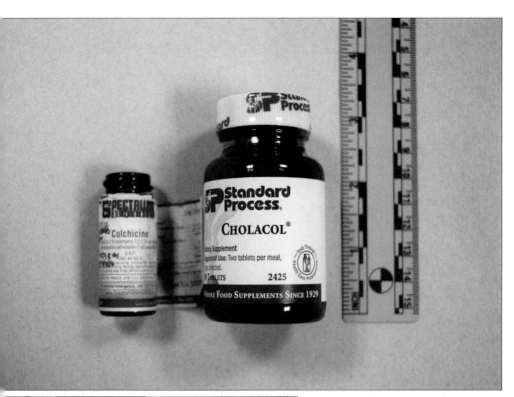

Conley's DNA, found on this small bottle of colchicine, was a key piece of forensic evidence used to convict her. *(Photo courtesy of the author.)*

Prosecutor Stacey Scotti, pictured here explaining a piece of evidence, worked with the lead prosecutor, Assistant District Attorney Laurie Lisi, and the Oneida County Sheriff's Office to secure a conviction. *(Photo courtesy of the author.)*

Mary Louise Yoder is missed not only by her family, but by her community, friends, neighbors, and patients.

self. Katie's negativity was always intentional and calculated; Adam's was overly emotional and responsive.

"I would wait for you for the rest of my life," Adam wrote not long after meeting Katie and falling in love. He was referencing a potential split. If Katie never returned, Adam added, "I would die sad and alone."

Continuing, he mentioned how if Katie stayed with him forever, "like I want," or decided to leave, he would "never be with anyone else."

Those two paragraphs, included in a one-page, double-spaced letter—in which Adam told Katie he loved her thirteen times, and apologized for not loving himself—gave Katie carte blanche over the relationship. There were other letters to follow, with more of the same pleading and self-loathing, low self-esteem. Adam poured it on, his confidence at its lowest, letting Katie know she held the keys to any chance he'd had for happiness and normalcy, simply with the touch of a phone call or text. This power she wielded was obvious when Adam had admitted, "I love you more than I love my family."

When Adam ended the relationship that August 2014, a total shift occurred in his heart. Katie did not have that magnetic vise-like grip over his emotions any longer. Katie must have realized she'd gone too far with the allegations of sexual assault and rape—and the way she prodded and poked at him. The tone Adam used in his texts afterward, along with his careful choice of words, let her know he had severed the bond, detached from her emotionally.

The dates are unclear because her iPhone notes were written and deleted (before being later recovered), but Katie made several additional notations on her iPhone *Notes* app after writing the August 24, 2014, sexual assault narrative. These notes could be viewed as a person's deepest, truest thoughts. One can construe them as unashamed, uncensored feelings and ideas the writer believes no one will ever see. Some of Katie's *Notes* app entries made sense on a surface level, while others would take time to decode.

For example, she wrote that "for a fact" Bill Yoder "will order [supplies for the office under] other people's names" and "Adam has given out his password to his parents." Concluding that three-line entry, she mentioned how Mary "wanted to keep working" while "dr. bill wanted to retire." The questions became: What do they mean? Why would she write them? What was her motivation and purpose?

Skipping a few spaces, she asked herself a question: "Could it be grainy like Truvia?" (Truvia is a stevia-based sugar substitute, a sweetener.) "If yes," she concluded that same thought, "office"—which was even more unusual, considering the context and what would happen to Mary in late July 2015.

Following those entries, the writing became a bit more cryptic.

"Spray adhesive."

A few spaces.

"Discover."

A few more spaces.

"En. 6055. 1990@g. Adamisgay. . . ."

Several more spaces.

". . . 200. 80. 140."

Katie mentioned the bathing suit she wore on the night of the alleged rape, writing how she still had it (thus dating the entry *after* August 24, 2014): "It was my favorite one."

The next note was about Mary. Poetically, Katie wrote, if "love could have saved" her, Mary "would have lived forever," followed by three heart emojis. She admitted how she could not "believe" Mary was "gone." Dated July 20, 2015, she then wrote, "Yesterday was so sudden and unexpected." Only, Mary wasn't ill on July 19, 2015, a Sunday; she left work on that Monday, July 20, the same day Katie dates this entry.

She called Mary a "positive light in the world" and noted how "lucky and thankful" she was the two of them had met. There had not been a day, Katie added, in which she did not want to go to work. She talked about how everyone "appreciated" Mary's "attention, stories, and laughter." Mary Yoder, according to Katie, would be remembered for her "light, energy, and strength . . ."

Katie concluded those thoughts by writing how she would best honor Mary's incredible life by emulating her "genuine, cheerful, and kind spirit . . . We love you, Dr. Mary."

41

A FEW DAYS BEFORE Christmas, 2014, Katie walked into the Hannaford supermarket in Utica. It was several weeks after Adam had all but cut off any personal, intimate communication with her. During the previous month, Adam was standoffish and cautious about his communication and what he said. Via text and rare phone calls, they discussed his Jeep, the weather, accounting, and other trivial matters.

Katie understood she needed to work harder if she wanted to ensnare Adam back into a relationship. One might even suspect she was furious after having dropped the allegations of rape, only to have Adam turn around and call her a liar, among many other vulgar insults and insensitive names. Still, as Christmas approached, Adam remained civil. He was talking to Katie again, being mindful of keeping his distance.

In Katie's OCSO statement withdrawing the charges, which she signed on November 18, she had said the "sexual assault complaint" she'd filed "regarding my ex-boyfriend, Adam Yoder, raping me, I no longer wish to proceed forth with criminal charges and I wish no further police action to be taken in this matter."

That entire episode seemed to be behind them. However, an invisible threat, which could explode into an argument at any time, was present during any communication. Adam worried constantly about what the rape accusation could mean for his life if it got out.

On December 22, 2014, while inside the supermarket, Katie purchased a $150 prepaid Mastercard. The last four digits on that prepaid Mastercard were 3288. She paid cash. Took the card from the cashier. Placed it into her purse. Walked out of the supermarket.

Nine days later, on Wednesday, December 31, 2014 (a workday), at precisely 11:26 a.m., someone signed into the Mr. Adam Yoder 1990 Gmail e-mail account created at Chiropractic Family Care on the computer Katie used—the same computer that had been used near this same time to set up a Google Voice account.

"Thanks for signing up for Google Voice!" the short e-mail confirmation noted, here is "your new Google Number . . ."

The password for the account was "Adamisgay"—which Katie had also previously written in her iPhone *Notes* app.

An e-mail from the Mr. Adam Yoder 1990 Gmail account—claiming to be from Adam Yoder—was then sent to Rosa Vargas, who worked for a company called ArtChemicals.

> *Hi, Rosa:*
> *I'm having some difficulty with the payment option. The card is Mastercard debit (the credit card number given, expiration date, and security code on back of card). Is it possible for you to run the card through manually?*
>
> *Sincerely,*
> *Adam Yoder*

Rosa had reached out to the same e-mail address two days before, at 6:16 p.m.

> *Hi, Adam:*
> *To start the process of your order we will need to get full payment. If you have any questions . . . please call us.*

She provided a direct phone number for the customer to call.

In her late thirties, Rosa had worked at Copper Harbor Company/ArtChemicals for a little less than a year. One of her jobs was to process orders. When an order came in, Rosa made sure the correct paperwork was in place; the item(s) in stock; and, important to completing the order, each item was completely paid for before she could finish processing it to ship.

Two days before the e-mail, on January 5, 2015, at 2:21 p.m., someone using the Mr. Adam Yoder 1990 Gmail account, signing in with the Adamisgay password, ordered one gram of colchicine. It was enough to poison dozens of people to death. The amount of colchicine it takes to kill one person is akin to about several dozen *individual* grains of sugar or sand—that is, granules about the same size as the sugar substitute Truvia.

The cost of that order was $120.98. With shipping, the total came to $136. ArtChemicals did not supply colchicine; orders for the toxin went to an outside vendor, Spectrum, which purchased the toxin and sold it to ArtChemicals, which then sold it to their customer. ArtChemicals company slogan is: "Chemistry for the imagination."

The company placing this particular order of colchicine, beyond the e-mail signed Adam Yoder, was Chiro Family Care. The address was 312 Oriskany Boulevard, Whitesboro, New York.

Same address as Chiropractic Family Care.

When Rosa checked the pricing from the vendor, she realized the price had gone up since the last time she'd checked (and communicated with "Adam Yoder"). The price was no longer what had been quoted in the original e-mail sent to Mr. Adam Yoder 1990 at Gmail. So Rosa called the phone number provided by "Adam Yoder" in that e-mail.

No answer. It seemed to Rosa she had been given the wrong number. So Rosa googled the business: "Chiro Family Care."

A different phone number came up, however, but the number was connected to the same address given in the e-mailed order from "Adam Yoder." *Must have been a typo? Or a shorter version of the company name?* Rosa thought.

Since the company names were so similar, Rosa never considered that they were different companies. And both, to confirm, had the same address.

Rosa called the new number.

A female answered. She didn't give her name.

Rosa introduced herself. Explained the situation and how the price had gone up on a recent colchicine order made from Chiro Family Care. The female Rosa connected with knew exactly what Rosa was talking about.

"No problem," the female voice said, referring to the price increase.

"I cannot process your order until it's paid in full," Rosa explained. "I'll have to generate another order for the larger amount."

"That's fine," the female said.

Rosa later described the person she spoke to as having "a female voice, soft, sweet, young."

The new price was $174.20. With shipping, the total came to $189.22. Rosa told the woman she could use PayPal. Or, while they were on the phone, she could take down any credit card information right then. Rosa would do whatever was easier.

The female said she'd make the payment online.

They said good-bye and hung up.

On that same afternoon, an e-mail from Mr. Adam Yoder 1990 Gmail was sent to ArtChemicals explaining how the customer— "Adam Yoder"—was having difficulty with the credit card payment (that new amount) online.

They eventually figured out the computer glitch. The customer would need to purchase a second prepaid card, this one in the amount of $200, to cover the new price (a second invoice generated, making the original invalid).

On January 5, 2015, at 6:32 p.m., that new prepaid Visa card used to complete this new transaction with the latest pricing was purchased at Hannaford. The new card ended in the number 0072.

Two days later, an e-mail from the Mr. Adam Yoder 1990 Gmail account was sent to Rosa. It explained how the person making the order was experiencing more difficulty completing it. Even with the new price and a new Visa card covering the entire invoice, there was still an issue.

Rosa shot back an e-mail response:

Hi, Adam,
I need a letter of intent and a copy of your business license—it's a
requirement.

ArtChemicals could not sell a toxic, regulated chemical, such as colchicine, without proof that the business was approved to purchase the toxin. Additionally, they required a letter (of intent) explaining what the chemical was going to be used for. Because it was highly lethal, sellers had to cover themselves. Handing out colchicine to just anybody was not only illegal but deadly.

When Rosa went to place the order from ArtChemicals with Spectrum, she ran into both issues. The letter of intent needed to be on letterhead from the company placing the order, and the business license number needed to be included so that Spectrum and ArtChemicals could verify the business existed.

On January 8, 2015, the prepaid Visa card ending in 0072 was processed as payment for the colchicine by a business called Copper Harbor Co., Inc./ArtChemicals.

The colchicine order was now paid in full.

Rosa reached out to Mr. Adam Yoder 1990 again, requesting the letter of intent and license number in order to be able to process and ship the colchicine. Rosa explained she needed the information faxed to her at once in order to be able to ship the toxin. On Monday, January 12, 2015, the following correspondence was sent at 9:05 a.m.:

Hello, Rosa,
I am sorry for the delay. Our fax machine is being serviced. The
business tax identification number is (provided). The NYS license is
(provided).

The Letter of Intent
Colchicine is used for encouraging polyhaploidism in plants. That
haploid induction is useful for creating genetically-stable inbred
plants and allows a faster turnover rate for research of specific gene ex-
pressions.

Because colchicine is so potent and we are a small, private operation, we do not need to order large amounts nor do we need to order often.

Please note: this phytochemical and/or its byproducts are not tested on humans or animals. We do not do resale. We do not intend for any research or development to be used therapeutically or diagnostically.

Rosa responded two hours later. She explained that ArtChemicals needed a signature to proceed. In addition, the letter of intent could not be pasted inside the body of an e-mail. It needed to be on company letterhead, and, as she'd explained once already, signed by a physician and faxed separately.

Two days later, the letter arrived at ArtChemicals on Chiro Family Care letterhead with Dr. William Yoder and Dr. Mary Yoder's names at the top of the letter next to the company logo, which was identical to the Chiropractic Family Care logo. A note at the top indicated that the fax was "intended for ArtChemicals (Attn: Rosa) and if the receiver obtained the fax in error, destroy this copy and contact office above . . ."

The letter faxed to Rosa included two signatures: Adam Yoder, Accounts Receivable Manager, with the Mr. Adam Yoder 1990 Gmail next to the name; and then Dr. Mary Yoder. The tax ID and business ID were included, along with a W-9 for the business, Chiro Family Care. Mary's signature was dated January 14, 2014. The business ID and W-9 numbers were identical to Chiropractic Family Care.

From ArtChemicals' end, it appeared Mary Yoder had signed off on ordering the colchicine. It was now ready to be shipped to Chiro Family Care.

Mary Yoder had, purportedly, signed for a toxin that would soon be used to kill her.

42

MARY YODER'S DEATH INVESTIGATION was not a complicated mass of erroneous facts and confusing details. It was not burdened by dead ends or rabbit holes. Once a competent investigator dug in and looked closely into how Mary died, paying close attention to the digital paper trail, answers presented themselves.

Detective Mark VanNamee was not even supposed to be involved. A colleague and good friend who sat near VanNamee in the squad room should have taken the call from Sharon Mills. But that investigator's shift ended at 4:30 p.m., so when Sharon's call came in at about four-fifteen, VanNamee and his colleague looked at each other. With a competitive, friendly sigh, VanNamee agreed to take the call.

"Sometimes a call comes in and you're on the phone for ten seconds," VanNamee recalled. "Other times, it's an hour. Sometimes you take the call, sometimes your colleague does."

Lieutenant Nelson was locked on one key element of the case: How did someone get hold of the colchicine, if Mary had not been poisoned accidentally? Colchicine is a prescription medication. It's carefully and closely managed, the OCSO learned. It is a controlled substance.

"We knew that colchicine could come from the autumn crocus flower," VanNamee said. That plant, with its beautiful and intoxicating purple-and-white six-petaled flowers, produced the toxin. "So you have to be *certain* it's not an accidental death."

Just as VanNamee started working the case, the ME and OCSO received a letter that changed everything. In late November 2015, someone was injecting himself/herself into the investigation, pointing the OCSO directly to Mary Yoder's killer.

"That changed everything," VanNamee said later.

The anonymous letter began by encouraging investigators looking into Mary Yoder's death to forward the letter to any acting investigators working on the case. The second paragraph said all there was to say about its intent:

> If the toxin found in her was colchicine, Adam Yoder, her son, is responsible. He told me he did it and moreover he told me how and where he put the rest of the toxin.

The next paragraph explained that the writer thought it was "odd" that Adam had driven back from Long Island on the day of Mary's death, arriving in town at 6:30 a.m.

> [It was] weird he'd drive down to Long Island and then go back North in the middle of the night, especially since he'd been so standoffish and mean to [Mary]. [Adam] functioned better by not seeing or talking to her . . . He felt she was unfair and he resented her, she should have helped him more.

The writer had seen Adam "a few days" before sending the letter and he had appeared "agitated and said he was the reason for her death." Adam wished he "could take it back."

The letter then outlined how Adam ordered the toxin online and put it in one of his mother's "vitamins when he was over" at his parents' house.

Several paragraphs laid out a case for why Adam Yoder was his mother's killer. He wanted more attention from Mary and felt he deserved it. He was visibly irritated that people "kept talking about his mom." He expected to be rewarded financially after her death, but had not been. When he realized he was not going to receive any money, he "regretted" what he had done and "became hysterical."

According to the letter, Adam told the writer that the bottle of colchicine was under the front passenger seat of his Jeep. He was going to keep it there until he figured out where to dispose of its leftover content. The writer described it as a "small glass bottle."

The person wished to remain anonymous out of fear. Being so close to Adam, the writer felt he was "capable of repeating this type of act."

Ending the letter, the writer related facts regarding the timeline of Mary's illness and how long she had been sick before passing away, before listing several of her symptoms. The writer once again drove home the financial implications:

Adam's monetary concerns are suspect because he is struggling financially and supported somewhat by his parents' assistance.

The letter concluded by pointing out that colchicine is a "very specific name" and the toxin that was "found in Mary Yoder was not released."

VanNamee finished reading the letter and put it down on his desk. He sat back, took a deep breath, and stared at his computer. It was time to call Adam and ask him to come into the OCSO for an interview.

43

A PERSON OF INTEREST, contrary to how derogatory the law enforcement phrase has become in the world of true crime, is a rather unassuming, precise euphemism for a witness and/or suspect. Internally, it is used by investigators to describe a person closely linked to the victim, or someone who may be connected closely to the victim by work, an intimate relationship, family, friend, spouse, and so on. "Person of interest" (POI) doesn't necessarily mean the individual is suspected of a crime. It may at some point, but in the initial stages of any death/murder investigation, POI could just as well mean "person we need to speak to."

As VanNamee later explained, Bill Yoder would be classified as a POI because he was married to the victim. After that anonymous letter arrived, however, the main person that the OCSO needed to speak to was Bill and Mary's son, Adam.

The anonymous letter pointed directly to Adam as his mother's killer, forcing the case into a new direction. After the letter arrived, VanNamee made a few calls. He decided to have Adam come into the OCSO for questioning. Before that, the detective requested a subpoena from the judge for E-ZPass records related to Mary, Bill, and Adam near the time of Mary's death.

E-ZPass is a white plastic apparatus about the size and shape of a deck of cards stuck to a vehicle's windshield near the rearview mirror, allowing subscribers to drive through toll lanes and across bridges without having to stop and pay. Yet, for an investigator, it can be akin to a GPS tracking device. With a look at those records, VanNamee could subpoena CCTV video from the toll booths/bridges that his witnesses used, in order to see if anything stood out. Additionally, the videos/records would provide insight into the comings and goings of POIs and their vehicles, not to mention dates and times.

VanNamee was now specifically interested in Adam Yoder's 1991 Jeep Wrangler, which the letter writer described in detail. As Van-Namee waited on the calling end of a ringing phone, he wrote down Katie's name as someone he needed to also speak with. As a POI herself, she had been with Mary, working, on the day Mary became ill. She had also dated Adam, VanNamee found out, on and off for years. By far, the main reason for talking to Katie was for the OCSO to gather intel into Adam Yoder's life.

"Hello?"

"Adam Yoder?" VanNamee said.

"Yes?"

"Investigator Mark VanNamee, Oneida County Sheriff's Office investigator. Do you have a minute to talk?"

"Of course. Sure. What can I do for you?"

"We're investigating your mother's death and we're hoping you could come in and speak with us."

"Absolutely," Adam said.

After hanging up, VanNamee thought about the call. Adam was eager and responsive. He was not unfriendly or alarmed by the call at all. What's more, he agreed to come into the OCSO—without delay.

The investigation into Mary's death was driven by leads. Currently VanNamee didn't have a manner of death signed off by the medical examiner. Was it homicide? Accidental? Suicide? Any of those could be a possibility. Experienced detectives like Van-Namee, who have seen nearly everything, focus on leads and data. Each piece—however significant—dictates where the investigation goes next, along with the folks that investigators speak to. There's no endgame in mind; it is a delicate, open-ended process. A good cop needs to be mindful and accepting of wherever the evidence leads.

The time frame surrounding when Mary ingested the colchicine was crucial. According to the US National Library of Medicine, National Institutes of Health (USNLMNIH), colchicine poisoning is difficult to detect by patient examination alone, if the examiners don't know what they are looking for. Regarding how long it takes for death to occur after a lethal dose is ingested, the available data are a bit vague.

There are three sequential, and usually overlapping, phases in colchicine poisoning: 1) Ten to twenty-four hours after ingestion, it presents as a "gastrointestinal phase mimicking gastroenteritis"; 2) Twenty-four hours to a week after ingestion, it includes "multi-organ dysfunction."

"Death results from rapidly progressive multi-organ failure and sepsis," the USNLMNIH research continues. "Delayed presentation, pre-existing renal or liver impairment are associated with poor prognosis."

The third phase explains how a patient can bounce back after being poisoned: Within a few weeks of ingestion, there is generally "a complete recovery barring complications of the acute illness."

A high fatality rate in this same study was reported "after acute ingestions exceeding 0.5 milligrams." The conclusion researchers came to, in what was a forty-four-year review, between 1966 and 2010, was how imperative it was "to recognize its features as it is associated with a high mortality rate when missed."[4]

Lack of knowledge (no fault of the doctors) and lack of proper treatment, based on not having enough research available, were contributing factors to Mary's death. Though it was clear by then that with the amount of colchicine she had ingested, Mary Yoder was dead on arrival. However, it was only through the work of a skilled, observant, and attentive medical examiner's office and Poison Control Center doctor that Mary's cause of death was even discovered.

4. https://www.ncbi.nlm.nih.gov/pubmed/20586571.

44

*B*Y JANUARY 15, 2015, the colchicine had not been delivered to Chiro/Chiropractic Family Care. So Mr. Adam Yoder 1990 Gmail sent out a terse note: "Is the order all set?"

Rosa answered an hour later that the order was all set and would ship shortly. She said she'd e-mail a tracking number.

Katie and Adam started communicating fairly regularly during this time. Their texts were amiable, but marked with a consistent sarcasm from Adam.

"Tea?" Katie texted on January 17, at 1:01 p.m.

"Why?" Adam asked. He was now guarded and suspicious where Katie's friendly gestures were concerned.

"Because. You're my friend. I like to hear you talk and have some tea and learn about games and math. Once a week or every other." Katie said it made her feel better. She was able "to breathe and relax and think and talk."

"I'm a friend with a complex [past] and relationship."

"Yeah. That's fine. It happens."

"You have other friends you can game with now," Adam said. "Which is also fine and happens."

They left it there.

On January 28, 2015, Rosa Vargas sent a tracking number and link to trace the shipment of colchicine to "Adam Yoder." The toxin was on its way to Chiro/Chiropractic Family Care.

Into early February 2015, Adam was feeling the past creep up on his emotions. He'd gone back inside his head to reanalyze the relationship. He was unable to let go of her sleeping with his friend. He couldn't get beyond it. She'd betrayed him in the most hurtful, spiteful way. On February 2, Adam texted how much it still hurt to even think about that betrayal.

"Do you regret it, Katie?" he asked, before adding, "I've always been the type of person that wants to know the truth no matter how much it hurts."

Katie's response didn't address the topic. She answered that Adam was "a constant in my life—you were everything. I don't think you know how much you meant and you're still important."

"You chose [my friend] and I'll never understand why. I'm not going to get angry or yell. I'm just asking."

Katie shot back a text suggesting the word "chose" had stirred something within her. She'd *chosen* Adam. "I loved you every day. I watched you fall apart and I was helpless . . . I'm sorry."

"That's *not* what I asked you."

"I think about it. I think about you. If life would've gone differently. I already know my regrets." She paused briefly. Then: "Where we would be?" She concluded her thought with four additional texts, all of which explained how Adam could call anytime and she would be there for him. "If you feel alone."

"I won't. Thanks. I asked you *one* question. That's all I needed . . . However, if you need me, I'm still here, just as I've always been."

"Thank you, Adam."

Later, near 8:00 p.m., Katie sent Adam a text saying she felt depressed. She was thinking about the relationship, their earlier conversation, and how great they had been together at times.

"Minus the days you were too busy fucking [my friend], of course," Adam replied. "I do not want to hear it."

"I told you I'd love you . . . Just know I love you, okay? You're loved and fine and okay."

Adam sensed a different motive for the text. Maybe Katie was going to harm herself? She'd done this before: texted feelings of despair and threats of self-harm before going silent. It was pure manipulation. She knew which of Adam's buttons to push and, more important, when. Hinting she might commit suicide would un-questionably produce a reaction from him.

"Katie. Please don't do this. Please don't disappear and scare me. Please. Katie?"

She did not respond.

"Please. If you love me, then don't do this to me again. You hurting yourself will not make me feel better. I don't know if that's what's going on, but please keep talking to me. Can you tell me you'll be okay?"

Katie replied with a request: "You want to just relax and take it easy tonight? Maybe just read or watch neat videos . . ."

Katie texted a few more times. She was unable to ensnare Adam, as she had in the past. It was clear to her that Adam had definitely changed. He was no longer a piece of clay she could shape with manipulation.

45

CLINICAL TOXICOLOGIST JEANNA MARRAFFA had been employed with Upstate Medical University, Upstate New York Poison Center, since 2001. She had worked her way up to assistant director. Marraffa specialized in pharmacology. She'd earned a doctorate before going into clinical toxicology, with her focus on poisons.

After viewing slides from Mary's autopsy, knowing all the tests for poisons had come back negative, Dr. Marraffa made the recommendation that changed the entire course of the OCSO's investigation. Speaking to Dr. Clark and the ME's office, Marraffa realized there was a colchicine level in Mary's system.

What tipped it off for Marraffa was the "chemotherapy evidence on autopsy." Mary had not been taking chemotherapy treatment. Yet, all the symptoms of poisoning were clear, Marraffa realized. It was only a matter of figuring out which poison had killed her.

Colchicine poisoning works in a rather simple manner, Marraffa explained—specifically, if you *know* what you're actually looking for. Cells in the body have a natural process of replication within the DNA. Too much colchicine cuts into that biological process (evolution) and interferes with the body's normal process of functioning and rebuilding. Colchicine stops white blood cells causing inflammation from getting to the areas in the body those cells need to—the reason doctors prescribe the toxin for gout. As much as it can help gout sufferers, however, there's a danger zone when taking colchicine as a treatment. It's one of those tricky medications, with a narrow therapeutic index, a short range between effectiveness and toxicity.

Another major symptom of colchicine poisoning is cardiac toxin, leading to unexplained cardiac arrest—i.e., a colchicine overdose.

Like in Mary's case.

Dr. Marraffa's findings were vital within the OCSO's investigation. Looking at the reports Dr. Marraffa had filed, it was clear to VanNamee that Mary had actually rebounded after a period in the ER. She was feeling better. Talking. Asking for things. Getting up. Walking. Then, the following morning, after a fall the previous night, Mary's condition radically declined.

This led to a new question: Had Mary's killer been able to feed her more colchicine while she was at the hospital? It was something to look into. But also, considering someone was accusing Adam Yoder of poisoning his mother, what happened on the day Mary became so violently ill and then died a day later?

VanNamee needed to construct a timeline of the events and see what, if anything, stood out.

46

*J*ULY 20, 2015, WAS a scorcher; the temperature at midnight was 81 degrees. When Mary Yoder left for work that morning, it was a balmy 91 degrees. Humidity was low at 53 percent. The sky was robin's-egg blue all day long, not a cloud anywhere. By Mary Yoder's tastes, this was a perfect summer day.

As the morning progressed, Mary was "her normal self." One of her longtime patients remembered going in for a 10:00 a.m. appointment. Katie checked the woman in, said good morning, and asked her to have seat.

For the past three years, since Katie had started working at Chiropractic Family Care, patients described her demeanor around the office in two ways: one, courteous, helpful, pleasant, quiet, and accommodating. Katie generally kept her hair pulled back in a ponytail and presented herself professionally and respectfully. On the other hand, others reported Katie being "set back" at times. Her personality occasionally stiff. Not cold or unwelcoming, but rather quiet and snobbish, as if she had much more going on behind her stoic manner than she was willing to share.

"Dr. Mary will see you now," Katie told Mary's 10:00 a.m. patient.

Mary did not let her patients wait. Your appointment was at ten, you checked in, and, within a few moments, Mary had you on the table. Generally, Mary worked on three patients at a time in the same room. This particular patient, Mary's first on that day, later explained how Mary worked on one patient, and while that patient recuperated, she'd move on to the next, alternating until they were done.

Every one of Mary's pre-lunchtime patients on July 20, 2015, reported her to be her usual jovial self. She never left the room while administering treatment—and did not appear to be at all feeling under the weather. Mary was talkative, kind, and concerned about the health of each patient she saw. She maintained a perfect balance of socialization and treatment.

Mary's last patient of the morning later said: "She seemed fine. The way she always was. She was pretty upbeat and talking about her upcoming vacation . . . and was excited about that. I didn't notice anything different."

After Mary finished her last patient of the morning, she did a bit of paperwork, then went to speak with Katie.

"I'm taking off to see my mother for lunch."

"Okay, Dr. Mary, enjoy your visit."

47

ADAM YODER DID NOT look good. On most days, Adam had a studious, maybe even a bit hipster, look about him. A handsome guy, with light red hair, he had a three-inch-wide swath down the middle of his head (paintbrush-long and straight, combed back), the sides of his head shaved tight to the scalp. Mary and Bill Yoder's only son sometimes wore trendy, owlish spectacles. Adam was in excellent physical shape, lean and cut, a runner's body—though he did not run on a routine basis. He dressed trendy, *GQ*-ish.

By December 2015, however, with his mother's unexpected passing, his family distraught, Adam's life had spiraled once more. Additionally, the OCSO wanted to speak with him about his mother's death.

"The husband is number one suspect in this type of investigation, not the son," VanNamee pointed out later. "That was our focus at this stage. You have to rule out the spouse."

Commonsense policework. Victimology. The A-to-Z process of excluding those closest to the victim.

If Bill Yoder was responsible, VanNamee thought, the guy was brazen and cold—on top of being stupid.

"Because what type of man would kill his wife and then send us a letter stating that his own son was responsible?"

The anonymous letters changed everything for the OCSO. VanNamee needed to take a look into Adam's life: "Is he the type of person who could have killed his own mother?"

The detective started with the family member farthest away from the situation: Liana. She was all the way down on Long Island, but she was a potentially good source—outside of the day-to-day activities—for a look into the family dynamic. So VanNamee called Mary Yoder's oldest child.

Liana explained that her husband was the head anesthesiologist at a local hospital. She had four kids. A doctor herself, she was temporarily not practicing and staying at home taking care of them.

"I'd like to sit down and meet with you," VanNamee offered.

"Well, with four kids," Liana explained, "I'd have to make arrangements. Can I get up there within a week?"

"If that's the best we can do, well, okay."

They hung up.

Minutes later, Liana called back: "I can be there tomorrow morning."

It wasn't until Liana met with VanNamee and broke down the Yoder family and business paradigm that Katie Conley became part of the investigation. Before then, the OCSO had her name on a list of people they needed to speak to. But she was considered a peripheral source, someone they would get to at some point.

After meeting with Liana, VanNamee drove to Cooperstown and interviewed Tammy. He learned that Tammy hadn't been in contact much with the family. She was concerned, of course. Upset. Mourning and wanting answers, like everyone else. But she couldn't offer much with regard to Adam, Katie, Liana, Bill, and Mary, or any day-to-day interactions.

"She was out of the loop," VanNamee recalled.

Since speaking to Liana and Tammy, based on the anonymous letter, Detective VanNamee applied for a search warrant on Adam's vehicle. If they were going to talk to him, they needed to search his vehicle.

The court turned the OCSO down.

"Anonymous information, the courts here in New York have unanimously determined, is inherently false," VanNamee explained. "They require additional information to obtain warrants, besides the anonymous source."

It was during a morning briefing about the case that VanNamee and colleagues had decided to make that call to Adam and offer him the opportunity to come in, same as his sisters.

"Three things made us do this. (A) We could not get a search warrant. (B) If the letter is inaccurate, Adam is going to come in willingly. And (C) If the murder weapon was inside his vehicle, he certainly wasn't going to willingly drive it to the sheriff's office and allow us to search his vehicle."

It was December 8 when VanNamee made the call to Adam and asked Mary's son if he could come into the OCSO.

THE MORE HE CONSIDERED the call, the less fearful Adam became about helping. The OCSO was looking into his mother's death. The family wanted this. Anything he could do to move the needle toward a resolution, Adam was all in.

"I had nothing to hide," Adam said.

As he drove to the sheriff's office, however, Adam felt a tickle of trepidation. *Why couldn't they discuss what they wanted over the phone? Why couldn't VanNamee come out to see me?*

On December 8, early afternoon, not an hour after VanNamee and Adam spoke on the phone, Adam arrived at the OCSO.

"That said a lot," VanNamee recalled. "The time it took him to come in."

The detective was interested in which vehicle Adam would show up driving: His Jeep Wrangler? Or would he borrow a car?

VanNamee's first impression of Adam was "that he came across a little odd. He felt socially awkward."

Still, in talking to Liana, VanNamee had learned one important fact—which became a key to the letter and Adam's potential involvement. "Adam was on Long Island when Mary became ill. And we proved how long and when he was there with the subpoenaed E-ZPass records."

If Adam had poisoned his mother, he would've had to devise an elaborate, time-release plan. He was six hours away from his mother when she ingested the toxin. Adam could not have personally given it to her in real time. Or timed it so perfectly for her to ingest while he was away.

"It just didn't seem possible."

Sitting, Adam explained how his mother coded all afternoon on that July day. Then she died. But it wasn't until September when the family learned her death was attributed to "a poison [called] colchicine, which is typically used to treat gout. I learned later that my mother never had gout. I never heard of this substance before."

"Okay," VanNamee said. "Can you tell us where you were, what you did, near the time your mother died?"

"I was on Long Island. I didn't have a job. I was there about a week. I came back soon as I heard she was sick."

VanNamee immediately thought back to the anonymous letter: *The person writing that letter had no idea Adam was gone that long.*

"I actually brought almond milk that my mom used to make her protein shakes out to the medical examiner's office in Syracuse. I don't think I brought anything else out there at the time."

"Where did you get the almond milk?"

"From my parents' business on Oriskany Boulevard in Whitesboro."

VanNamee asked Adam to go over the time period near and around Mary's death and recall what happened in the days, weeks, and months afterward.

Adam mentioned Long Island again. Taking care of Liana's kids. Being at her house for a birthday party. He was on Long Island when he heard his mother was in the hospital and fighting for her life. He rushed back home to be with her after receiving a call from his father.

"When did you get back into town, Adam?"

"I arrived at the hospital near six a.m. on July 22, 2015. I drove through the night."

"What happened next?"

"My father told me my mother was on life support."

VanNamee informed Adam that based on new information the OCSO had obtained, they believed someone was trying to frame him for his mother's death.

"What?" he said. "What do you mean?"

Adam came across as shocked by this revelation. He wanted to know how the OCSO could draw such a conclusion.

Investigator VanNamee mentioned the anonymous letter.

"Can I see it?" Adam asked.

VanNamee left the room. He sat with his lieutenant. They decided to show Adam a section of the letter where his name was mentioned. The letter contained certain information that the OCSO did not want Adam to know or put out into the public domain.

"I can show you portions of it, but not the entire letter."

"Okay," Adam said.

VanNamee showed Adam a section of the anonymous letter detailing how the OCSO would find colchicine inside his Jeep.

"What? How can this possibly be happening?"

Then VanNamee showed Adam where, specifically, his name was written in the letter.

"He turned pale white," VanNamee said later.

"I was scared and angry that someone was doing this to me," Adam commented.

Adam immediately handed over his iPhone and showed the OCSO text messages between him and his father, as well as additional text messages. He told VanNamee he was an open book.

"Can we search your Jeep, Adam?"

Adam thought about it. Someone was framing him. Things had gone from a conversation about his whereabouts and a timeline of events to someone accusing him of killing his mother.

"I'd like to consult with an attorney before I allow that."

VanNamee understood.

"I had just discovered . . . that someone was intentionally trying to frame me," Adam explained later. "I'm scared. I've never been in [this] situation before—never been interrogated by the police. So it seemed like the smartest thing for me to do was to at least consult a lawyer before moving on."

VanNamee put Adam in touch with public defender Kurt Schultz before leaving the room.

"Do you have any knowledge of this being in your car?" Schultz asked Adam.

"No!" Adam said.

"Do you think it's in there?"

"No."

"Let them look. If you're not involved in this, let them do it."

After speaking with Schultz, an attorney with the Oneida County Public Defender's Office, Adam told VanNamee it was "in the best interest of the investigation" that he allow the OCSO to search his Jeep.

Adam took them outside.

After snapping on a pair blue latex gloves, one of the OCSO's forensic investigators pulled out a bottle of colchicine from underneath the front-passenger seat. It was wrapped in cardboard packaging. A receipt from where the toxin had been purchased online was alongside it.

Adam stepped to the side as they searched. He lit a cigarette. When they pulled out the bottle of colchicine, he stood stunned, the cigarette dangling from his lips, his eyes bulging.

"I've never seen that before," he said. "It was certainly put there by someone else."

48

O<small>N</small> F<small>EBRUARY</small> 6, 2015, the bottle of colchicine supposedly ordered by Adam Yoder was delivered to Chiropractic Family Care. Like most packages delivered to the office, Katie Conley signed for it.

In the *Notes* app on Katie's iPhone, eleven days later, a note was created at 4:27 p.m. "Here for this" was the title. "Grow light? Light for chickens? DAAD scholarship??? Arnica gel. Milk cartons*** Breather***.5=/kg LD est. .9kg 180lb-81.6 kg. Security. Ugly red computer. Personal phrase-cheese."

What did this mean?

Taking the "180lb" notation alone and pairing it to the fact it was translated down into 81.6 kg, with .9kg before it, it seemed as if the author of the note was trying to calculate the exact amount of colchicine needed to kill a 180-pound person. All of the other writing was perhaps subterfuge, words and phrases shielding the true purpose of the note.

W<small>HEN</small> A<small>DAM</small> <small>PULLED</small> <small>THROUGH</small> that sudden stomach illness in April 2015, he thought about the possibility of Katie putting something in the Alpha BRAIN supplement pills she'd given him. He began to consider how odd it was she kept pushing him to take the supplement and how adamant she was about it once helping her studies. Stewing about this, however, Adam concluded Katie could never have taken things that far.

In May, just before Mother's Day, Mary Yoder grew increasingly concerned about her son. She was texting Adam regularly. Asking him what was going on. "How are you? Is there anything I can do to help you?" Mary had always been there for Adam. Helping him out of personal and financial jams. Giving sage, motherly advice.

Adam told his mother he was admittedly dealing with the stressors of life in an unhealthy manner. But he would get through it. Same as he had managed most other times.

"[My parents] could tell visibly I was off. I was struggling with some of my own things, so I preferred not to really talk about it . . ."

This caused a divide between Adam and his parents, especially Mary, who encouraged Adam to open up and talk through his problems, whatever they were.

Although they argued a bit, and had a disagreement on Mother's Day, Adam made it over to the house and had a pleasant dinner with his parents. Mary had spoken her piece about Adam's "issues" and they left it there.

When June came, Adam was more determined than ever regarding not engaging in any type of intimate relationship with Katie. They could remain friends, whatever that turned out to be. But any chance of rekindling a romance was now gone forever. With their relationship completely severed, Katie realized she had only one way to keep the channels open and remain in contact with Adam.

The loan.

According to Katie, Adam had not made an effort to pay her back. She routinely contacted him and asked what he was going to do about it.

"You have to pay me," became a common text Adam started to receive from Katie, once he made it clear the relationship was over. She'd conclude by adding the number: $22,000.

"Can we meet and discuss?" Adam texted near the end of June. They agreed to meet at a local pizza restaurant outside Utica.

Adam claimed the agreement he had with Katie was for him to begin paying her back after he got out of school and started working. The deal included Adam taking a percentage from each paycheck and depositing it into an account she'd set up. They agreed on a fair interest rate.

"That's what we talked about, Katie," Adam said, reiterating.

Katie looked at him—and broke down crying.

"I'm afraid," she said. "I'm just afraid that you will leave and I will never see you again."

Katie was still stuck on the idea of reconciliation. She could not let go.

"That's *not* what I'm trying to do, Katie. I just need to finish my degree so I can start working and pay you back this loan." Then he made himself clear: "We will never be together again in that way."

Katie cried.

"We can still continue to be friends," Adam promised.

Katie shed tears during the entire lunch. As Adam sat and listened, he could not believe she'd hijacked the meeting, setting it up under the pretense of the loan, before making it about their relationship.

Katie later stated any type of consensual sexual relationship with Adam, along with an intimate, personal relationship, ended in September 2013. They remained friends, she added, but it went no further. She wanted nothing more, she claimed.

This was patently false. They had reconciled several times after that date. A plethora of corroborating evidence supported this. In fact, Adam had difficulty keeping track of how many times or the dates.

As he thought about it later, from almost the moment he met Katie, she had shown signs of malignant narcissism and personality disorder. After they were introduced at Katie's high-school graduation party, Adam sent Katie a Facebook message. He was interested in her, he wrote. He wanted to get together.

Adam did not receive an immediate response. He'd believed all the flirting and talking they'd done at the party would turn into something. But after making his move on Facebook and getting no response, he moved on.

"After her graduation party, before starting college, I learned Katie had taken off for Germany," Adam said.

Weeks after receiving the Facebook message, Katie finally responded. "But she never addressed the things I had written to her in my original message," Adam recalled. "So I disregarded her message. She wasn't interested. This was clear to me."

Adam had met a young girl in the interim. He was twenty then.

She was sixteen. They had sex. "Shitty decision, obviously I regret it, but that is the truth, and that is what happened. I won't run from my mistakes. I was lonely, suffering from depression. I made the decision to do that. I am not happy about it. I have owned it."

Katie found out about the tryst. "And, strangely, she acted as though I had cheated on her," Adam said. "Like we were together the whole time. It was weird. She actually used this against me, brought it up often, during the course of our entire relationship.

"We were not anything. We were not together. I didn't even know her. I just broached the topic of getting together in my Facebook message and did not even get a response to it."

The way Adam later analyzed the relationship: "It was pretty much all downhill from the beginning—I just didn't see it."

KATIE WAS AN AVID traveler, having reportedly vacationed in Ireland, the Bahamas, Canada, "and across America in several cross-country road trips." She and her family were avid campers and liked to take vacations together.

A website dedicated to Katie advocated that those closest to her "can attest to [Katie's] kind, generous soul." They added that she'd always been "witty, supportive, friendly, and outgoing." A majority of people writing on the site agreed that Katie knew how "to make someone smile . . . [was] always willing to help others, as that is how she was raised."

After Adam became ill in April 2015, Katie kept texting, inquiring about his symptoms, what doctors were saying, and how he was feeling. She seemed genuinely concerned.

"Your doctor still thinks it's a regular bug?" she texted one afternoon. Adam wasn't giving her much information other than scant details. His texts were succinct. Impersonal.

"Can you tell my mom I have an appointment and I'm at the doctor's now," Adam responded, ignoring her question.

It was April 26, 2015. Three months before Mary was murdered. Weeks later, Katie continued pushing Adam to discuss how sick he had been and what illness doctors figured it had been. She would not let up about it. She wanted details. Was it a bug? Food poisoning?

Adam could not understand why she was so fixated on his illness and what had caused it. As he thought more about her odd fascination, however, partly in jest, he texted: "And so, what I'm saying is, if you poisoned me, I'm afraid we can no longer be friends."

Katie did not respond.

Adam then considered the date he became ill. Then texted: "And I had taken my second dose of Alpha BRAIN the night before."

No reply from Katie.

49

AFTER FINDING THE BOTTLE of colchicine in Adam's Jeep, along with the receipt from where it had been purchased, the OCSO investigators were positive someone was trying to frame Adam Yoder for the murder of his mother.

"And that's when we focused on Bill Yoder," VanNamee explained.

As they began to look into Bill's life, the first interesting lead became Bill's involvement with Kathleen Richmond, Mary's sister.

"We have to find out when the relationship started," VanNamee said during a morning briefing.

Lieutenant Nelson agreed.

The timing of the relationship was vital. If evidence existed that the romance started before Mary's death, VanNamee surmised, "There's your motivation for Bill to kill his wife." And if the guy had enough bravado to kill his wife, the possibility existed for him to take things a step further and frame his son for the crime.

The OCSO also took interest in the fact that Adam had become very ill back in April. "The same symptoms my mother later experienced," Adam had explained to VanNamee.

Mary's son was certain his illness corresponded with taking an Alpha BRAIN supplement Katie Conley had given him and later pushed him to take. He wasn't suspicious of Katie; he was more or less just pointing out how odd it all seemed in hindsight.

"Might be just a coincidence," Adam suggested.

Might not be, VanNamee thought.

"Let's secure that bottle of supplements," VanNamee told forensics.

They also wanted Adam's laptop.

"All yours," Adam said.

The OCSO next set out to interview Mary's sisters, two of whom gave statements saying they had no idea who could have murdered their sister. It just didn't make any sense. Mary had no enemies. Everybody loved her.

"So then we come across the information that Bill is now seeing Mary's oldest sister, Kathleen," VanNamee said. "And we followed that thread. How could we not?"

After securing the bottle of Alpha BRAIN, VanNamee and his team discovered something. Adam was firm: "I took two pills, the second one made me ill."

The bottle they confiscated was thirty tablets. After counting, they came up with twenty-nine.

"If Adam took two, that's twenty-eight," VanNamee told Nelson.

"Right."

"So there were thirty-one pills in the bottle?"

They looked at each other.

ON DECEMBER 18, VANNAMEE called Katie. He explained that the OCSO was preparing to conduct an interview with Bill Yoder and needed her help. Katie had knowledge of the inner workings of the office. She was also there on the day Mary became ill. She personally knew Mary and Bill, along with Bill's comings and goings within the day-to-day structure of the office setting. Had Bill been at the office, at any time, on the day Mary became sick? Had Bill (or Adam) received that package Katie had signed for from ArtChemicals, or stopped by the office to pick it up? Had Bill and Mary been talking by phone on the day she became ill? Were they the type of couple that argued? Was there a secret, or a rift, between them Katie might have known about?

By now, the OCSO knew the colchicine had been shipped to the office. They also knew from where it had been ordered.

Bill could have easily placed the order—and made it appear as though Adam had done it from Katie's workstation computer. He could have stopped by the office to pick up the package.

"How are products ordered?" VanNamee asked Katie.

Katie explained the procedure.

VanNamee had asked Adam about the e-mail account used to order the toxin. To which, Adam had said: "That e-mail address looks like two of my personal e-mail accounts combined together." Adam said he'd never set it up. Had no idea it even existed until VanNamee had brought it up.

"Have you ever seen a Gmail e-mail account used by Adam Yoder?" VanNamee asked Katie.

"No," Katie said. "I know he has a college account. He also has a 'Mr. Adam Yoder' account, but there is no '1990' at the end."

VanNamee spoke to Katie for several hours on December 18 and 19 at the OCSO. She came across as honest, positive, and eager to answer questions.

"She struck us as . . . innocent. She was extremely helpful."

Those first interviews with Katie, Bill, Adam, and others closely connected to Mary were about gathering information. At one point, while speaking with Katie, VanNamee put a blank sheet of paper on the table in front of her and asked if she might sketch out a floor plan of the office. After she did that, he asked which sections of the office she spent most of her day in. Where Mary spent her time. When Bill and/or Adam came in, where did they go, what did they actually do?

After a few additional inconsequential questions, VanNamee cut Katie loose.

"We'll be in touch."

"Sure, glad I could help."

Bill was next. VanNamee called him.

"We'd like to speak with you when you have a moment—preferably as soon as possible."

Bill drove to the OCSO immediately, without delay or asking why. He wound up inside the stationhouse for eight hours. He provided answers to every question asked, turned over all of his computers, iPhone, and iPad without hesitation.

"Anything I can do to help you," Bill said.

"We appreciate that, Mr. Yoder. We understand this is a difficult time."

"They came after me," Bill said later. "I felt like a suspect for certain. I was more than willing to help any way possible. I had nothing to hide."

Now the OCSO had all incoming and outgoing text messages from Bill's iPhone, along with e-mails. All of which dated far beyond and after the date Mary had died.

"We learned immediately that all of the e-mails and text messages between Bill Yoder and Kathleen Richmond were still on Bill's devices and computers," VanNamee explained. "Meaning that he did not delete anything connecting him to Kathleen Richmond."

For investigators, that fact alone told them if you're trying to hide an affair/relationship—or at least when it started—you'd almost certainly delete texts and e-mails dating the start of it. If Bill had put together such an elaborate plan to kill his wife—ordering the toxin ten months in advance, writing and sending two anonymous letters—the deletion of e-mails and texts would not be something he would overlook.

"And we put it together via that electronic paper trail that Bill and Kathleen started communicating about ten days *after* Mary passed away," VanNamee said. "That was huge."

One of the most telling texts they'd discovered on Bill's iPhone was the first time he went to visit Kathleen days after the Celebration of Life. It was obvious from the texts Bill sent to Kathleen on that day that he had no idea where she lived. Bill texted Kathleen and asked her to stand on her porch and wave her arms so he could find her house. He knew the street, but not the exact house number or location.

To VanNamee, this type of behavior didn't sound like a man who had been carrying on with Mary's sister before Mary died.

"If that's *my* girlfriend," VanNamee observed, "I sure as hell know where her house is."

A few days after Bill Yoder was interviewed, during a morning briefing, VanNamee and the OCSO learned forensics had discovered female DNA underneath one of the stamps on the anonymous letter. As VanNamee heard this, he thought back to the initial interviews he'd conducted with Katie. It was something she'd said. The comment struck him.

"She had explained to us that she actually placed a stamp on each envelope going out of the office. They did not have premade envelopes, like most businesses."

The OCSO was still focused on Bill Yoder; they had not ruled him out. From their view, Bill could have planned the homicide and then seduced Kathleen. Or planned the entire wave-your-arms-so-I-know-which-house-you-live-in scenario to throw off investigators. Additionally, Bill and Kathleen could have planned the crime together. Within the scope of any homicide investigation, especially with a victim of Mary's reputation and standing, no possibility was overlooked or tossed out until it was excluded by corroborating evidence.

All that being said, their finding female DNA under the stamp of the anonymous letter somewhat changed the OCSO's focus. Only one female closely involved in the circle of witnesses was being questioned at the time.

"Why don't I call Katie again?" VanNamee put out during the next morning briefing.

"Do that," Nelson said.

"Bring her in, put a little pressure on her, and ask hard questions."

Nelson agreed.

The OCSO had applied for eighty subpoenas. They had computer forensics working day and night, looking for any possible link to any of their suspects. Information was now beginning to trickle in.

"Katie, hi, it's Detective Mark VanNamee with the OCSO. I was wondering if you'd mind coming up to the office and providing us with a DNA sample?" He explained further how they were looking for "elimination DNA." They needed to exclude everyone they could as a donor connected to DNA they'd recently discovered.

Katie hesitated.

"It would really help us out."

"Um, I guess," Katie said.

When she arrived, VanNamee noticed Katie had something in her hands.

"What's this?" the detective asked.

Katie had brought the envelopes and letterhead they used at the office.

"Thanks, Katie," VanNamee said. "Really appreciate this."

The OCSO had not asked Katie to do this. Katie was now offering information and evidence—a telltale sign, VanNamee knew from experience, indicating the person has something to hide.

"This is our letterhead and the type of envelope we use," Katie said, showing VanNamee. "I just wanted to show you."

"Thanks, Katie. This is a great help. Can I ask you something? When was the last time you saw Adam?"

"Oh, um, I guess it was September," Katie said. She talked about the day Adam had picked her up at school and they went to the office to collect any potential contaminated items of interest so Adam could bring them to the ME's office. Katie said the conversation became contentious between them as Adam grew angry and bossy while inside the office. It made her uncomfortable. He was stressed and yelled at her.

"So about three months ago?" VanNamee clarified.

"Yes."

That was about it for the moment, VanNamee said.

Katie turned to leave.

"We'll call you soon," VanNamee said. "Thanks again for bringing the envelopes and letterhead. Great help to us."

"Sure, no problem," Katie said. "My pleasure."

50

*T*HE LATEST COMPUTER FORENSICS came in. Investigators told VanNamee that one of the IP addresses logging on to the Mr. Adam Yoder 1990 Gmail account had been traced back to Katie Conley's home address. That was in October. If she hadn't seen Adam since September, meaning he had not been over to the Conley residence in October, how could he have logged into the account from that IP address?

On December 21, VanNamee called Katie again.

"You think you have a minute to stop in and sit down with me? Won't take long."

"Yes, sure. I can do that." Katie didn't sound thrilled.

Before she arrived, Nelson and VanNamee decided VanNamee would be more frank and accusatory. He would ask specific questions based on the new evidence the OCSO had received. Van-Namee was specifically interested in Katie's response to how Adam could have logged on to his Gmail account from Katie's house if she had not seen him since September.

Katie walked in, again without a lawyer. She was directed into an interrogation room. She wore a gray hoodie, large tortoiseshell glasses, and blue jeans. She sat with a bottle of water and a box of Kleenex in front of her, her hands on her lap. Katie stared at her hands and the wall after VanNamee sat her down and excused himself, leaving her alone. Bored and impatient, Katie picked at her fingernails. She looked frightened. Her body slumped over, shoulders drooped, upper body curled into itself.

VanNamee returned. He explained he was looking to get more into why Adam could have killed his mother.

A motive.

"You're free to leave anytime. I'm going to take a statement, but that's just for me . . ."

As VanNamee spoke, Katie acted strangely. She started to hyperventilate. Cry.

"I'm scared . . . I'm scared," she said.

VanNamee mentioned how, because he was going to be sharing evidence from what was an open case, policy dictated he read Katie the Miranda warning. "And you've probably seen this in the movies and on TV? Do you understand?"

"Yeah . . . yeah," she answered through tears and quick, repeated, short breaths, as if lifting weights.

"You're not in *any* trouble. I just need you to be honest with me, okay?"

After reading the Miranda warning, VanNamee asked Katie if she was willing to continue talking to the OCSO without an attorney present.

Katie hesitated.

VanNamee asked again.

"Yeah," Katie uttered, nodding her head, wiping tears from her eyes. By now, she had a tissue balled up in one hand, which she stared at occasionally.

VanNamee asked why she was so scared.

"Adam's really smart."

Within a few moments, Katie admitted to writing the anonymous letters.

VanNamee asked how she knew where to send the letters. He was curious why she didn't send a letter to the state police. Why choose the OCSO over the state police? How could she know the OCSO was looking into Mary's death?

After a long back-and-forth, Katie agreed she was "guessing" the case was within the OCSO's jurisdiction. The ME's office, they both agreed, was an obvious choice.

Katie explained how Adam had made an admission on the day they were at the office back in September. After freaking out inside the office, while driving her back up to school, he said he put the colchicine he'd used to kill his mother underneath the passenger seat of the Jeep. Katie said she realized she was essentially sitting on the murder weapon.

"Did you ask him to show it to you?"

"I didn't want to see it."

"Did he tell you how he got it?"

"Yeah."

VanNamee had a difficult time understanding and hearing Katie. She spoke softly, with a high-pitched voice. It was as though she was constantly on the verge of tears.

Beckoning her to speak up and continue, Katie said: "He said he . . . he . . . had it sent to the office."

Katie insisted, before recalibrating her answer to "pretty sure," she "saw him that day" when the package arrived from ArtChemicals. The allegation was that Adam had shown up at the office and was looking for a delivery in his name.

"[Did he] take the package?"

"Yeah, yeah," she said.

VanNamee pulled out a document and set it in front of Katie. He mentioned the Gmail account.

"You knew what the password is, correct?"

Katie nodded her head.

"What password did *you* use to close this account?"

"I don't remember exactly what it was . . ."

They discussed the password. Katie would not commit to an answer. So VanNamee asked: "You did log into it, correct?"

"I was hoping he didn't change the password."

"You logged into the account from your house, correct? I need you to be honest with me. I can't have you telling me I never logged into this account . . . and I get more of the IP addresses back and I realize you *have* logged into it. . . . If you want me to help you, I need you to help me. You follow me?"

That comment drew a long pause from Katie. She shifted in her seat. Then became irate: "I'm trying to help you!"

"Did you *ever* log into this?"

"It was on my phone."

Katie said she knew it had been logged into on other devices.

VanNamee wanted to know how she would know such an important piece of information.

"I've seen Adam on it."

He would come into the office during business hours and log on to the account, she added.

Katie rubbed her palms on her thighs, trying to get comfortable in her chair. "I'm trying," she said "How do I know you believe me?"

"I need your help proving it was Adam."

This shook Katie up. "But what if you *can't* prove it's Adam?"

"Who do you think he made it look like this is?"

"I'm afraid he put it back on me."

That one comment shifted the interview into a new direction. VanNamee asked Katie if she felt Adam was going to make sure she was responsible for the homicide.

"At the office [that day], he said if anyone was going to get in trouble, it was going to be me."

"For what?"

"That I'm 'connected to everything,' he said."

They discussed Adam for the next several minutes. Katie admitted she had been trying to get Adam to talk about what he did, but he stopped giving her information in September and refused to discuss details after that.

"Let me ask you this," VanNamee said. "The package comes to the office. You said he picked it up. Did you open it? Did you touch it?"

"No," Katie said.

"So, when I say that your DNA will not be on the bottle because you didn't open it, is that accurate?"

"Unless it's the one that I saw on the back counter."

"Okay, who did you give *that* bottle to?"

"I didn't give it to anyone. It was sitting there . . . It was spilled over."

Katie said she cleaned it up, put the bottle back in its cardboard container, and then placed it back in the box it had arrived in.

Katie was referring to a bottle of Cholacol, not colchicine. The

Cholacol bottle found at the office during a search was twice the size of the colchicine bottle found in Adam's Jeep. Cholacol contains concentrated bovine bile salts and collinsonia root to aid in dietary fat metabolism and absorption. It's not a powder, like colchicine. The Cholacol bottle contained ninety tablets.

Two different substances in different-size bottles.

Katie was saying she never touched the bottle of colchicine. This was exactly what VanNamee wanted to know—because the bottle of colchicine found in Adam's Jeep contained traces of female DNA. The OCSO was now certain the DNA found on the colchicine bottle under the seat in Adam's Jeep would trace back to Katie Conley.

51

*G*ETTING INTO KATIE'S PHONE proved to be the most productive discovery of the investigation, to date, for the OCSO. Studying the iPhone's contents closely, the OCSO learned Katie had been lying about certain facts during those first few interviews VanNamee had conducted with her. For example, on December 21, when VanNamee walked into the interview where Katie was nervous and crying and unsure of her answers, he was armed with so many inconsistencies in her story, he could have taken the interview in any direction. Yet, he allowed Katie to talk. Got her version of the events down.

The most competent interrogators don't come out of the gate poking a finger into a suspect's chest. They gradually work contradictions into the conversation and see where the conversation goes. Katie had no reason to be evasive or to avoid the truth—that is, unless she was hiding something.

"There was nothing she needed to lie about," VanNamee explained. "If you knew Adam had that Gmail account, then tell us Adam had that account. Why lie and say you don't know about it? Why be ambiguous and elusive?"

Two computer forensic specialists from Utica College figured out the Mr. Adam Yoder 1990 Gmail account's password: Adamisgay.

When VanNamee received this information, his first thought became: *What guy would make that his password?* In that respect, it felt fitting a female looking to frame her ex-boyfriend would create the account. In getting to know Adam, VanNamee believed he would never try to throw them off with the password.

Another interesting fact VanNamee found out was that this particular Gmail account had been created in September 2014, ten months before Mary was poisoned. Would Adam have planned his mother's homicide that far in advance? "Policework 101" told Van-Namee that if a son was going to kill his mother, based on the relationship Mary and Adam had, it would have been a crime of passion and opportunity. Furthermore, when VanNamee looked into Adam's life during September 2014, the guy was in no shape, mentally, to plan such an elaborate crime.

Continuing with Katie on December 21, VanNamee stayed on the topic of honesty and the Gmail account. He wanted to know why, when they looked inside Katie's iPhone, this Gmail account had turned up.

Katie squirmed. Her face pale as dough. She played with the tissue in her hand. "I . . . um . . . I got rid of it," she said. Meaning, she'd deleted any connection to the Gmail account from her phone, once she realized it was there. She was scared Adam had put all of the information in her cell phone so the homicide would come back on her.

"I understand, but I cannot have your phone showing up at *all* on the IP address," VanNamee said.

Logging into that e-mail account once or twice, VanNamee continued, he could buy. You log in and check it out, realize maybe Adam had gotten into your phone. So you delete it. But the OCSO had subpoenaed a year back on Katie's phone.

"I cannot have you logging in more than once," VanNamee reiterated. "Like you've been logging into it all along—you follow what I'm saying?"

Katie titled her head to the right, played with the tissue, mumbled, "Yeah . . . yes . . ."

"Have you logged into it before? I just need an honest answer. It's okay."

She picked at a fingernail. Had a hard time staring VanNamee in the eyes. "I'm just scared . . ."

"Why?"

Katie evaded giving a direct answer. She would not commit. "I'm not sure. I don't know."

VanNamee took it a step further. He wondered, when she said in an earlier interview she didn't know about the account, had she lied, or was she being truthful?

"I thought I recognized it."

VanNamee changed courses, as he often did during the interview. He focused on May 2015, bringing up how sick Adam was at the beginning of the month. As he talked about Adam's illness, he worked the idea of the FBI being able to test hair. Like, for example, if you used marijuana, a test could be performed to see how long you'd used it.

"They're going to test Adam's," the detective explained. Then he gave Katie an out: "Do you think it's possible that he attempted to poison himself with colchicine then?"

"I would say yes, only because he specifically said there were some similarities between him and his mom . . ."

"So you think he researched colchicine in order to come up with this plan to use it on his mom? Right? He must have looked it up somewhere, right?"

"Right," Katie said, nodding her head. This suggestion made her feel more at ease. She perked up a little. Seemed more interested in talking.

VanNamee asked about Adam using such a dramatic, painful means to commit suicide, if that had been part of his plan.

Katie said it made sense in one respect. In another, however, she said, "I don't know why he would try to poison himself."

"He got a bottle of supplements from you?" VanNamee asked, changing subjects.

"Yeah . . . he got a bottle of supplements, like a drink mix."

"Did he ever tell you how many of the supplements he took?"

"No."

"Did you ever tell him how many to take? Five at a time? One at a time?"

"No, it's on the bottle. I think it's like one to two maybe?"

Mark VanNamee had a knack for interrogation. Not every detective does. He knew when to let go of a subject and when to latch on to another. He understood how to project empathy and sympathy in order to make an interviewee feel comfortable. The trick was to gain Katie's trust and to allow her to back herself into a corner of her own lies. Interrogation is an art. You paint that corner with facts and steer your subject into a position of being surrounded by it. VanNamee projected the aura of a cop who knew more than he was sharing, on top of having the answers to the questions he asked. He was willing to go from one topic to another for as long as it took to land on the truth. Katie liked him. It was obvious in her body language and the questions she asked. She felt more relaxed as the interrogation continued, due to the fact that VanNamee, smartly, always gave her an out: *Adam did it.*

They discussed whether Adam had shared with Katie how he administered the toxin to Mary. By a bottle of water? Or by something else . . . ?

"Um, ah, I . . . vitamins, or something he put it in," Katie said.

"When his mom passed away, did you know where Adam was?"

"I think he was going down to his sister's, or he was planning on it."

"But he hadn't gone down?"

"I do not know."

"Do you think it's possible someone *other* than Adam did this?"

"Like Doctor Bill?"

VanNamee nodded his head.

"I guess Adam would have known . . ."

"Would have known what? That Bill did it?"

"Yeah."

"Why?"

"Because Adam knew what [the toxin] was."

The question of why Adam placed the colchicine under the seat inside his Jeep and held on to it came up next. This didn't make any rational sense to VanNamee. Adam could have discarded the bottle anywhere. Tossed it in a river or a lake, into a Dumpster. Why keep it underneath the seat inside his Jeep?

Katie said he was likely planning to kill someone else.

VanNamee countered: There wasn't enough colchicine left in the bottle to kill another person. Then: "Let me ask you *this.* Is it possible someone *planted* that in his Jeep?"

"I guess it's possible."

"I can tell you right now, in the FBI's studies we went back on, guys don't hang on to the murder weapon, because that's how they get caught."

This sparked an intense reaction from Katie. She lit up. Sat straighter. Shoulders propped up and square. "Right," she said defensively. Then an odd statement: "But *guys* also *don't* use poison."

That response got VanNamee's attention.

Katie paused. Stared at the detective. Laughed. Twisted her head in a snooty gesture—and finished what she'd set out to say: "They say it's a *lady's* weapon."

"'They say it's a lady's weapon'?" VanNamee repeated, shocked Katie would say such a thing under the circumstances.

"Yeah," Katie reiterated. She stared at the detective without flinching, a brazen and confrontational glare. Her mood changed. Katie wasn't the shy, soft-spoken country girl anymore. She blinked her eyes slowly, repeatedly, purposefully. She placed an elbow on the table, crossed her legs, clasped her hands together.

With all of these movements and a renewed energy in the room, in addition to her body language, Katie Conley had altered her consciousness. Locked it into place. She was glib. Her self-serving nature was obvious. Clearly, the interview had stimulated her. She'd gone from the cowering victim of an overly aggressive cop to a woman now taunting that same investigator.

VanNamee stared at Katie. "That [lady's weapon] comment," VanNamee said later, "changed everything for us."

VanNamee believed that Katie had admitted to murdering Mary Yoder with that one callous comment. It showed Katie had a grandiose sense of herself—not to mention a lack of empathy for Mary Yoder and her family.

52

*D*URING THEIR TEXT EXCHANGE in May 2015, Adam joked about Katie possibly poisoning him. He pointed out how he had taken the Alpha BRAIN supplement the night before his illness. As he thought about it, that teasing comment became sobering. In the context of what was happening within the investigation, Adam began to see it as a potential revelation.

"You're doing really well and I'm happy for you," Katie had texted, after Adam brought up her giving him the supplement and the timing of his illness. "I think of you often and hope you're happy."

"Thank you. I hope you're happy, too."

"Okay," Katie shot back, "but seriously, do you *think* it was food poisoning?"

"No. Not food poisoning. A nasty virus . . . it has completely destroyed me from the inside. Then, after emptying my entire system excessively, shut it right down."

"You could have been on some medical show. You could've been on *House*."

"Seriously . . . this virus was a mean . . . motherfucker."

"On the plus side, since you beat it, you now have the antibodies for it."

On May 11, 2015, Katie texted to say she was ill herself: "My own stubborn little bug." She included a list of symptoms, which were

similar to what Adam had been describing in the four weeks leading up to this day.

By June, Katie was feeling like herself again. In her *Notes* app, she
created a list of miscellaneous items she needed to buy, along with
several Internet sites she wanted to visit. Within that, quite randomly, she wrote: "I like my men like I like my tea. Thrown into the
Boston Harbor." She followed that statement up with: "particularly
interested in the evidence of systematic patterns."

A few days later, after not hearing from Adam, Katie sent an un-
solicited text: "Thru June: $22,839.99 ASAP."

"Are you telling me to come up with 23K this month?"

"No, I'm letting you know the current balance."

"Are you leaving? You said you were leaving this summer. ASAP is
not a date. That figure and current balance is comically high." He
wondered how many additional "things" Katie had added to the
total—items she'd specifically told him she didn't want to be paid
back for. "You're amazing! Wow."

"Compounding interest," she snapped back, before demanding
the money by the end of the month.

Adam called the deal "disgusting." On June 6, he asked Katie if
she wanted to meet after work. He needed to sort the loan out,
once and for all, concluding, "It will be the *last* time you ever get to
see and talk with me in person after this. So take it or leave it."

"That sounds like an ultimatum. Unfortunately, I am not available today."

They stopped speaking. Throughout the remainder of June, neither initiated any sort of lengthy, meaningful exchange. If there
had been a slight chance of Adam rekindling what they'd once
had, starting out as friends, it was never going to happen. He was
unwavering about his desire to sever the relationship forever.

Katie realized this. She understood it was over. Her texts give the
impression she was trying to punish Adam in some way for not
wanting to grant her another chance. He had flatly rejected her.
He could not have been any clearer.

On July 6, 2015, two weeks before Mary Yoder was poisoned,
Adam texted Katie, reiterating his feelings: "We spent a final miser-
able year together. You pushed hard to be with me from around
December to August, if I remember correctly."

"It didn't work out," Katie later observed. "So we changed. Nothing would have changed the outcome of this. Nothing."

"I'm not saying it definitely would have, but we will *never* know now."

"No, we won't."

On July 15, Adam left for Long Island to spend time with Liana, his brother-in-law, nieces, and nephew. He did not tell Katie he was leaving or where he was going.

Five days later, on July 20, 2015, at 7:57 p.m. (the day that Mary walked into her house sick, dashing for the toilet), Katie texted her. Oddly, Katie asked Mary if she could take Friday, August 14, off, never saying why.

"I really do like this job and appreciate all you do (and Dr. Bill). Hope it's just a passing bug and you feel 100% tomorrow."

Mary never responded.

In under forty-eight hours, Mary would be dead.

53

*D*ETECTIVE MARK VANNAMEE HAD a suspect for Mary Yoder's murder sitting in front of him. She had just told him how ladies preferred poison as a means to kill.

Katie's snide facial gestures told the seasoned detective she was now engaged in a game of cat and mouse. Waiting. Watching. Planning her next move. It had taken VanNamee just thirty-three minutes, fifty-seven seconds into the interview to get here. His instincts had told him when they started, it would happen; he didn't think it would occur so soon.

"Katie was a tough interview because unless you had her painted into a corner, she would give you *nothing* she could not try to explain away," VanNamee later said. "As taught in many interview schools, a suspect's lie is the most important statement if you can *prove* it's a lie, due to the fact that the lie shows the criminal trying to cover up portions of involvement in a crime."

The relevant question for the OCSO now became: Why lie at all? VanNamee knew Katie was not telling the truth regarding certain facts. What would a lie get her? The only reason a suspect lies, VanNamee knew, was because she felt the truth would not serve her purpose.

The corner Katie talked herself into, perhaps without realizing it, was full of factual evidence VanNamee had at his disposal. Katie did not know this. Most investigators never ask a question they do

not know the answer to. In VanNamee's opinion, Katie was display-
ing signs of antisocial personality disorder and extreme narcissism.
Those who display a pattern of disregard for right and wrong, persistent lying, arrogance, impulsiveness, lack of empathy and remorse,
along with other symptoms, fall within the antisocial/sociopath
spectrum.

VanNamee was beginning to develop a true sense of who Katie
Conley was. After all, she could have stood up, said she'd had
enough, and walked out. Or demanded an attorney. Yet, Katie continued trying to convince the detective that Bill and/or Adam
Yoder had murdered Mary.

The conversation shifted back to Adam. VanNamee asked Katie's
opinion regarding what punishment Adam should receive if, in
fact, he'd murdered his mother.

Katie had no response, falling back into the passive, soft-spoken
victim role.

VanNamee showed her facsimiles of the envelopes each anonymous letter had been posted in. Then asked a question: "Did you
type them on the typewriter at your office desk?"

"Yeah."

He showed her the anonymous letters. Asked the same question.

"I don't know."

"You *don't* know where you typed this?"

"No."

"This is kind of a *big* deal, Katie."

She looked down at her hands.

VanNamee wondered if Katie had typed both letters at home, on
her laptop, or perhaps the office computer, adding, "Katie, I know
you know *where* [the letters were] typed."

It had only been a month.

"Um . . . I . . . um . . ." Katie was stumbling, before blurting out:
"At school."

"Are you sure?"

After a lengthy back-and-forth about those IP addresses showing
Mr. Adam Yoder 1990 had been logged into from Katie's parents'
house and Chiropractic Family Care, Katie insisted Adam had done
it remotely. He knew how to hack into computers, she insisted.

VanNamee hit her with a few facts. If it had been done remotely, computer forensics would have uncovered evidence of hacking. They had not. So VanNamee gave Katie the opportunity to admit she had logged in as far back as November and December 2014, when the colchicine was ordered through Rosa Vargas and ArtChemicals.

"It could have been," she admitted.

Katie was unwilling to completely admit she knew about the Mr. Adam Yoder 1990 Gmail account and had logged into it. Van-Namee wasn't having it. He knew how many times she had logged in, when, and where. The IP addresses were connected to her iPhone; the times and dates connected to IPs at the office and her home. In addition, VanNamee knew Adam was nowhere in the area. If he had logged in, computer forensics would have found out where and when. The OCSO had gone through Adam's electronics, including his iPhone and laptop. The guy was an open book. He had not lied about anything.

VanNamee changed tactics: "How did you know about colchicine? When was the first time you *heard* about it?"

"Adam . . ."

"When?"

"A while ago. A long time ago. I don't know . . . Maybe like . . . um . . . a year ago? I really don't remember."

"What did he tell you about it?"

"He asked if I ever heard about it."

VanNamee would not accept the suggestion that Adam Yoder had randomly brought up colchicine during teatime one afternoon. How was it Adam had taken a sudden interest in colchicine? Where had he discovered the toxin?

"He asked me . . . how he could get some."

"He asked *you*?"

"Yeah . . . but . . . um, I had never heard of it."

Katie had already told the OCSO she'd heard of colchicine. Van-Namee knew she was lying.

The more she talked, the deeper the hole Katie dug. She mentioned how, at the hospital, when Mary was fighting for her life, "Adam seemed concerned, but Dr. Bill didn't seem concerned at all."

The latter part of the statement, VanNamee knew, contradicted what five witnesses at the hospital had already told the OCSO. Katie was trying to change the narrative. She now wanted to focus the investigation on Bill.

The money Adam owed Katie came up. VanNamee wondered if maybe that's why Adam murdered Mary—to get a payout and pay off Katie. It was another crumb VanNamee offered. When suspects lie, they generally don't lie about larger facts. Instead, they inadvertently get caught in the smaller, overlooked facts difficult (or impossible) to remember. Like Katie saying Adam was going to pay her back by the end of summer and didn't care how he was going to get the money. Text exchanges between Katie and Adam, which VanNamee had access to, proved a different version of that statement.

About seventy minutes into the interview, VanNamee took a short pause. It felt as though he had reached an impasse. So he excused himself. He left Katie alone for ten minutes.

She picked at her fingernails, checked her phone, sat comfortably with her legs crossed. By now, it was 4:06 p.m. She'd been at the OCSO for several hours. The door opened. Katie turned.

It was VanNamee's boss, Lieutenant Robert Nelson. He wore a dark blue suit, white-striped shirt, and blue tie. Nelson sat down directly across from Katie. She followed him with her eyes as he sat.

Nelson was more direct. A different interview style from Van-Namee. He did not mince words. He placed his elbows on his knees. Leaned in toward Katie.

"You're our letter writer, right?"

"Um . . . yeah, but . . ."

"But *what?*"

"I'm just trying to help . . ."

Nelson broke it down. The OCSO had a problem. Using his fingers to count off each, Nelson said: "We're looking at one of three people here. The husband, Adam, or you!"

Katie needed to help the OCSO rule herself out, Nelson reaffirmed, same as they were offering Adam and Bill. It was a process that, Nelson suggested, Katie was slowing down and obstructing.

The Gmail account came up. "That is a problem," Nelson said, "because *that* comes back to you."

Katie put her hands under her butt cheeks, moved her body toward Nelson. As he spoke, she kept repeating the same word.

"Right. Right. Right."

Nelson explained the OCSO believed Katie set up the account, used it, and was now trying to distance herself from it. But why? "We need to know."

Katie sat. Staring. Silent.

Nelson outlined a few facts: Katie had pointed at Adam, then Bill; knew about the colchicine in the Jeep, and the colchicine had been delivered to the office; she had written the anonymous letters. These were important pieces of evidence, Nelson explained, which Katie was doing her best to step away from.

"Why are you distancing yourself?" Nelson asked in his short, harsh style of interrogation. He wasn't Katie's friend. He wasn't willing to provide her with an out of any kind.

Katie remained quiet.

Nelson then offered Katie the opportunity to take a CVSA, Computer Voice Stress Analysis test, adding, "To see if people are being truthful with us. Two of the questions we'd like to ask you—One, did you order this colchicine? Two, did you put this colchicine under Adam's car seat?" He paused. "How are you going to do on those two questions?"

"Well."

"'Well'? Okay."

Nelson went through each question again. Asked Katie what her answers would be.

Katie said "no" and "no."

Nelson was convinced Katie had committed both crimes: poisoning Adam and killing Mary. "I mean, you had a grudge against Adam for what he did to you."

"I don't have a grudge."

They got into the alleged rape, and Nelson mentioned how angry it must have made Katie. How her rage could have been a possible motive for her to make Adam ill and to then kill Mary. He tossed in the word "accidental," to perhaps give her some way of justifying it all.

Katie didn't bite. "I'm not angry about it."

Nelson wanted to know why Adam would tell her he killed his mother and where he put the murder weapon. The investigators were struggling to make sense out of this allegation. Why would Adam trust Katie with sensitive information that could put him in prison for life—particularly at a time when they were so at odds with each other and broken up? Their texts were contentious and heated at times.

From their correspondence, it was clear Adam was scared of sharing anything personal with Katie. She had accused him of rape and assault. So the OCSO was now expected to believe Adam would, during this combative period, go to her and admit to killing his mother? And show her where he'd hidden the murder weapon? Using common sense alone, Nelson implied, the allegation was baseless.

"I think it's a control thing, a power thing . . . ," Katie started to say. But as she spoke, perhaps without meaning to, she moved the focus back on herself.

Every time she tried to bury Adam, Nelson countered with "certain facts" the OCSO had, which "come *right* back to you." He pointed at Katie's iPhone sitting on the table in front of them. "That is *you*! Adam cannot control that. That phone is connected to *you*."

Katie said, "Right . . . right . . . it is connected to me, and I'm afraid that it is never going to be connected to Adam at all . . . I can tell you and it's never going to be enough."

"Well, we have to corroborate things."

"I know, but I am afraid it is *never* going to be enough."

Nelson wanted to know when Katie had spoken to Adam last.

She grabbed her iPhone and scrolled. "December sixth . . . he was talking about his dog. And then he said, he wasn't going to talk about what happened."

54

ON DECEMBER 17, 2015, the week before Katie sat down for her first lengthy interview with the OCSO, a friend had texted her. It was near 8:00 p.m. They began the exchange discussing how behind Katie had gotten with finals. How she'd reached out to a professor and he was going to help her catch up. Her friend sounded upbeat, in a good mood. She wondered how Katie was feeling these days.

It was an empathetic gesture. Katie's friend assumed the murder of Mary Yoder, a woman Katie had professed her love for, would have sent Katie into a dark place. The past several months must have been hard to deal with.

Instead, Katie complained about the investigation and how the OCSO had been pestering her.

"Yikes," her friend texted. "Are they still considering you a suspect?"

"Development on the dr. case," Katie shot back. "On Monday, the investigators called me fifteen times and showed up at my house. Persistent! I went and talked w them and gave a DNA sample. I hope they appreciate my valuable finals time!"

Such a revealing comment. So crass. So devoid of empathy. Mary had been murdered. The Yoder family was grieving and in shock by all the latest revelations. The OCSO was pushing back at the information Katie had shared, focused on her as a potential suspect. In the midst of this, she was talking about "valuable finals time."

As Katie and her friend texted further, Katie mentioned Adam: "I'm circumnavigating him! I was getting nowhere and he was being so rude all the time."

Answering that question, her friend asked again if Katie was still a suspect.

"No. I think they know I'm just doing my job. Work and school. Work and school. They're looking at the husband."

"Okay, just being sure you didn't poison her," her friend wrote back in jest, ending the text with a wink-face emoji.

Katie did not respond to that comment directly; she continued talking about how behind she was with finals.

Throughout the next several days, Katie wrote several significant comments in her iPhone. To investigators later on, it was obvious how Katie, through her *Notes* app, seemed to be planting seeds: "Strange—Adam asked if my phone was still connected to his. I think it is bc not everything on there is mine."

In another comment, she made it appear as though she was going through invoices at the office one afternoon. When she came to one in particular, she wrote out a rhetorical (random) question: "When did [the woman's name] bring thieves toothpaste, ordered Jan 16." It didn't make any sense.

The OCSO investigators were also interested in a statement she'd copied into the *Notes* app in mid-November 2015: "A warrant cannot be issued on an informant's tip unless the officers state the reasons that led them to believe the informant are credible or that the information is reliable on this particular occasion."

A quick Google search for the first fifteen words proved Katie had copied and pasted the passage from the National Criminal Justice Reference Service's website. Specifically, a document from the *Iowa Law Review* titled "Probable Cause, Good Faith and Beyond." The piece focused on a Supreme Court discussion regarding "probable cause standards." Katie was studying the proper legal language to use in constructing the anonymous letter so the OCSO would have probable cause to search Adam's Jeep.

As they looked even deeper into Katie's iPhone at several items she'd authored the same week, they found excerpts from the anonymous letter. Katie had practiced how to write out a particular phrase correctly: "AY k his mother. He put something called cokillsin. AY k his mother. He put something called cokillsin in one of her vitamins when he was at her house for Father's Day. . . ."

55

*K*ATIE WAS DOING THE best she could to deflect and impede the OCSO's investigation. Her focus now was placing blame on either Adam or Bill. As Nelson had explained to Katie, telling the truth wasn't hard, and being honest was going to set her free. If she did that, the OCSO could move on. If Katie was not involved, they could find the person who killed Mary Yoder.

Katie, however, had a different plan.

"I'm afraid it is never going to be attached to Adam," she repeated to Nelson. Her voice went up an octave as she said this. She became animated. Irritated.

Nelson sat and thought: *There is no other explanation available for Katie to talk her way out of logging into the Gmail account from her iPhone and her mother's house.*

"Tell us when you set up the account?"

"I didn't set it up."

"Yet you know how to log in and get the password to it?"

"Right."

During her first interview with Mark VanNamee, Katie had said she did not have any idea what type of toxin killed Mary. VanNamee told her it was colchicine. She denied ever having heard of colchicine (despite having written "cokillsin" in her *Notes* app the previous month). Now she had not only admitted knowing colchicine killed Mary, but she had logged into the same account (on multiple occasions). She had left an electronic trail that computer forensics could then look at and trace how the toxin had been ordered.

Nelson asked why she had done that.

Katie opened a bottle of water in front of her. Took a quick sip. Then, as Nelson echoed that she needed to "help" explain the Gmail account, and why she was distancing herself from it, Katie slammed the water bottle down on the table: "I'm *trying* to help!"

Katie had momentarily lost control.

Nelson was getting to her.

The lieutenant brought up the CVSA again, the voice stress test. Why not take the test and be done with it?

"I know that you cannot protect me from Adam."

"From *Adam*?"

"Yeah."

"What is Adam going to do to you? Why is Adam going to come after you? We can protect you from that. That is not impossible."

Katie then said again: Adam killed Mary.

Nelson asked how she knew. "We still have to prove certain facts. We have to rule people out . . ."

It had been five months since Mary's murder. Adam hadn't threatened Katie or given her the impression he was going to hurt her. To the contrary, he had told Katie to stay away from him. Why would he risk hurting her now?

Nelson broke into a lengthy soliloquy regarding how often Katie had lied to the OCSO. How each time she spoke to the OCSO, she gave up something new, in between several lies. A person uninvolved, Nelson pointed out, would have *no* reason to lie, backtrack, and distance herself from certain facts in a murder investigation. Nelson was having a difficult time getting beyond this.

"I'm trying," Katie said again, while slapping her hands on her thighs, twisting her head toward Nelson, getting louder.

Nelson stood. Walked out.

Katie kept her eyes on the lieutenant. As soon as the door closed, she picked up her phone. Her thumbs jackhammered up and down on the screen. To VanNamee, watching from a video monitor in another room, clearly she had become agitated and anxious.

VanNamee walked in a few minutes later.

"I cannot stay too much longer," Katie said, putting her phone away before VanNamee sat down.

VanNamee had a stack of papers in his right hand. He was hoping Katie could explain a few things they had just found out—and ask a few more questions—before she left.

Katie wasn't sure about this, she said.

"Can you at *least* do the voice stress test? It won't take long."

"I think I'm a little nervous for that."

"Why?"

"I'm being connected to everything and I am afraid it's not going to come back on Adam at all." She used her hands to reiterate this point.

VanNamee pushed hard for Katie to take the voice stress test. Katie rejected the idea. She was too nervous.

The OCSO's main concern, VanNamee explained, was how many times Katie's iPhone had been connected to accessing the Mr. Adam Yoder 1990 Gmail account. This number told them she had continually lied about that particular thread of the investigation. For example, VanNamee added while working in a bit of new information: "I am concerned about your phone coming back to trying to set up a PayPal account to order this thing."

Katie turned her head to one side. She spoke, but had a hard time articulating what she wanted to say. She then mentioned how someone had likely set up a PayPal account in Mary's or the business's name.

"This is where the downfall is," the detective added, "people don't realize that their phone leaves the trail . . ."

"No, no, I know that," Katie responded.

"So you're one hundred percent sure it's *not* going to come back with your number or your IP address?" VanNamee asked, referring to the PayPal account. "I need you to be honest."

"No. No. I am sure. I am being honest."

VanNamee knew which phone number/IP address the PayPal account had been set up from and later accessed. Or he would not have asked the question. But Katie wasn't hearing him. She was too focused on trying to place the blame on Bill and Adam.

They talked about Bill Yoder. Katie couldn't provide anything useful.

VanNamee went back to the stress test and how accurate the device was, saying he had done "hundreds of these things. That's why we don't use a polygraph anymore, because this is ten times more accurate."

Katie wanted nothing to do with it. She seemed on the verge of tears. She bounced a bit in her chair, waved her hands around, repeatedly took nervous sips from her water bottle, screwing the cap on and off. Meanwhile, she kept repeating how she was going to be blamed for the murder because Adam had set it up that way.

VanNamee pressed for fifteen more minutes, focused on the test, which would help investigators "get [her] out of the way."

Katie became so agitated and jumpy, she stood and paced, stared out the window, played with her car keys.

"I'll be back," she said when VanNamee pressed for a date and time to take the test.

"Give me one second," VanNamee said. He walked out of the room.

Katie took out her phone and scrolled.

Nelson walked in. "So you *don't* want to take the test?"

"No, not right now!" she said, irritated. "No! If it was, like, three hours ago . . . but I have an engagement to get to."

"Well, do you feel that you're *not* going to take it because you're *not* going to pass it?"

"No!"

The lieutenant described how they had established that Katie was connected to the letter, and the letter had outlined detailed accusations. They needed to talk that through as soon as possible. Nothing in her life should be more important than clearing her name. What "engagement" could possibly usurp the significance of being charged with murder?

Nelson demanded a date and time. The implied impression was that of a detective investigating a murder, asking a person of interest when she was coming back to continue answering questions and take a lie detector test. If Katie should have ever flipped the "I want a lawyer" card, it was in this moment. But instead of asking for a lawyer, she said she couldn't give them a time or date.

Nelson explained that the evidence did not point to Adam or Bill Yoder. All of it had come back to Katie and her iPhone.

"I know," Katie said as the interview concluded, and she walked out of the building.

56

*T*HE OCSO STRATEGIZED CAREFULLY after the December 2015 interviews with Katie. She had backed herself into such a tight spot with so many lies, there seemed to be only one way out of it.

The voice stress test.

Would Katie, as she promised, submit to the test?

"We needed to tread very lightly with Katie, because we wanted to keep her talking," VanNamee said later.

The goal was to have her sit down and take the test—without walking into the OCSO with a lawyer.

Meanwhile, outstanding subpoenas, which the OCSO had filed, were continuing to come back. They had more information than they could unpack at once. In addition, VanNamee wrote additional search warrants for Katie's house and phone. Although they had seen some of what was on her phone—a cursory search while she was at the OCSO, and information from IP addresses computer forensics had collected—VanNamee and Nelson wanted to look at any files or apps she had deleted.

In the meantime, Bill Yoder was still a suspect. He had not been cleared. On December 23, the OCSO asked him to come back in for a sit-down interview. Bill dropped everything and drove to the OCSO that morning. Sat down in the interview suite.

"I'll help any way I can."

Neither VanNamee nor Nelson conducted the interview. But they sat with Bill in advance and talked.

"I don't believe this is an accident, Mr. Yoder," VanNamee told him.

Bill turned pale. The confirmation of his wife being murdered stunned him.

"We need your help."

"I'm an open book." As they talked, Bill turned everything he had over to the OCSO: cell phone, laptop, iPad. "Whatever you need." Bill then explained the relationship he was currently in with Mary's sister, Kathleen.

Without telling him, the OCSO had already been over to speak to Kathleen. "Bill brought that up to us," VanNamee recalled—which was important. Bill came across as having nothing to hide. He talked about his entire life.

At one point, VanNamee said he was in the middle of writing a search warrant for the office. It was a warning. The warrant would take some time, but they were going to be turning the entire office upside down. If evidence of murder existed, they would eventually find it.

"We were interested in Bill's reaction to this," VanNamee recalled.

"You don't need a warrant," Bill said. "I'll give you permission right now to go in and do whatever you need to. You want to go there today, I'll take you myself."

"He didn't suggest a day or a week later," VanNamee recounted. "He said 'now.'"

They took him up on it.

57

*I*N LATE DECEMBER, KATIE agreed to return to the OCSO for the voice stress test. When she arrived, VanNamee stepped out from his office to greet her.

"These are my parents," Katie said, introducing her mother and father.

VanNamee struck up a conversation.

"Do you think she's involved? Should we get her a lawyer?" one of Katie's parents asked.

"We're not saying she's involved," VanNamee said. "We just need to talk with her."

Before the test began, VanNamee, Nelson, and the officer conducting the test met. No matter what the test revealed, they were not going to tell Katie that she was lying.

"We made a choice that those words would not come out of our mouths," VanNamee said. "The goal was one more interview. Her parents could have taken her home, lawyered up, and said you are never speaking to our daughter again."

Katie sat down. Got settled in the chair. The test began. As she recited her name alone, "her stress levels were off the charts," Van-Namee said.

Because Katie had such a faint, low voice, adjustments were made to counteract it. As soon as they dialed in Katie's voice and pressed forward with the test, *Deception Indicated* lit up across the computer screen. Confirmation: She was lying.

Per their plan, neither VanNamee nor Nelson told Katie how she'd scored. Instead, they presented her with new warrants and confiscated her phone. "We're going to be heading over to your residence to take your computers and anything else we deem important to the investigation."

Katie and her parents were speechless.

"Katie, listen," VanNamee told all three of them, "you passed the voice stress test."

58

*I*N THE EARLY PART of February 2016, after a respite in pressure put on Katie over the holiday season, the OCSO received a multitude of subpoenas back from Google. One important piece of information they learned was that on January 12, 2016, a new e-mail address was accessed from the Conley residence: ACyoder@ gmail.com.

They also were interested in the money Katie had loaned Adam. The OCSO wondered where Katie would get such a large amount of cash.

"It wasn't like five hundred bucks," VanNamee said. "It was fifteen, twenty grand. Where did she get that kind of money? Here's a girl who lives at home, goes to school, has a job that pays a small wage. But she loans Adam all this money and then, in January 2016, [she] buys a three-year-old Honda Accord."

"When they searched Katie's bedroom," one law enforcement source claimed, "a large bag of cash was found in her room."

"We have no idea where she got it," VanNamee said.

VANNAMEE GOT HOLD OF Bill Yoder. He asked Bill about any cash potentially missing from the business.

"I would not be able to tell you," Bill said. "I have no idea."

The Yoders were the type of people who ran a business because they were passionate about helping people. If you didn't have money to pay for treatment, they'd work it out another way. Bill and Mary never kept a close eye on the books.

"It's clear Katie was embezzling money from the business," one law enforcement source said.

After having a chance to study the books for the time period Katie worked at Chiropractic Family Care, Bill Yoder agreed.

The more the OCSO looked at the receipt recovered next to the bottle of colchicine in Adam's Jeep, they understood the electronic trail and how the colchicine was ordered and paid for. Through that receipt, VanNamee found Rosa Vargas, which put him onto the Hannaford supermarket. This led to the prepaid credit cards and a PayPal account.

"We contacted Copper Harbor, the company that actually had the colchicine. They told us a payment was attempted from a Pay-Pal account, but was eventually paid for with a prepaid credit card . . . and we came to find out there were *two* prepaid credit cards. One was loaded onto PayPal and the other was actually sent to Copper Harbor–ArtChemicals with the correct amount."

This was all done within a few days of the prepaid credit cards being purchased—which pointed the OCSO in the direction of the supermarket and a possible video of Katie walking in and buying the two prepaid cards.

Looking at a map of the area around the Hannaford super-market, VanNamee noticed something. If you left the Yoder office and drove toward Katie's house, which she did every workday, Han-naford was directly along your path. Both prepaid credit cards were purchased within one week of each other. The dates and lag time in between dovetailed perfectly with the electronic trail the OCSO received regarding when and how the colchicine was purchased.

In the opinion of the OCSO, Katie purchased the prepaid cards and the colchicine. Her iPhone and several deleted files they had recovered corroborated the theory. Through that, a timeline match-ing the timeline of ordering and purchasing the colchicine was cre-ated.

VanNamee and Nelson wanted Katie back in the chair, talking. "But before we do that," VanNamee said, "I need to do one thing."

The Hannaford videos had been deleted by the time the OCSO

tracked down where the prepaid credit cards had been purchased. VanNamee had an idea, however. He took several blank DVDs, printed Hannaford supermarket labels with the dates the cards had been purchased, and stuck them on the blank DVDs.

"I could then take those DVDs with me into an interview with Katie. She would believe we had video of her purchasing the cards."

This was a risky move, however.

"Because what if she sent her sister into the supermarket, or a friend, to purchase the cards for her? We didn't really know."

VanNamee came up with a foolproof plan for that specific contingency. It would cover him in the event Katie did not purchase the cards.

Katie returned on February 5, 2016. Again, she was without a lawyer. The OCSO knew this was likely the last chance they would get to break her.

Katie entered the OCSO by herself. She was dressed in a puffy red winter jacket with a hood, black jeans, and bright-colored sneakers. She wore glasses. Her dark black hair, thick and stylishly trendy, flowed down past her shoulders. She seemed agitated. Restless.

VanNamee wore a bright blue shirt and black slacks. He had a harder edge to him this time, giving Katie the impression time was running out.

"Hey, Katie. How are you?"

Katie didn't answer.

"Come on in. Let's get this done. I really want to help you, Katie. But you have to help us."

Katie sat down.

VanNamee pulled up a chair across from her and sat down. Their knees were corner to corner. He then spread several papers over the table between them.

"You ready, Katie?"

"I guess."

The detective started by telling Katie he was going to be taking a deposition of her statement. Anything she said was going to be on the record. The last two times she'd sat in this same interrogation room, the OCSO had recorded the interviews. VanNamee explained he was doing the same.

Katie calmed herself. She looked at the detective and appeared willing to help.

VanNamee apologized, but said he could not get around this next step. "I need to read you your rights."

Katie nodded.

As VanNamee read Katie her Miranda rights, she bowed her head, put her hands in her lap, and closed her eyes, as if the detective was reading a prayer. With that out of the way, he pulled out the facsimiles of the anonymous letter (two pages) once again, same as he did the previous December, and placed them in front of her. He asked Katie where she wrote and printed the letter.

"School," Katie admitted.

VanNamee knew it was a lie. So he explained rather matter-of-factly how the two of them needed to go through the letter, line by line. Each sentence. Maybe each word. As he began, VanNamee asked Katie if she recalled writing several sentences, which he read aloud.

Katie looked at him, turned pale white. She shuffled nervously a bit in her chair and began breathing heavily.

"Katie, you okay?"

"Sorry . . ."

"Katie, we're going to get through this. You're my best witness."

Katie hyperventilated. Her chest heaved in and out. Her breathing became loud and labored. She started crying. "I'm so scared," she uttered in that quiet voice she could turn on and off.

"What are you scared of?"

No answer.

"What. Are. You. Scared. Of. Katie?"

"If Adam knows . . . if Adam knows . . ." she said, barely able to get the words out.

For the next minute, Katie continued hyperventilating and crying. Her shoulders dropped. She slouched over.

I've got her, VanNamee thought.

The detective moved his chair directly in front of Katie. This, he knew, was when a suspect generally gave it up. Katie seemed to be on the verge of admitting whatever was weighing on her conscience, causing all this visceral stress. Her body was reacting to the guilt she felt. An instinctive response to hard evidence is telling, VanNamee knew. It was completely involuntary.

"Puzzles," VanNamee said, pouring it on. "We're putting puzzles together and we already *know* where ninety-five percent of the pieces go."

"Okay . . . okay." Katie rocked in her chair.

"I'm going to cut to the chase in a hurry, okay?" VanNamee said.

Katie appeared to be getting sick.

"Do not puke on me, Katie!"

It took a few minutes, but Katie was able to regroup. She removed her glasses, rubbed her eyes. Took a prolonged, deep breath. Then covered her entire face with her hands, before letting out a deep, high-pitched sigh.

She asked for water.

VanNamee made it clear that if she helped him, she would not have to worry about Adam any longer, giving her the impression they were still going after her ex-boyfriend.

After that, VanNamee pulled out the first draft of the anonymous letter. He explained how they believed she had modified the final draft she had sent to the OCSO and ME's office. The changes in the opening lines were important to VanNamee. In the original draft, which VanNamee pointed to with his index finger, Katie had written that Adam was drunk when he admitted he had killed his mother.

"And we noticed on your phone in the *Notes* app, you wrote yourself a note saying, 'don't say drunk.'"

As they looked at the final draft, there was no mention of Adam being drunk. It appeared as if Katie had been writing fiction, editing and redrafting the letter, making it up in her *Notes* app as she went along.

Why would she do this? It either happened the way it did, or it didn't. The truth does not change.

"This isn't my letter," Katie said.

"I'm absolutely *sure* it's your letter."

"Neither one of these," Katie insisted, explaining how both the first draft and the draft she sent to the OCSO and ME's office were not the same letters she had written.

As they continued, Katie remained certain neither of the letters was a facsimile of what she had sent.

VanNamee pulled out photos of the tape ribbon from the typewriter at the office. It was an old-school typewriter. You hit a key, and it left an imprint on the ribbon. He showed Katie certain phrases and words straight from the letters.

After discovering the ribbon at the office during their Bill Yoder–sanctioned search, the OCSO knew Katie had lied about where she typed the letter. Why lie about such a thing after admitting you wrote the letters?

Katie did not respond to the photos of the ribbon.

VanNamee explained a typo on the envelopes sent to both places and how that same typo was executed from the typewriter at the office, because the ribbon had the same typo imprinted into it.

"No," Katie said.

They argued about when she sent the letters. Katie was sure she'd sent the letters in September. VanNamee said the date was not in dispute. It was an immutable fact. She had sent the letters on November 20, 2015. They had more than enough proof to corroborate the date with an electronic trail from the post office attached to it. Why was she pushing back on this?

It did not matter what VanNamee said, what evidence he presented, Katie would not agree she sent the letters in November.

"I didn't do it on a typewriter," she added.

VanNamee became frustrated. "Let's talk about something else."

Katie stared, didn't respond.

"We know that you had the *CamScanner* app in your phone. When they forensically broke down your phone, the *CamScanner* app was there."

Katie had deleted it. When forensics went into the App Store on her iPhone and searched for the *CamScanner* app, there it was. Because she had purchased it—even if she deleted the app—a cloud icon with an arrow pointing down (so she could re-download the app at any time) was fixed in the store. Once you purchased an app, you owned the app. It was always available, even if you deleted it. In addition, in the stored password portion of Katie's iPhone, every app on the phone had a listing, whether deleted or not. There was no way to delete an app completely from an iPhone. It was impossible.

More puzzle pieces.

Why was the *CamScanner* app important to the OCSO investigators? A mountain of inculpatory evidence pointing to Katie setting up a shell company—Chiro Family Care—to order the colchicine was inside the app. Another document she had inside her iPhone was titled "Diagnosis and Treatment of Colchicine Poisoning," downloaded from the Official Newsletter of the California Poison Control System. The article covered everything from diagnosis, treatment, epidemiology, and pathophysiology.

The OCSO investigators also recovered a text from Katie to Adam on August 7, 2015, in which she wrote: "Can you please delete my phone backup?" Thus, a few weeks after Mary's murder, Katie demanded all the contents of her iPhone be deleted from Adam's laptop, which she'd suddenly realized had been downloaded after she'd plugged her iPhone in to download an audiobook.

Beyond several other items forensically recovered, there was also a photo of Adam and Katie together at a restaurant. Cheek to cheek, Adam held up a beverage. He looked incredibly uncomfortable and sad. Katie is smiling ear to ear, looking happier than she'd ever been. This photo was taken, the OCSO investigators learned, not long after Katie had made those rape allegations against Adam.

Even more evidence of her guilt, Katie had a W-9 filled out in Bill Yoder's name under the Chiro Family Care company she created, with Mary Yoder's stamped signature. In the account settings of the *CamScanner* was the Mr. Adam Yoder 1990 Gmail account, so the *CamScanner* itself was registered to that specific e-mail address. All of the documents sent from Katie's iPhone to Rosa Vargas to order the colchicine had the *CamScanner* logo on the bottom. That watermark was visible only to the recipient of the documents.

59

As THE INTERVIEW CONTINUED, the New York State Police Forensic Investigation Center (NYSPFIC) was testing the DNA sample, which Katie had willingly given, against potential DNA found on the colchicine bottle and receipt inside Adam's Jeep. The bottle had been wrapped in a piece of corrugated cardboard, rolled up around it, and stuffed under the seat. It was part of the packaging the bottle had been delivered in. On the wrapper itself—a fact VanNamee did not know during this interview—the NYSPFIC would soon find a match to Katie's DNA.

Still, what they did *not* find on the wrapper, bottle, or receipt became as equally, if not more, important.

Adam Yoder's DNA.

Even though the OCSO did not have the DNA results back from the NYSPFIC, VanNamee and Nelson felt Katie Conley planted the bottle of colchicine inside Adam's Jeep. In a matter of days, they would have the science to back it up.

Katie looked at all of the evidence VanNamee placed in front of her, taking it in.

"Katie, twenty-year-olds are glued to their phones. Someone didn't take your phone and accidentally scan these [documents]."

Katie looked up at VanNamee, then down at the paperwork.

"These are the documents that were used to purchase the colchicine," VanNamee reiterated. His voice was more empathetic and calm. He was trying to reason with Katie: *Look, we have you nailed here with forensic computer science . . .*

She didn't respond.

"Somebody snapped [images of] these [documents] with *your* phone," VanNamee said. A statement, not a question.

She looked at the facsimiles of the documents again. "How?"

"Katie! Here's where we're at a crossroads in this case. We've done a lot of work, okay. And we *know* that your phone is used quite a lot for items in this case."

Katie stared at him.

A rather amusing piece of information—in an ironic twist—came to light when the OCSO finished going through the contents of Katie's iPhone and computers. At one point during the period when she bought the colchicine, Katie had actually tried to use a 10 percent off Internet coupon code to purchase the toxin. The website wouldn't allow it. But the fact that she had tried left an electronic trail. Same as every document she'd scanned with the *CamScanner* app, each move she made on her iPhone had been tracked and saved.

Would Adam, if he had stolen her phone and framed her, actually try to use an Internet coupon? Would he use the *CamScanner* app? And finally, with technology being what it is, who would use their phone to purchase a weapon to commit a murder? Adam had studied computer science. He knew how IP addresses and the mechanics of metadata on an iPhone and computer worked.

VanNamee questioned Katie for over an hour about the letters, documents, *CamScanner* app, and additional digital evidence she'd left behind. He presented images and explained how no one else could have logged on to the accounts but her.

When he asked which password she had used to close the accounts, Katie laughed. "I don't know."

"You cannot close an account without knowing the password," VanNamee said. He paused. "I don't ask questions I don't know the answers to."

Katie smiled.

They debated back and forth. Katie played stupid—like she had no idea how all of this evidence had ended up on her iPhone, which was her only move at this point. VanNamee kept his cool and continued presenting unimpeachable evidence to see if she would own up to any of it. He explained how they had obtained it, what it told them, and how they were going to use it against Mary's killer.

Katie listened. But didn't utter a word.

VanNamee then went into how, during difficult homicide investigations, investigators usually get a break at some point: A big piece of the puzzle tying the rest of the picture together. Something telling them "the who" of the murder. In this case, VanNamee explained to Katie, it came in the form of recordings from Hannaford supermarket's CCTV.

This was a risky move on the detective's part. The OCSO did not have surveillance video of Katie purchasing the prepaid cards used to buy the colchicine. If VanNamee said, "*We have you on video buying those prepaid credit cards,*" and Katie knew she had not bought them, he would have played a card and revealed the OCSO's hand. The bluff would backfire. So VanNamee, quite smoothly and cleverly, devised a fail-safe plan to present the blank DVDs he tossed on the table in front of Katie.

He took out the DVDs (props) and slid them in front of Katie. He explained what they were. Pointed to the fake Hannaford labels pasted around the center hole.

A stunned look washed over Katie's face.

"Tell me," VanNamee said, putting his scheme in motion, "who is *not* on those DVDs?" Then, without waiting for her to answer, he added: "It's not Adam!" He pointed to the DVDs. Paused.

Katie looked at him.

"Who purchased the prepaid cards?" VanNamee asked.

Katie stared at him. "I don't know."

"*You* got them," VanNamee said, emphasizing the word "you" by pointing in her face.

Katie shook her head no.

"If you purchased them, *you* are involved in this." VanNamee moved his seat a little closer, getting directly in Katie's face. His tone changed. "I'm telling you, Katie, there is *no* way around this. I've let you sit here . . . I've let you tell me, 'I don't know how that got on my phone.' . . . Okay! We're at a crossroad now. You know I do not ask a question I do *not* know the answer to. *You* purchased those credit cards, didn't you?"

"Yes, yes," Katie responded. She sounded unemotional. Stoic. For a few minutes, she didn't move.

VanNamee went back to the *CamScanner* documents, hitting her with: "You said you purchased these credit cards, and I know they were used within a day . . ."

Katie whispered, claiming she bought the cards for someone else.

"Who did you give those cards to then? If that's the road we're going to go down, let's keep rolling this stone . . . okay?"

"I don't know . . ."

"There's two of us in this room, Katie, and we *both* know who purchased this colchicine. There is no *doubt* in my mind who purchased this colchicine."

"I don't know . . ."

"You admitted to me you purchased that credit card. The very next day, it is e-mailed to purchase the colchicine . . ."

"Yes . . ."

VanNamee mentioned the stone they were rolling. He asked Katie if she was tired of pushing it.

Katie stared at him.

"That credit card was used to purchase the poison."

Katie shook her head no.

"If you're the one who purchased the credit card, *you're* the one who purchased the poison."

"No!"

"Help me."

"I did not . . . but you are never gonna believe me."

VanNamee increased the volume of his voice. He wasn't going to cower. Not now. He was too close. Katie was on the verge of a confession.

"But if I don't know an answer," she said, "I can't give you an answer. I. Don't. Know."

"It's a straight-up lie, Katie."

"It's not a lie."

"It's a lie!"

"It's *not* a lie."

"Then if you didn't do it, you *know* who did it."

"I don't know."

This went on for ten minutes. VanNamee asked if she was going to stick with "I don't know."

Katie said that was all she had to say.

"I don't think you want to get in trouble for this," VanNamee offered. He stepped his tone down to a normal level.

Katie smiled and laughed, waved her hands over the evidence sitting in front of her on the table. "Look at all this."

"Yeah. It's pretty overwhelming when you look at it."

Katie continued to smile.

"Pretty overwhelming," VanNamee repeated.

"It's scary," Katie said.

"Scary because it clearly points to *one* person."

"Right, but I don't know how."

In a near whisper, VanNamee said, "It clearly points to *one* person. We are not going to have a problem with that."

After a brief moment of silence between them, the detective went back to the credit cards.

Katie now said they were gift cards, before turning and facing the window to her right, away from the detective. She was crying again.

"This is my future . . . ," she whispered.

"Let me help you get your story out. You're not some monster who did this out of the blue."

She took off her glasses, wiped tears. VanNamee adopted a more sympathetic position. He said he was sorry. He wanted to help. The best thing to do now was tell the truth. He asked what she would want her future children to do in this same situation.

Katie continued to cry. "I've worked so hard . . ."

"You're one of the hardest-working people I have ever met. What happened, Katie? What is causing all of this emotion? I'm willing to go to bat for you. What would cause somebody to risk everything to do this? What made a bright, smart girl risk *everything*?"

Katie bowed her head. Put two fingers into her eye sockets and massaged. She then folded her hands together.

VanNamee could tell she was contemplating how to explain herself. "I talk to Adam a lot. He's beyond hope. If this is about Adam, I am completely on your side of the fence, Katie."

She leaned on her left hand, elbow on the table, rubbed the side of her head.

"Own up to the mistake and let's move on. That's how life is."

Katie played with a strand of her hair. No doubt she was just moments away from admitting it all. VanNamee had her backed into a corner. Katie was thinking deeply, seriously, about how to talk herself out of it without taking blame. VanNamee expected her to minimize her role. Blame someone else for pushing her into a place where she needed to react.

Adam.

"I don't have kids," Katie said through tears, after VanNamee asked again if this was what she would want to teach her future children.

"Katie, you're going to have kids without a doubt."

She put one hand over her face.

"Let's make this right. Let's move on from here. Let's get you to graduate college this May and you having a family."

VanNamee took a closer look at Katie. She was now hiding her face behind her hands and hair.

"What, are you *laughing* at me?" VanNamee said, noticing Katie was not crying anymore, but chuckling.

"No. That just sounds so good and normal."

"Put your past behind you. Your past cannot become your past until you face the facts behind it." VanNamee then asked her to help him understand what happened.

"I don't think I can help you," she said.

"Why?"

Between several silent breaks, VanNamee came across as Katie's friend. He said as long as she stayed with the truth, he could take it into his boss and fight for her.

"I don't think anything can help me," Katie said.

"I don't believe that."

"Well, it's *my* life on the line."

"Do you think you're in less trouble for *not* telling us the why?"

No response.

VanNamee asked the same question two more times.

"You can't help me," Katie said.

"How am I doing, Katie? Am I on the right base path, or am I wasting my time here?"

Katie didn't answer.

"I can assure you that not everybody will see you as a victim, but I do."

Katie sat still and stared at the floor.

In the end, Katie withstood VanNamee's blitz of interrogation, which he'd backed up with indisputable evidence standing on its own merit.

PART IV

TRUE LIES

60

*T*HERE WAS ONLY ONE path for the OCSO after reaching an impasse with Katie. She was not going to admit to planning and killing Mary Yoder. As June 2016 ushered in some rather pleasant upstate New York weather—a mild and warm early summer—the community of Utica stirred, wondering what was going on with the case. For people around town, it was difficult to find someone who believed Katie Conley could have committed murder. Katie was a twentysomething college student. By all outward appearances, she was an upstanding, kind, and generous person, reared from a well-known and well-liked family.

The allegation was outside the bounds of acceptable, expected behavior. How could someone who'd never been in any trouble commit such an evil, scornful act? As residents talked, town gossip focused on Adam and Bill. One story had them conspiring to kill Mary together; another claimed Bill had been involved with Adam in growing a marijuana supercrop, which gave them access to colchicine, which was used to grow weed into an uberplant. People even speculated that Bill was a major drug dealer who'd had mistresses for years and found himself in a precarious financial situation.

None of these rumors found any footing because all of it was fallacious. In reality, Adam had moved out of town. Bill was devastated without his wife. He was trying to move on with Kathleen, but the mere thought of Mary turned the guy into a chest-heaving faucet of tears. Now to be told someone you trusted, someone you allowed into all aspects of your life, someone who *claimed* to love Mary, could have killed her? It was more than overwhelming for the entire Yoder family.

"She was excellent with my children," Liana Hegde recalled. "We could not believe that Katie, who laughed and joked with us, cried with us, a woman my children looked up to, someone my brother loved at one time, had been this *other* person the entire time."

61

*I*N A NONDESCRIPT ROOM inside the OCSO, during the final interview Katie had given in February, a computer recorded the interview. Several people were huddled around the monitor, watching
and listening. Oneida County Vehicular Crimes bureau chief and
ADA Stacey Scotti, ADA Laurie Lisi, and several members of the
OCSO's investigative team were among those looking on in real
time. Prior to that February interview, after Detective Mark
VanNamee knew Katie was coming in to talk, ADA Laurie Lisi
approached Scotti.

"There's going to be a lot of forensic computer work," Lisi said.
"I need you to come on board to handle the portion of the case
dealing with evidence collection, including the collection and
swabbing of the letters and the submission, along with anything
having to do with the computer forensics—tablets and phones, the
typewriter ribbon."

Forty-one-year-old Stacey Scotti was thrilled by the opportunity.
A local, Scotti had graduated from Whitesboro Senior High
School. She left the area to attend Dickinson College in Carlisle,
Pennsylvania, graduating four years later magna cum laude, with a
degree in sociology. From there, Scotti went off to Villanova University School of Law, receiving her Juris Doctor in 1997. A year
later, she was admitted to practice law in New York, and, on July 6,

1998, she joined the Oneida County District Attorney's Office as an ADA.

With diligence and professionalism, Scotti had overseen the county's Vehicular Crimes Unit for several years before Laurie Lisi asked her to join the team prosecuting Katie. If you decided to drive drunk or gassed up on some sort of illegal substance in Oneida County and got pinched, you'd meet Stacey Scotti inside a courtroom. With her dirty-blond hair sweeping past her shoulders, petite frame, and dogged attitude, she was a force to be reckoned with amid the oak bench seats, gavel, and witness stand. Don't let her small size fool you. She's a tenacious fighter in a courtroom.

Laurie Lisi knew the case against Katie was going to be built and then hinge upon computer forensic science. There would be thousands of pages of data to sift through, study, and compare to other facts the OCSO had generated. Not to mention any new evidence the OCSO developed from several outstanding warrants. It would take a dedicated, sharp, focused attorney to search and discover evidence that would have otherwise slipped through the fingers of a less experienced mind and eye.

Scotti lived with her dog, Libbey, just down the road from the Conley residence. She would spend hours scouring data, studying Katie's iPhone and computers, along with whatever else computer forensic experts dug up. She was tasked with breaking down the components of what, when, where, and—most important—how. She went in search of additional inculpatory evidence. Everyone involved knew it was there; she would find it.

"I was asked to handle all of those components of the case and prepare us for trial," Scotti said later. "There was so much material. I jumped right in."

At the time, Scotti didn't know many details about the case. She'd heard things around the office, of course. Spoke to Laurie Lisi and Mark VanNamee here and there. But she had so much day-to-day DUI and drug court work on her desk, she hadn't given it too much thought. And because Katie's case involved a grand jury investigation, most of the policework was sealed.

"Once ADA Lisi apprised me of the case details," Scotti said, "it was difficult to wrap my brain around it at first." Scotti meant, *Why would Katie Conley do this?* This was a question the entire community, including the Yoder family, was asking. "But once I settled in and started reviewing the evidence, I knew—it was clear to me—that she had done it. And I *knew* computer forensics was going to be the key."

62

THE FIRST HURDLE THAT Laurie Lisi faced was indicting Katie. Without an indictment and subsequent arrest, there would be no trial.

A grand jury convened on June 1, 2, 9, and 10, 2016. The prosecution presented 124 exhibits, including a dozen or so screenshots from Katie's iPhone, the manual typewriter evidence from the Yoder office, ArtChemicals documents and accompanying computer records, all of the IP addresses they had at the time, the anonymous letters, along with a host of other critical evidence. Seventeen witnesses—including Bill Yoder, Rosa Vargas, Adam Yoder, Lieutenant Nelson, Detective VanNamee, forensics experts, Jeanna Marraffa, the PCC expert who had figured out colchicine had killed Mary, along with several others—were called to the stand.

The evidence spoke to how thorough and detrimental the case the prosecution was building against Katie was. The grand jury testimony transcripts numbered in the 800-page range.

By June 13, 2016, a secret grand jury hearing the evidence presented by the Oneida County District Attorney's Office indicted Katie and she was arrested. Twenty-three years old, Katie was charged in county court with murder in the second degree, one count of forgery in the second degree, two counts of falsifying business records in the first degree, and two counts of petit larceny. If found guilty, Katie would be imprisoned for the rest of her life.

A bone had been thrown into the community: Katie was heading to trial for the murder of Mary Yoder—that much was now certain. She could now get up on the stand and say "I don't know" all she wanted. She could claim she had no idea how a mountain of computer forensic evidence wound up on her iPhone, computers, and sat in her iCloud. She could hoot and holler all she wanted that Adam Yoder killed Mary and framed her. She could concoct any narrative, including Bill Yoder was some sort of pot dealer, running around with Mary's sister long before Mary's death. But at the end of the day, it was up to a jury of Katie's Oneida County peers—which would soon play a vital role in the case—to decide if all those accusations were invented by salivating, tunnel-visioned cops.

As both sides prepared for trial, said to be a year away, Katie's defense got busy. They hired a private investigator, who later submitted a complete report of his findings.

The PI zeroed in on Adam's cousin David King. Adam had moved in with him on August 22, 2015. According to the report, Adam "told [Dave] he was only going to stay for a few days." For some reason, the PI thought it important to note Adam "had never informed [Dave] that he (Adam) was a suspect in the case."

In interviewing Dave King, the PI wrote, one particular night in early December 2015 stood out to him. Dave recalled waking up to "two men talking downstairs." He knew one voice was Adam's, but he did not recognize the other man. When Dave got up a few hours later, Adam was gone. He had "left laundry in the dryer and washer, all his clothes, toothbrush, and shaver." It took Dave a while to get hold of Adam. When he did, Adam explained the police had asked him to go down to the OCSO—and while searching his Jeep, they found colchicine.

"What probably really happened," the PI speculated, "was the police asked Adam for consent to search his car, he refused. Once they left, he left."

Like a lot of the report, this turned out to be a false narrative—a completely ill-informed, entirely hypothetical assessment of Adam's life.

As the report continued, the PI explained Dave King's feelings about the situation. Adam's cousin said that at first he did not think

Adam could have been behind Mary's death: "But now all the things turning up, and . . . through phone calls and text, he feels now Adam could be some type of participant in this."

For the next few paragraphs, the PI ran down a list of Adam Yoder's faults and personal issues. Dave called Adam a "liar" and said "he feels Adam would lie for his father . . ."

Notably, at the end of the report, the PI mentioned that Dave had never met Katie. He also said Adam had complained to his cousin about how "mean" and "domineering" she was, and that she "demanded he take money from her."

Beyond that, the PI came up with nothing to help Katie prove her innocence.

63

*T*HE ONEIDA COUNTY COURTHOUSE on Elizabeth Street, in downtown Utica, is an imposing building. Whitewashed stone, it was built in 1901, renovated in 1975. If you stand in front, and stare up at it from the street, an ominous feeling washes over, suggesting that you'd never want to find yourself inside one of its courtrooms facing a judge.

With just under 250,000 residents, 90 percent of whom are white, 6 percent black, the county had a large pool of available jurors. With all the local media coverage that the case had garnered—mainly television and online—many considered how difficult it was going to be to find an impartial set of twelve jurors and alternates who had not heard, read, or thought about the case.

Michael Dwyer, acting justice of the supreme court, a longtime judge known for his objectivity, presided. As each prospective juror walked through the door and sat down to be questioned and possibly chosen, Judge Dwyer commented that they had "tied a record," in his opinion, for not having "one smiling face." The comment relieved some of the mounting tension in the room. Put most at ease during voir dire.

By April 24, 2017, a twelve-person jury—made up of more males than females—and several alternates had been chosen. After all of the pretrial motions, arguments, and courtroom banter concluded, on April 25, *New York* vs. *Kaitlyn A. Conley* began, with jury instructions and opening arguments.

Katie sat next to her lawyer, Christopher Pelli, who had spent his entire life in Mohawk Valley. Pelli had a professional, polished look; he was a handsome fortysomething. Pelli had dealt mainly with personal injury and traffic law, but he also had a solid reputation in criminal law.

"I learned early on the importance of a strong work ethic, and good communication," Pelli stated publicly.

He believed there were "far too many innocent people in jail," a cultural trend that juries were mindful of in 2017. A momentum within an injustice movement was happening across the country. More and more innocent people were being rescued and cleared by DNA, new forensic science technology, and bogus witness statements. Streaming giant Netflix's *Making a Murderer* and the NPR podcast *Serial* had pushed these incidents of police and prosecutorial misconduct into public discourse. Juries now wanted more than a smoking gun. There was little room for giving the prosecution the benefit of the doubt any longer.

In days past, juries could overlook one or two questionable pieces of testimony or a lack of forensic evidence and still convict. In the climate of 2017, prosecutors and defense attorneys understood that mostly every thread needed to be buttoned up. No one wanted to be even remotely responsible for the chance of a defendant spending years behind bars, which could never be gotten back, only to be set free on future evidence everyone had gotten wrong or overlooked. The bar was high. Juries did not walk into courtrooms anymore already siding with the prosecution—no matter how impartial they said they were during voir dire.

While attending Syracuse University School of Law, Pelli worked for the New York State Office of the Attorney General under Dennis Vacco and Elliot Spitzer. That type of prosecutorial insight was going to be an asset for Pelli in Katie's case. Knowing, in some respects, how your opponent thought was staying one step ahead.

For prosecutors, the burden of guilt when presenting a mainly computer forensic science case floated higher as technology and television dominated how the public opinion of murder has been shaped. Juries have become apprehensive about convicting on largely circumstantial evidence, with no direct piece of the puzzle assuring guilt. Computer forensics is data. It is not a fingerprint, blood, bodily fluids, or video surveillance. Juries want DNA, or the computer equivalent, most believing DNA is infallible. They also want to *understand* a case in a way that proves beyond any possibility that the accused is guilty. The narrative has to be straightforward and direct. Nothing complicated.

This public view becomes a double-edged sword for prosecutors, because technology today is a resource with unlimited potential to prove guilt, but also to confuse. As a prosecutor in a case such as Mary Yoder's murder, you had better be able to connect the virtual dots to the accused—via solid, corroborating evidence. If not, you ran the risk of jurors feeling that digital evidence can expose many things, but it cannot *show* who was actually at the other end of a computer connection or an iPhone, unless there's a direct link.

LEAD PROSECUTOR LAURIE LISI had been admitted to the bar in 1984. She had more years practicing law then Katie had been alive. Lisi sported a short bob cut, with straight bangs covering her forehead, her golden blond hair reaching just below her ears. She wore trendy, fashionable glasses with black frames and red lipstick. Lisi had a reputation of integrity and determination; the cases her office presented were ironclad or else they never saw a courtroom.

Outwardly, Katie dressed like a fresh-faced coed: blazer, skirt or pants to match, flats, her dark hair tied back in a ponytail, glasses, a subtle sheen of makeup, red or plum lipstick. Katie's sisters, stepmother and father, several friends, were on hand for proceedings, sitting behind her. One of Katie's friends or a sister was seen occasionally fixing Katie's hair, whispering in her ear, laughing with her.

The team supporting Katie had initiated a *Free Katie Conley* website, depicting Katie as a wholesome country girl who loved animals and family and all things classically good in the world. They stood in unison, believing Katie had been wrongfully charged and targeted. Three of Mary Yoder's sisters belonged to Katie's team. They believed that Katie was innocent of all charges, and made no secret of their feelings. They had gone so far as to accuse Bill Yoder of killing his wife. In town, signs were stuck in the ground everywhere: FREE KATIE CONLEY; SHE'S INNOCENT; WRONGFULLY CHARGED.

The entire city of Utica seemed to be behind this young woman who appeared to be the perfect scapegoat for a prosecution with tunnel vision. It seemed they had dug too deep an investigative hole and were looking to hang the murder of Mary Yoder on anyone who fit.

Opening statements began with Laurie Lisi, who introduced a metaphor, referencing "the serene philosophy of the pink rose" and how "steadying" it is. "Its fragrant, delicate petals open fully and are ready to fall without regret or dissolution after a day in the sun." That process took place every summer, Lisi explained. "Summer, summer. It will always be summer." For Mary Yoder, she concluded the thought, "it will *always* be summer."

The outspoken prosecutor described Mary Yoder's love of gardening, tying the pink rose to her. Then she talked about Mary's final day on the planet. She walked jurors through the entire day, into that night, the next morning, and, finally, Mary's heart-wrenching, painful, untimely death.

Lisi moved on to the blood samples taken by the Poison Control Center as the team established colchicine as the weapon used to kill Mary.

Then Lisi brought Detective Mark VanNamee into her opening narrative as she explained how doggedly he pursued the case, first looking at Adam, then Bill, finally drawing the conclusion that Katie was Mary's killer. The evidence was too strong and obvious to ignore. Not to mention, of course, Katie's bizarre behavior at times during the interviews VanNamee had conducted.

Defending Adam and Bill, Lisi explained how they could not have possibly killed Mary because their actions displayed two devastated family members willing to provide the OCSO with anything they needed, whenever they needed it.

This opened up the opportunity for Lisi to raise the red flag of the Mr. Adam Yoder 1990 at Gmail account, the first of many oddities that led VanNamee and his team into a virtual rabbit hole. Their investigation ended, always, at Katie's fingers on the keys of her computer or iPhone, purchasing the toxin.

The prepaid cards.

The Hannaford supermarket trip to buy them.

ArtChemicals.

Rosa Vargas.

The anonymous letters.

After that, Lisi made an important point, based in fact, delivered directly from Katie's mouth. During her first interview, Lisi pointed out, Katie had said she did not know Adam's passwords or that the Mr. Adam Yoder 1990 e-mail account even existed. After being backed into a corner, however, with pressure from VanNamee and facts, a few interviews later, Katie admitted, *Oh, yeah, I know that's Adam's e-mail.*

The point was: Why the ambiguity? Why the pushing back on Katie's part? Why had she been so secretive and combative? So emotional? So determined to walk the OCSO into a dark room of confusion? And, most important, why was Katie not doing everything she could to help find out who was responsible for Mary Yoder's murder—her boss and friend, a woman she claimed to have nothing but high praise and love for?

"The evidence that will be presented to you will connect Kaitlyn Conley to colchicine that was used to kill Mary Yoder," Lisi said matter-of-factly. "It is simply just another piece of evidence that points the finger at this defendant as the person who is solely responsible for the *intentional* murder of Mary Yoder."

Intentional murder. Lisi was saying Katie thought this through, planned it, plotted, and executed those actions for the purpose of taking Mary's life.

For about an hour, Lisi went through the state's most powerful pieces of evidence—how the fatal drug was purchased at the hands of Katie and no one else. Smartly, as she spoke of evidence, every once in a while, Lisi reminded jurors about the type of person the prosecution found Katie to be: "There also will be evidence presented in this trial demonstrating that even after Mary Yoder's death, Kaitlyn Conley was not done causing havoc on the Yoder family."

Although it's not imperative or a legal requirement for the prosecution to prove motive, Lisi knew jurors needed to hear her thoughts about it. And what a surprise many in the gallery received: "Motive is not an element of any of the crimes that Kaitlyn

Conley is charged with . . . Motive is rarely, if ever, an element of *any* crime . . . There's no reason for her to have done this—in fact, what she did was lose a good friend and a job and an employer."

Then a warning: "Do not base your verdict in innuendo, on rumors, on hearsay, on mere speculation. That is not what our criminal justice system is about . . . Don't throw away your common sense."

Christopher Pelli was dressed in a shiny gray suit; his full beard and mustache, brown-framed glasses, gave him the look of a distinguished science professor. Pelli was there to defend the rights of his client, everything else was noise and static. He understood the task was an uphill battle. After all, Katie had admitted to buying the credit cards used to purchase the colchicine—a fact that would be difficult to explain away.

Pelli told jurors there were simple, obvious reasons for much of the prosecution's evidence, adding how, "This case is entirely about motive . . . The question is, who had what to gain from Mary's death? . . . There's no reason for her to have done this!" He paused. Then, stepping out of what was a gray area, he brought in his chief suspect: "It's Dr. William Yoder who is guilty of this horrific crime."

Silence from the gallery.

Then whispers.

There were people in the courtroom—both Conley and Yoder family members—who had taken the statement to heart. Many court attendees had bought into the rumors that Bill was some sort of scoundrel who had spent all of the Yoder money and had pissed away his and Mary's retirement funds, had a harem of concubines, and was a drug dealer who hated his wife. This defense was typical and predictable: If not Katie, who could have murdered Mary? To take Katie out of the equation, her defense needed an alternative. In this trial, it was going to be Bill Yoder. Christopher Pelli made this clear within a few minutes of getting started.

He then went on to say the romantic relationship that Bill had initiated with Mary's sister, along with his obsessive pursuit of money and fame (his book), became Bill's motivation to poison his wife. On top of that, Pelli argued, Bill had a history of growing marijuana: "Colchicine is used during marijuana growth." And in the paperwork sent to ArtChemicals for ordering the colchicine, Pelli contended, raising his voice a notch, guess what? It referenced plant growth process, which Katie could not have known about.

Except, Pelli failed to say, she could have learned about it with a Google search. According to her iPhone and computer data, Katie spent a hell of a lot of time doing just that during the months leading up to Mary's murder.

"Basically, the government is telling you that they don't have a very good case," Pelli said, shrugging his shoulders in a mocking gesture. "They don't know *how* the poison got into Mary's system and they don't know *why*."

Both of those particular statements were nonsense. Looking on with professional disdain, coupled with glee, Laurie Lisi and Stacey Scotti were fully prepared to present evidence to prove how the toxin entered Mary's system.

64

*T*ESTIMONY BEGAN THE FOLLOWING morning, April 26, 2017, at ten-thirty. A person sitting close to the front of the room, with a clear view of Katie, shared an interesting observation. To this person's utter amazement, as this source sat and looked on, every so often Katie would point her chair toward the jurors, namely the males. She would smile her charming schoolgirl grin, and then spread her legs partially open, revealing she was not wearing stockings underneath her short skirt. This moment, and there were many similar to it, played like a scene straight out of *Basic Instinct,* the 1992 thriller. In this film noir, Sharon Stone's character, while questioned by male detectives, gives them the same shot, an unmistakably clear view of her vagina up her skirt.

"I looked over at her . . . and there was nothing," said one woman who sat in the gallery, and had been close to Katie at one time in her life. "Katie had no emotion whatsoever."

After a short break, ADA Lisi began with the ER director, setting up Mary Yoder's arrival on that morning. The witness went through the medications Mary had been given and the symptoms she presented.

The state then brought in a number of medical and forensic witnesses to show how, after not being able to figure out what had made Mary so ill, it was narrowed down to colchicine by the PCC.

Liana Hegde sat in the witness chair next. Liana, a beautiful woman, bore a striking resemblance to her late mother. She brought an emotional side of the state's case into the trial. She explained how her mother was the matriarch of the family, the adhesive keeping everyone connected. Liana could not hold back the tears at certain times. She came across as a strong, independent woman who had lost not only her mother, but her best friend. Throughout her direct testimony, Liana was able to date the narrative, explain to jurors where Adam and Bill were and how they were reacting to Mary's death. A doctor herself, Liana then laid out how she became the liaison between the family and the ME's office. The point was that Bill and Adam Yoder were shocked, saddened, and transformed by Mary's death. Both men were as eager as the rest of the family to find out what had killed her, all while in a miserable state of mourning.

Not halfway into Liana's testimony, the day had gotten away from the judge and it was time to recess until the following morning.

Liana finished her direct on April 27, 2017. Then Chris Pelli stepped in, making a beeline toward Adam. He asked Liana if she'd ever loaned her brother money. The motivation behind this line of questioning was to set up a plot proving Adam was desperate, broke, unstable, and not in his right mind during the months before and after Mary's death. The defense needed a backup villain. Adam was the perfect secondary stooge.

At one point, Pelli also used Liana to implicate his chief person of interest: Bill Yoder. "Is it fair to say your [aunts] suspected your father of being involved in this?"

Liana wasn't biting. "You'd have to ask them. I knew there [were] suspicions later on. I did not know at the time. They did not share those ideas with me. They actually told me directly they were suspicious of their other sister . . ."

Toxicology took up most of the remaining day, as it was important to explain how colchicine was difficult to detect when no one knew what they were looking for. But once the PCC figured out colchicine was the likely killer, the testing proved it. From there, it became a matter of figuring out how Mary had ingested the toxin.

The second day of full testimony ended with several of Mary Yoder's final patients coming in. They told their stories of what they had witnessed. All of these eyewitnesses mentioned how Mary was fine one minute, her normal self, but late afternoon—after she came back from lunch—Mary Yoder became a person none of them recognized.

65

*D*URING A BREAK IN proceedings the following day, a friend of Mary's, a longtime patient, heard laughter outside the courtroom doors. Loud, rambunctious banter, almost as if a group of coworkers was celebrating an office birthday. She stood up from her bench seat in the courtroom, walked through the doors, and shuffled around the corner. She spotted Katie, several of her family members, and a few others, laughing and joking and playing around. For one of Mary's good friends, it was an appalling display of disrespect.

Yet, it showed how Katie did not seem to be taking any of this seriously. At times, she would sit inside the courtroom next to her lawyer, with a stoic, intense gaze, as if scared her freedom could be taken away. Then she'd retreat into the hallway, out of jurors' view and earshot, and transform into a carefree twentysomething. She'd ham it up with her family and friends, as if none of this was bothering her. The narcissism Katie demonstrated was blatant and rude. A woman had been murdered—and the person accused of that vicious crime was laughing and joking around.

"I knew Katie very well," that same source said, "and I realized there were two sides to her. One of them smart and introverted and shy—the other cold, calculated, and narcissistic."

Dr. Jeanna Marraffa, Poison Control Center assistant director, was the expert who figured out colchicine had killed Mary. Dr. Marraffa gave jurors a complete perspective regarding poisoning and toxicity in the body. It should be noted—and several had—that without Dr. Marraffa getting involved, Mary's killer might have walked away and Mary's death would have been ruled accidental.

After several additional witnesses, most of whom explained how Mary felt and acted on the day she became ill, Bill Yoder walked in and sat down. It was April 28. Bill would spend the better part of the entire day in the witness-box.

Bill was seventy-one. He looked good, but sad, under some stress knowing he was going to have to relive the most horrifying moments of his life. Bill came across as a guy with a tough exterior, who realized how important his testimony was to the overall scope of the prosecution's case.

Leading up to trial, Bill had been the subject of a constant online character assassination. Social media had not been kind. He was a killer and a cad. A man who had plotted and planned the death of his wife. A moneygrubbing cheater who initiated a romance with Mary's sister months before Mary died.

None of this was true.

The prosecution told Bill not to respond to any of the allegations—it would only make matters worse. Bill held back, hard as it was, and withstood the barrage of insults and erroneous accusations without fighting back.

After going through his professional credentials, stopping occasionally because a torrent of tears overcame him, Bill talked about the day Mary walked in ill and never got better. Then he discussed how she had died, after coding many times, her family surrounding her. Bill was an intensely emotional man, unafraid to let his feelings show. It was clear to everyone: in his voice, composure, and demeanor.

There were no surprise revelations from Bill during his direct. He set up the narrative of Mary's illness, answered questions regarding his relationship with Mary's sister, and gave jurors a clear picture of losing the love of his life so suddenly and unexpectedly. Through Bill's testimony, ADA Lisi was able to enter key exhibits into the record—including e-mails and texts and reports. Clearly, Bill had started his relationship with Mary's sister in the weeks after Mary's death. The evidence that Lisi presented proved it.

Concluding his direct, Bill detailed how orders were made from the office, a task Katie had always taken care of. Bill had not created a shell company, Chiro Family Care. That had been done without his knowledge. The signature on the documents used to purchase the colchicine, Bill confirmed, was Mary's. ADA Lisi asked Bill where the signature stamper was kept.

"In Katie's desk," Bill answered.

Then Bill was questioned about the typewriter, which he had purchased when they opened the business.

"In the reception area where Katie worked," Bill answered after being asked where the typewriter had sat.

Lisi wondered how long it had been there.

"Thirty-five years . . ."

In explaining his relationship with Mary's sister, Bill said, quite emphatically and emotionally, "I had nothing left in my life . . . Just felt pain and sadness every day. And I'd learned firsthand that everything could be ripped away in an instant, and I saw this chance for a little companionship and human warmth and just a little bit of happiness. And I thought, you know, I might be gone tomorrow . . . I didn't want to wait around until everybody thought it was politically correct."

During his direct, Bill must have said something that angered one of Mary's sisters sitting in the courtroom. As he spoke, she burst into temper-filled shouting, tossing in one or two curse words, many in her vicinity later alleged.

The sister was instantly silenced by a scowl from Judge Dwyer. But after turning his attention back to Bill's testimony, the sister stood up, flipped the middle finger toward Bill and the judge, and stomped out of the courtroom.

Beginning his cross-examination, Chris Pelli went right after Bill. He accused him of dating Mary's sister before having met Mary in 1975. (This was not Kathleen Richmond, whom he would date after Mary died.) Bill said he had no recollection of this whatsoever.

"Isn't it true that Mary set you and [her sister] up on a blind date?" Pelli asked.

"I sure don't recall that. No."

The marriage was next.

"Is it true on that day [you were married], you expressed to Mary that you expected the marriage would be an open marriage?"

"No," Bill said. Then: "We discussed that question sometime *before* we were getting married."

"Okay, you were the one to bring that up?"

"Yes, I did."

As Pelli worked in how Bill and Mary moved to South Carolina after getting married and having Liana, he mentioned a photograph, which he then entered as an exhibit.

After having Bill look at it, Pelli asked him to describe what he saw.

Bill pointed to Liana, just an infant, in the photo.

Pelli asked what was in the background.

"It looks like a little . . . an old shed."

"The marijuana plants that you admitted to growing with Mary in South Carolina"—which Bill had no problem divulging on direct examination—"they were behind that shed?"

"No. There was a big brush field that adjoined our property, so they . . . they weren't even close."

This talk about Bill and Mary growing weed in the 1970s, while living in South Carolina, went on for some time. It was meant to shame Bill. Place him under a bad light. To make him appear to be a morality-free pot dealer. If growing and selling pot was not a problem for him, then perhaps killing his wife would not be, either.

Pelli also wanted to make the point that Bill knew about colchicine because it was sometimes used in marijuana plant growing. As Pelli chronicled the way in which Bill and Mary grew weed, it became clear that Mary's sisters who supported Katie had given him all of the information. In the end, however, Bill testified that he had no trouble selling weed to two of Mary's sisters and mailing it to them.

Bill answered all questions, no matter how humiliating, how degrading, or how unimportant they seemed in the scope of his wife's murder. He came across as truthful and honest. One of Pelli's major issues was immunity: The prosecution had given Bill immunity from ever being prosecuted for his wife's murder if he testified on its behalf.

"No, I was not aware of any immunity. I was just testifying," he said, striking the entire accusation down.

The hits kept coming. After prompting, Bill explained how, once a month, he would drive up north by himself and rent a house (or hotel room) so he could work on his book in private. He needed to get away from the hustle and bustle back in Utica.

After warning Bill that perjury was a crime, Pelli saw an opportunity: "Isn't it true that on many of those occasions . . . you met another woman?"

"Not at all."

Pelli brought in Bill's grand jury testimony and pointed out where Bill had talked about how many times he had seen Kathleen, Mary's sister, before Mary's death. The conversation went back and forth, and Pelli did nothing more than confuse the issue entirely, which might have been his strategy.

Ultimately, all Pelli's cross-examination did was bring into the record more confusion over who was on trial: Adam, Bill, or Katie. Bill was smeared and attacked, made to explain his intimate thoughts about marriage and love and sex, along with the meaning behind personal texts he'd written to Kathleen. Pelli tried to find some sort of hidden affair (before Mary's murder) within the text messages, but it just wasn't there.

At one point, the state of Adam's mental health came up. Pelli asked Bill if his son was bipolar. Bill said he didn't know. Adam had alcohol problems, Bill suggested, and after his mother's death, he suffered from anxiety and depression. "He was very devastated," Bill testified.

Then another peculiar line of questioning: "Okay, Bill, this will be the last of the embarrassing questions. Are you a member . . . during the time that your wife was alive, of any Internet . . . porn sites—"

Bill didn't allow Pelli to finish before butting in. "No."

". . . where stories were submitted . . ."

"I was never a member of anything, no."

After a break, Pelli came at Bill again with a personal question. He asked if he could recall the first time he had sexual relations with Kathleen, Mary's sister.

"I don't remember the date, no. I wasn't keeping a journal."

After that, Pelli asked Bill if he'd ever entered the office through a back door. Again, the defense attorney was implying that Bill was acting mysterious and creepy during those days before and after Mary's death. Bill replied that he went into the office through the back door when he didn't want to be disturbed.

Mary's three sisters, who were in the courtroom for most of the testimony, frequently broke into loud outbursts. The judge had to tell them numerous times to be silent. To the shock of the gallery, Judge Dwyer threw one of the sisters out of the courtroom for the remainder of the day. She then sat in the hallway.

When Bill finished his testimony, he walked out and passed her. He was in tears, wiping his eyes, unaware that she was there.

"Well, Bill, that was *quite* a performance," she allegedly said, according to Bill's recollection.

Startled, Bill began to reply, but two cops in the hallway rushed over. One led Bill away, the other stood in front of the sister.

"You're not allowed to harass the witnesses," Bill overheard the cop tell her.

Later, when the two police officers reported the incident to the judge, he banned the sister from the courtroom for the remainder of the trial.

66

*A*FTER A WEEKEND BREAK, Detective Mark VanNamee and additional law enforcement investigators ate up the next few days, bringing the trial into May. This allowed Laurie Lisi to enter the interviews the OCSO had conducted (and recorded) with Katie, along with all of the evidence they had uncovered up to that point: the anonymous letters, the bottle of colchicine, the receipt, Katie's DNA found on the packaging and bottom of the colchicine bottle, and several important items from the office.

The state's next major witness was Adam Yoder. He wore a checkered, button-down blue shirt. His goatee was carefully groomed, and his reddish-blond hair was slicked back against his pale complexion. Adam's gaze seemed troubled, serious.

He walked in on the morning of May 2, 2017, to finish his testimony. His testimony on the stand had been cut short the previous day because of time constraints. Adam was leaner than he had been. He came across as sullen, beaten. He rarely gestured toward Katie.

It had been some time since Adam had moved out of town. He was living a life far away from the chaos that had taken over his life. He had distanced himself from a woman who had been, clearly, obsessed with keeping him. The scowl on his face spoke to how much Adam still blamed himself for allowing a romantic partner to step into their lives and kill his mother. It weighed heavily on him. He was harboring the burden of his mother's death.

Laurie Lisi asked Adam to explain his relationship with Katie and how it had progressed: the back-and-forth, the breakups, the reunions, the fights, the make-up sex, and the countless contentious texts. Then she led Adam into talking about that bout of "flu" in April 2015. Mainly, she concentrated on how it came on after Katie had given him a bottle of Alpha BRAIN supplement.

Katie had repeatedly encouraged him to take it. "She told me it's there to help. Basically focus and boost memory. She said make sure I take it consecutively and consistently, because it works better over time . . . She told me that she had been taking it earlier in the semester. She hoped it would help me during finals." However, after taking the supplement, Adam became severely ill and remained so for weeks. He couldn't understand what was wrong.

At the time he became sick, both he and Katie were students at SUNY Polytechnic Institute. He said they met once a week for coffee or food, but he and Katie were not in a romantic relationship then. He needed to remain friends. It was important to him not to sever the relationship entirely and walk away bitter. Beyond that, Katie had accused him of rape; keeping her close was a way to deal with any fallout from such a horrible, reputation-crushing accusation, if it ever got out.

At this stage of the state's case, they did not have all of the data back from Katie's iPhone and computers, so the illness was mentioned only as a speculative aside. The prosecution had so much data to look over, and new evidence was coming in every day. In addition, the DA's office was not aware that inside Adam's laptop was a complete computer snapshot of Katie's iPhone. It contained all the deleted files and thousands of images, many of which had been deleted. Adam knew because he had discovered it, but carelessly—perhaps because he had so much on his mind—he had not thought to share the information with the DA's office.

Beyond the sudden illness and a personal snapshot of his tumultuous relationship, Adam provided context, giving the jury an intimate look into Katie's behavior. He outlined a timeline. He said he did not know that the bogus Gmail account existed until detectives told him. He had nothing to do with setting it up. Did not even know the password—Adam Is Gay—until he was told.

Notably, Katie only shed a tear once throughout the trial. She cried when Adam, pressed about their relationship, responded to Laurie Lisi by answering: "Katie was not a good girlfriend." Mind you, the medical examiner and other expert witnesses had testified and detailed the immense amount of pain Mary Yoder had gone through. Her suffering. The intensity of all those codes and how hard she fought to stay alive.

Yet, throughout that, Katie played with her hair, unaffected. She sat and stared at each witness without an emotion. It was only when she heard Adam describe how bad a partner she had been that Katie found it within herself to shed a tear.

Chris Pelli began his cross-examination by having Adam admit that before he dated Katie, he was in a sexually active relationship with a sixteen-year-old girl. He was twenty then, committing a crime, but was never charged. The question and answer was a blow to Adam's character by the mere mention of it. Still: What did a stupid, criminal decision by a twenty-year-old have to do with the evidence the state presented against Katie?

From there, Pelli's cross-examination focused on text messages Adam had sent to Katie before and after his mother's death, from February 2015 to November 2015. In February 2015, Adam explained, he and Katie were not in a relationship but still met from time to time.

Pelli pointed out that Adam, even then, was texting "I love you" and "We should just start fresh and try again." That November, Adam had texted: "I miss you and I still love you. I just want you to know that."

Despite such intimate texts, Pelli implied, Adam claimed he did *not* want to get back together with Katie. It was difficult for Adam to break free from what was a codependent relationship.

Adam agreed. He had no intention of being in a romance with Katie. He'd been down that road several times and it never worked. He still loved her, but he knew he could not be with her.

Pelli tried to create a divide between Adam and his mother, using text messages to illustrate it. He attempted to shape misunderstandings and routine mother-son squabbles into some kind of dark, twisted, hidden hatred that the guy harbored for his mom. None of it was there, however.

Then Pelli mentioned the drugs Adam had taken: Adderall and

a few others. Adam said yes, he had taken those medications. He was also asthmatic and used an inhaler.

This type of testimony was generally tossed aside by attentive jurors, who realized there were agendas on both sides. Adam was a distraught, biased witness. As far as Katie's team showing how Adam could have killed Mary, the evidence to corroborate the theory wasn't available. Murder takes motive, opportunity, and action—none of which could be proven in *any* way pertaining to Adam, or even Bill, for that matter.

The remainder of the trial consisted of expert and character witnesses. They laid out a scenario that showed how Katie Conley ordered the colchicine from her iPhone and home computer and then used it to kill Mary Yoder. There could be no doubt that she framed Adam Yoder for the crime. Even though many gray areas remained in the evidentiary chain—for the sole reason the prosecution did not have enough time to study everything—the state made a compelling case for murder.

Rosa Vargas, for example, walked into the courtroom and owned the entire space. In a fictionalized version of her entrance, Rosa might have dramatically flung the courtroom door open, surprising everyone, while snapping gum and blowing bubbles. The real-life Rosa sported green hair, with matching fingernail polish, wore skintight pants and a fringe-edged blouse, and rocked an eccentric, over-the-top vibe.

Despite her trendy Hollywood look, Rosa gave jurors an impartial, credible side of the truth from a person who had no obligation to anyone involved. She offered cold facts, backed up by documentation, all of which did not support the defense's claim. Rosa carefully testified how determined the woman she spoke to over the phone was to get her hands on that colchicine. The description of the customer's voice also matched Katie's.

The next several days consisted of technical computer experts, forensics, and additional law enforcement officers. Some of their testimony was cumbersome, but crucial. It reflected how much the investigation relied on computer forensics. The experts outlined the significance of e-mail accounts, Google, phone apps, and how computer and phone metadata worked behind the screens, which we all rely on today.

The interviews with Katie played a large role, too.

By May 9, 10, and 11, the defense put up a weak case of trying to shift the blame onto Adam. Katie's lawyers used witnesses like Adam's cousin Dave King to try to bury him.

Katie never testified. Kathleen Richmond, Mary's sister and Bill's new girlfriend, did, however. Pelli called Kathleen to perhaps see if he could squeeze anything out of the widowed romance and give jurors a reason to question Bill's motives.

After only a few questions, Kathleen said she and Bill did not hook up romantically until September 2015, nearly two months after Mary passed. "We were grieving together and we gravitated to each other."

Kathleen had lost her husband and her little sister within a year or so. Pelli tried to get Kathleen to say she and Bill were involved before Mary's death, but it wasn't happening. The facts weren't there to support the allegation. Pelli had zero corroborating evidence: no e-mails, texts, phone calls, or letters.

Pelli asked: "Didn't you tell [your sister] that you'd been close with Bill for the past couple of years?"

"No. I said we'd been friends for many years . . . It was nothing different from the last thirty years."

That other sister was called next. Pelli wanted to know how Bill was acting after Mary's death, specifically at the Celebration of Life.

"[Bill] just seemed sort of distant," she said, as if it was suspect for a guy who'd just lost his wife and soul mate of four decades to be acting erratic and off.

Pelli also wanted to know what she thought after investigators called her in and explained the case they were building against Katie.

"Okay," she replied. "I'm willing to accept that maybe Katie had something to do with this, but I cannot believe that she acted on her own." Mary's sister went on to explain how discouraged she felt after investigators seemed to be only focused on Katie. According to her, they did not want to hear additional theories about what *could* have happened.

"It was obvious I did not agree with their theory," Mary's sister testified. "I thought [they] were going to tell me something about

[Katie's] character or her past, and [they] didn't do that. You know, all this [was] just computer logistical stuff."

Moving on, she explained that once, in 1981, she'd received a bag of weed from Bill in the mail. Then she digressed, recalling how she suddenly remembered telling investigators when she met with them: "Couldn't someone have hacked or, you know, gotten into the computer stuff or the phone stuff? It was like they weren't . . . they really didn't want to hear anything that I might have offered at that point in time."

At times, the court had to stop testimony because she became too agitated and nervous. Laurie Lisi was able to get the sister to admit she had told investigators she never suspected Bill or Mary of having an extramarital affair. As a heated, prickly back-and-forth ensued, the smart prosecutor pointed out how upset the sister became after the OCSO failed to provide her with a motive for Mary's murder.

"And is that one of the reasons why you didn't agree with their theory?" Lisi asked.

"No. I don't think it was because . . . um, well, yes. I mean, it makes no . . . it made no sense—"

"Just 'yes' or 'no'?" Lisi insisted.

". . . that Katie would do this, that a young girl would do this— was not even just Katie—out of the blue."

The statement put an exclamation point on Lisi's argument that this sister had demanded a motive, a reason why, and the OCSO was not coming through.

Lisi paused. She looked at the witness. Then, with squinted eyes, the prosecutor repeated the witness's comment as a question: "'Out of the blue'?"

The sister did not respond.

"No further questions." ADA Lisi sat down.

Both sides offered closing arguments on May 11. By 2:26 p.m., the judge was reading the jury its instructions. Pelli had motioned earlier in the day for the court to dismiss the case, which was immediately denied.

Many leaving the courtroom were scratching their heads. They wondered what, exactly, had taken place. There didn't seem to be a focus for the defense, besides Bill or Adam Yoder committing the murder.

The prosecution's case was a strong circumstantial presentation, but perhaps it lacked the pithy explanation that juries yearned to hear. Additionally, so much evidence still needed to be looked at. Although confident, both Laurie Lisi and Stacey Scotti wondered if they'd offered that *aha* moment to convince jurors that Katie was their killer.

67

MURDER TRIALS IN SMALL towns are a bit different than those in big cities, where televised talking-head attorneys bang on about speculative evidence and hearsay on a public stage. There's a certain close-knit community atmosphere within the former. It's almost as if those in town who pay attention have personal skin in the game; they have an intimate connection to the accused or (rare as it is) the prosecution. Katie's trial had garnered big headlines, some talk on the cable shows, with NBC's *Dateline* in the courtroom to report on it.

None of it, sadly, had to do with the reason why everyone was there: Mary Yoder. As in many high-profile murder trials, the victim had taken a backseat to sensationalism.

After all, one has to ask: Did the Jodi Arias case gain all that international attention because of murder victim Travis Alexander? Or was it the absolute bloody, horrific nature of the crime itself?

Neither.

It was Jodi.

Arias had a cunning, charming ability to manipulate situations and people. She was a psychopath adept at portraying the innocent, beautiful, girl-next-door ingénue, who became a media martyr. There were striking similarities between Katie Conley and Jodi Arias.

The way they thought was similar. How they acted. Their obvious narcissism. How they paraded themselves in public, as opposed to behind closed doors. Their psychology. The way they both believed that as long as they told a lie long enough, to as many people as possible, that it *should* be believed because *they* said it.

Community members take sides when small-town murder occurs. They debate details at local diners, the post office, while fueling up at the gas station. Theories are individual and personal. People make judgments. They feel directly attached to some of the players. Many in Utica and Oneida County had known Mary Yoder personally. Many more knew the Conley family and viewed Katie as an upstanding young member of the community.

You look at Katie and her sisters, father, and mother, and what you see on the outside—without knowing anything about them—is wholesomeness. It's easy to be sucked into the charm, some of which is genuine. Like Mary's sister who had testified on Katie's behalf, and said she just couldn't *believe* a young girl such as Kaitlyn could commit such a horrible crime.

It's all perception. It's how some people are able to present an image of who they want you to think they are. It's how we see, sometimes, only what we want to see.

Likewise, you look at the Yoders and see some of the same characteristics. They are a hardworking, upper-middle-class, honorable, kind, and generous family. Well-educated professionals. The outstanding difference between the Conleys and the Yoders: the Yoder family lost the one member who held the rest of them together.

All of these facts and opinions attracted NBC's *Dateline* to the case. According to the Yoders and the prosecution, the TV team chummed it up with Katie and her family. This murder was the ideal *Dateline* narrative. It checked every production box the show called for.

Chris Pelli had placed a blemish on the Yoder family name from the get-go, and had done a good job of it. It was in the suggestions he'd made, the questions he put to witnesses. The speculation and gray areas left without complete explanations. The answers from witnesses didn't matter. Once a bell is rung, it's impossible to *un*-ring it.

In dissecting it all, still without knowing any of the intimate details, one could draw any conclusion he or she wanted, and justify the choice. For a jury facing the burden of guilt or innocence, the same is true. The men and women making up a jury feel, judge, and develop theories and questions. The difference is juries sit through every moment of testimony and have the opportunity to look at and weigh every single piece of evidence.

Heading into deliberations, Katie sat in the courtroom, seemingly content and self-assured. If you studied Katie's life, you saw through the conservative dresses, the country-girl—strolling-in-the-meadow hairstyle, and her innocent mien. An angry, dark woman, whom nobody truly knew, lurked inside Katie. She was a woman who had done things most in her camp would never believe, no matter how much evidence had been presented to prove it.

On the afternoon of May 12, after the judge called everyone back in, Katie looked hopeful and undaunted. The rumors were true: the jury was having trouble. This was no slam dunk, as some might have expected. In order to get over to the prosecution's side, there were a great many computer-technology and high-tech bridges to cross. So much so, it became a bumpy walk. On the flip side, if you wanted to toss reasonable doubt onto the table and claim you were unsure whether it was Adam or Bill who was involved, that bridge was easy to get over.

The judge indicated he'd received a note from the jury. They had requested evidence regarding Bill Yoder's testimony regarding "the first time he heard colchicine toxicity, how he first learned about it."

Not a good sign for the prosecution.

The jury also wanted to know what Mary had eaten on the morning of her illness. Which could mean they were looking for a way in which to blame her death on anyone but Katie.

Finally, in the same note, the jury asked for the "poison control expert testimony" on the time frame of "colchicine reaction on the body,"

This was certainly a sign there were several jurors looking to see if the possibility existed that Bill could have put the toxin in Mary's breakfast.

Colchicine toxicity symptoms can arise almost immediately, subtle as they might come on. Testimony by experts claimed there is not enough research available to give a more exact window of time other than eight hours for the onset of fully bloomed symptoms. The first symptoms one experiences if poisoned by an overdose of colchicine are persistent nausea, abdominal pain, vomiting, and diarrhea—all of which Mary experienced late that afternoon, near three to four o'clock.

If jurors looked at the testimony and evidence, this second question could have been answered with Mary ingesting the colchicine while at work. Bill Yoder testified Mary did not eat breakfast. The opinion of the prosecution was that Mary had a Shaklee protein shake that afternoon for a pick-me-up. Inside the tin of powder she kept in the office was a dose of colchicine sprinkled over the top by the only other person in the office—Katie Conley. Katie had access and opportunity, along with knowledge of the Shaklee powder being in the refrigerator.

And, perhaps most important, she had motive.

Then the jury asked to see Katie's interview with Detective Mark VanNamee.

After the video played, Judge Dwyer adjourned for the weekend. He gave his verbal warning regarding talking to people and looking at news/media reports or engaging in social media conversation and Web surfing.

"See you all on Monday morning."

As everyone left the courthouse, an incident took place outside, in front of the building. "It was beyond comprehension," said one Yoder family member.

Christopher Pelli had driven "his fancy sports car," as several described it, to court. He'd parked it on the street in front of the DA's office. As they had done every day of the trial, the Yoders had waited inside the courtroom for the Conley family and Katie's supporters to leave first, to avoid a run-in.

"But when we went outside," said the same family member, "Katie and her sisters were posing for pictures with the car, taking selfies, laughing."

It spoke to the utter lack of appropriateness, understanding, and empathy displayed by Katie throughout the trial.

"Never in my career," said one member of the prosecution, "have I ever seen a family act like this—especially during a murder trial."

68

O_N MAY 15, 2017, a chilly Monday morning, 48 degrees, with puffy, marshmallow clouds slowly moving east, the sun poking in and out, the jury arrived and met for a short time. The foreman then indicated they had additional requests. "We need the definition of 'intent,' as described in the charges."

Laurie Lisi and Stacey Scotti looked at each other. *Damn.*

Pelli sat back in his chair and took a deep breath.

Then this: "We feel that we do not know what to do. We cannot reach a mutual agreement."

Clearly, there was a holdout or two.

This gave everyone on Katie's side a fuzzy feeling of success, but not necessarily victory. The jury was deadlocked. They were unable to reach a group decision. A verdict of not guilty was definitely off the table, that much was certain. Yet, there was still a problem— and a good chance Katie was walking out of the courtroom, on bond, with her freedom.

The judge read the note. He addressed the jury. Clear and direct, Dwyer told them: "If you cannot reach a unanimous verdict . . . a new trial will have to be scheduled before a different jury."

Dwyer went on to say this type of indecision was not uncommon. Most juries were, however, able to reach a unanimous verdict after further deliberations. It seemed to Dwyer that the jury, not yet deliberating for a full day, wanted to give up.

After ordering the jury to continue, Dwyer said: "Start with a fresh slate . . . Have the courage to be flexible. Be willing to change your position if a reevaluation of the evidence convinces you that a charge is appropriate . . . Be honest with yourselves and with the other jurors . . . Frankly, it wasn't intended to be easy."

Jurors went back in for an hour and indicated they needed to speak to the judge. It was 11:29 a.m., the second day of deliberations. They were still hung on the definition of "intent." They wanted to understand burden of proof on the state to show Katie had acted intentionally, consciously, and knew her actions could take a life.

It's almost humorous to follow this stumbling block: How could somebody purchase prepaid credit cards, order regulated poison online, spend months manipulating documents and forging a fake company, before devising a plan to place the poison in something she knew the victim would eat or drink, and it *not* be intentional?

The jury was looking for any way out of this.

Dwyer advised the jurors that the law permitted each to consider the acts and conduct of Katie before, during, and after the commission of the crime. In other words, downloading *CamScanner,* forging Mary's signature, manipulating documents to create a company, writing anonymous letters accusing her ex-boyfriend of killing his mother, mailing them to law enforcement, were "acts" by Katie clearly showing intent.

Was the jury trying to say they believed Katie wanted only for Mary to become ill? If so, the statement didn't matter within the scope of the charges because Mary *had* died.

The judge wasn't having any of it. He explained the long version of "intent" and sent them back into deliberations.

An hour and fifteen minutes later, the jury came back.

The judge suggested lunch, adding how he would appreciate it if they continued deliberating after some food.

By 4:00 p.m., the jury surprised everyone, suggesting they were still discussing the case and wanted to return the next morning to continue deliberating.

First thing the following morning, May 16, they asked for a dry-erase board, markers, and a large pad of paper.

"To create a timeline."

This said a lot. They had entered into a discussion, obviously, regarding who had the opportunity to kill Mary and when the ingestion of poison occurred.

At 4:00 p.m., the jury asked for "testimony on what days of the week Miss Conley worked while at Chiropractic Family Care."

On May 17, deliberations continued all day. The judge dismissed the jury late into the afternoon. When they returned on May 18, deliberations went until lunch. Near 1:00 p.m., they came back and announced: "We, the jury, after taking a break, are still never going to be able to reach a unanimous verdict."

Both sides accepted the jury's decision. Agreed to call it hung, and requested a mistrial.

"You've worked longer than any jury I've ever had, and that is twenty-two years," Judge Dwyer said with both respect and frustration. Katie's father, wearing a red-white-and-blue, stars-and-stripes flag tie (which he wore quite often), sat directly behind his daughter. He laughed, a smile washing over his entire face. Wearing a blue-and-white, leopard-patterned dress, her hair pulled back into a braid, Katie looked relieved. Bill and Adam Yoder sat in the first row of seats, directly in back of the prosecution. They appeared confused and shell-shocked, obviously devastated. The evidence seemed so clear.

Outside the courtroom, soft-spoken Chris Pelli talked about the mistrial as a victory, but not worthy of celebration. He uttered the old cliché: "We won the battle, but not the war."

Laurie Lisi was not surprised. She knew after a day of deliberations the jury was struggling. "I thought we had a strong case," Lisi told a local reporter. "I *believe* we have a strong case, and I'll be ready to go in the fall."

June 2, 2017, was the next court date.

69

*K*ATIE'S FAMILY SPOKE TO local media, providing a statement not long after the mistrial had been announced.

"It's been a long four weeks, the family has been through a lot, and we are strong and we know she is innocent. And we love [her].

"A mother knows . . . her child."

It was said that a majority of the jury sided with a verdict of not guilty, but there were several unconvinced holdouts.

On June 2, Judge Dwyer told a packed courtroom the case would likely see retrial in September or October, three months hence. That was enough time, Stacey Scotti and Laurie Lisi felt, to dig into all the evidence and find whatever else they could.

"Most of our demise in the first trial was that there were too many men on the jury," Stacey Scotti said. "She'd come in with her short skirts on, no panty hose, and just sit there batting her eyes at the jury the whole time."

Even more alarming to Scotti throughout the first trial, "We could not help but feel like we had probably missed stuff with the computer forensics. Katie was just so casual throughout the entire trial. Giggling, checking her phone, braiding her sisters' hair during breaks."

Scotti then made a devastating accusation: "At that time, we were unaware someone on the jury had a connection to her family. I know that it was nagging at me constantly, every single day during the first trial and deliberations. As the jury deliberated, Katie did not seem to have a care in the world, and Laurie and I were sweating bullets. At some point during the first trial, we heard rumors there was a Conley family connection to one of the jurors."

The Conley family soon announced Chris Pelli would not be representing Katie in the next trial. The family had retained local hotshot defense attorney Frank Policelli, a guy with over thirty years' experience in the courtroom.

FRANK POLICELLI STRUCK AN imposing figure: dark, expensive-looking suits; bushy, thick black eyebrows; a receding hairline leading up to a thick shock of gray hair; blue eyes. Policelli is tall, intimidating, and serious—aggressive to Pelli's passive. Policelli had tried cases in nearly a dozen different states and had a reputation for being uncompromising, a trait that usually bode well for his clients.

As the summer of 2017 began, Stacey Scotti dug in. She brought home all the computer forensic evidence and began to sift through it whenever time permitted. It became an almost obsession, certainly a challenge she welcomed. It was a mountain of data and metadata. As she stepped into the case and immersed herself in the evidence, what had bothered Scotti from the beginning was Katie's erratic behavior during her relationship with Adam.

As Scotti went through the hundreds of pages of texts between the two of them, Katie's manipulation, lying, teasing, taunting, and testing of Adam became utterly obvious. She lied to him repeatedly. Made herself the victim time and again. She played with Adam's emotions. Shamed him. She knew exactly which buttons to push to get a rise, and then to rein him back under control whenever she felt he might be slipping away.

The texts regarding Katie's pregnancy claims illustrated the impact she had on Adam, and how she could masterfully pull his strings. When Katie had told Adam about being pregnant, she suggested—without coming out with it clearly—that she'd had an abortion. This had infuriated Adam. And Katie knew it would. Then she went on to tell him she'd suffered an ectopic pregnancy, went to the hospital, and had it taken care of.

"We subpoenaed hospital records in a fifty-mile radius outside the county, into Albany, and found no record of Katie *ever* being at a hospital for this so-called ectopic pregnancy."

What's more, the entire trip to the hospital and back home, according to Katie's texts, took sixty minutes. "You're not going to be bleeding out from an ectopic pregnancy and be home in an hour," Scotti commented.

The prosecution theorized that Katie had felt so scorned by Adam leaving her for good that last time, on top of him being with someone new, she retaliated by poisoning him and killing his mother. Then she set out to frame him for it.

"Her DNA was on the sleeve over the bottle of colchicine, which is put there so the glass doesn't break, as well as the bottom portion of the bottle," Scotti recounted. "Her argument was that it had been 'transfer DNA,' because she'd spent so much time in Adam's Jeep and around him."

Scotti knew that Katie's DNA explanation was nonsense, but beyond all reason, the scorned young woman was determined to make Adam's life hell. The ultimate revenge.

Katie wanted to get even and make him pay for leaving her. It was all rooted in her absolute need for power and control.

"And look, if Katie would have not sent [the] anonymous letter, she would have never gotten caught," Scotti emphasized.

The jury did not buy the prosecution's argument, however. Now the DA's office had to make sure that the proof, which they believed they now possessed, was presented clearly, without a lot of computer forensic noise squelching out the important facts. Moreover, the prosecution believed Katie knew what was on her iPhone that they had missed during the first trial. That was one of the reasons why she had been so unconcerned during proceedings.

"The computer forensic analysis programs had updated since the first trial, so we had them 'rerun' the most important pieces of evidence to see if we could uncover additional files."

Scotti was chatting with Adam one day while prepping him for the second trial. "Let's go through everything again," she suggested. She mentioned Katie's iPhone. Laurie Lisi sat in the room, looking on, listening. They talked through it, step by step. Had they missed anything important? There had to be something.

"Katie's phone had backed up to my personal laptop," Adam said.

Scotti and Lisi looked at each other in disbelief.

"She was downloading an audiobook," Adam continued. "I told you about this."

"Um, no, you *did* not, Adam," Scotti said.

A complete snapshot from the time frame of the murder, including the entire contents of Katie's iPhone, everything she had deleted, was sitting inside Adam's laptop.

Immediately, Scotti made that her focus. She had forensics pull out the metadata so she could run keyword searches.

"Unfortunately, keyword searches will only capture words that have been searched or inputted by the user. Once I started perusing the backup of Katie's iPhone, however, it was at that point I realized she had a habit of taking a screenshot all the time when she was online. I figured out then that I would have to go through every single image to see if any were relevant to searches or activity connected to Katie and Mary."

One night, Scotti was at home, files spread across her bed. Her Labrador, Libbey, was sitting nearby, staring up at her. A laptop sat on her thighs. She scrolled methodically through every single screenshot, e-mail, text message, and miscellaneous file that the OCSO had not had access to when Katie turned her phone over before the first trial.

There's a piece of the puzzle here, Scotti thought. *I just need to find it.*

"Between the images and the [thumbprints], there were over twenty thousand to look through. You have to understand, every time a photo is taken, the phone automatically creates a thumbprint. The thumbprint is not accessible to the user, and the user doesn't even know it is being created. When a user manually deletes a photo/image, it does not delete the thumbprint. The thumbprint is maintained by the device until it runs out of room to hold any more, and then they are automatically deleted by the device."

The user, however, would be under the impression that once he or she has deleted an image, it no longer exists.

"That is an important detail, because it means the user would have no way of knowing the thumbprint was still available. So when

I found a thumbprint only, I could conclusively determine that [Katie] had manually deleted the image."

The deletion indicated the image was likely something important.

So now the prosecution had a backup of Katie's entire iPhone, which dated back to those months before and after the murder. A backup Katie had pestered Adam on multiple occasions to get rid of.

Scotti loaded the backup onto an office laptop and took it everywhere she went. Whenever she had a free moment, she scrolled, looking for evidence. As Scotti scoured through the files, there were nights when she fell asleep repeating this process, only to wake up with the computer still on her lap.

She'd jump right back into it.

"I would also do this all day long at the office."

While sitting one afternoon behind her messy office desk, piled head high with files and folders and evidence and testimony from the first trial, Scotti came upon a screenshot that stunned her.

"On Katie's iPhone was a screenshot of an Internet search for 'world's most dangerous toxins.'"

This one screenshot energized her to keep searching.

"I literally could not believe what I was seeing," she recalled. Everything pointed to Katie searching the Internet for the perfect poison to use in a plot to poison Adam and then, eventually, Mary. And as she thought about the first trial, Scotti realized, "It all made sense as to [Katie's] level of carefreeness during trial. She had cause to be laughing at us because she knew about all this data on her iPhone we did not have.

"We could never win the first trial, and she knew it, and we could tell she knew it."

In total, the prosecution had millions of files to mine evidence from. They could never look at each file individually, so focus became important.

Another image Scotti discovered, which she eventually printed and hung on the wall inside her office, reminding her how Katie actually thought when no one was looking, said so much about motive and intent.

It was an image of a black-and-white drawing found on Katie's iPhone. The artist is Chiara Bautista. The pencil drawing is of a mermaid poking out of the water, her fish tail curled up in back of her. Naked from the waist up, the exotic mermaid holds a raven's skull in her hands, most likely the head of her dead lover, as sun-like rays beam out around it. Her long, thick, flowing hair is curled down her back in the shape of an S. In the water, to the mermaid's right, facedown, is a man. His back torso, from neck to legs, is visible. The man is obviously dead. A sword/dagger penetrates the center of his back; the handle and a portion of the blade are sticking up. There is a hibiscus-type flower floating near the two characters.

Scotti stared at this image.

On the bottom, the title read: "The Breakup."

"I thought it was completely appropriate for who she is," Detective Mark VanNamee said later, speaking of the drawing. "It demonstrates her proclivity toward violence when things do not go her way. We had not discussed it with her because she had lawyered up long before the image was located during that search by Stacey Scotti between the two trials."

This drawing points to how Katie viewed breaking up with a romantic partner. The man—in this drawing—obviously had to pay a price.

Scotti kept at it, searching until her eyes became, on some days and nights, so fuzzy she had to stop. In one file, she noticed how Katie had gotten into Adam's Facebook account and had made screenshots of his list of blocked people. Her name was, of course, on the list.

"Her resentment of him, as I began to see what she was doing on her iPhone and on the Internet, was so deep and longstanding."

As each day passed and Katie realized Adam was not interested any longer, the resentment she harbored manifested into anger.

Then rage.

Scrolling through it all, Scotti developed a motive as Katie became more obsessed with getting even with Adam for letting her go. Her bubbling revenge was implicit in so many of the websites she visited and toxins she researched. Not to mention her *Notes* app, where all the notes Katie had written to herself detailed a murder plan.

When this new evidence was placed next to what they had already presented during the first trial, it was obvious to Scotti just how guilty Katie now came across.

With help from OCSO investigators, Scotti created a timeline and chart, detailing every piece of evidence pointing to Katie planning and plotting to poison not only Adam but Mary. Mary's name was rarely mentioned. If you were to search Katie's iPhone and look for a person Katie was most interested in killing, Adam came up. Beginning in the fall of 2014, after the entire manufactured rape claim didn't work, Katie was hell-bent on making sure Adam paid a price for abandoning her.

"What better way to pay him back than to take away the *one* person who meant the most to Adam," Stacey Scotti concluded.

70

FRANK POLICELLI COULD EXHIBIT a brash and in-your-face side at times, but he was able to tone it down and come across as likable and polite. Policelli was fighting for the freedom of his client. He was going to do whatever was necessary, within legal parameters.

As the second trial started, during his opening statement, Policelli focused on the specific charges. This was the burden that a second, more gender-diverse jury faced. At times, Policelli was able to convincingly rein in what he viewed as a flawed investigation that took too long to begin and went no further than targeting his client. He accused investigators of wearing blinders, aiming for Katie, and failing to read in between the lines of how Bill and Adam Yoder could have conspired to kill Mary together or alone.

Here we go again, Stacey Scotti thought, rolling her eyes, sitting, listening.

If that was Katie's only defense, it had run out of steam. The first jury, perhaps Policelli felt, might have believed the Bill or Adam theory, which was why it had hung itself. Yet, by this point in the case, without any tangible evidence to back up such substantial allegations, it seemed impossible for one to draw this same conclusion. The evidence—all of it—pointed to Katie Conley. No one else. Particularly all the new material inside Katie's iPhone, which Stacey Scotti had uncovered.

Katie had purchased the credit cards at Hannaford supermarket, which she *admitted* to Mark VanNamee on videotape during interrogation. Indisputably, those cards were used to purchase the colchicine, a purchase well-documented and time-stamped by computers, backed up with data and testimony.

Green-haired Rosa Vargas had made this clear during her direct testimony in the first trial—a narrative she would repeat here during the second. While acting as the contact in selling the colchicine, and getting the proper paperwork in order, Rosa had dealt with only one other person. It was a soft-spoken female who matched Katie's voice and who had answered the telephone at Chiropractic Family Care.

What additional evidence did a jury need than those facts alone? Why would Katie purchase prepaid credit cards and buy the toxin? These were facts that could not be explained away by accusing Adam and Bill Yoder of the crime.

The OCSO had conducted a complete and thorough investigation into Bill and Adam Yoder and excluded them. The long trail of computer forensic evidence—on top of Katie's own admissions—pointed them back to her.

Still, during his opening, Policelli insisted: "William Yoder testified before a grand jury [and] received immunity . . ." Then, regarding the colchicine, "Adam Yoder gets the package . . ." These defamatory claims could not be corroborated with factual evidence.

The prosecution could have objected throughout Policelli's opening, but for the most part, ADA Laurie Lisi allowed him to beat what sounded like a worn-out drum.

"Adam Yoder was a manipulator. He used this girl, Katie Conley . . . Adam Yoder was a chronic alcoholic addicted to Adderall, who took opiates . . . and he was on the hot seat because in July of 2014 he raped her . . . Mary knew about the rape. [Katie] told that to VanNamee, but VanNamee, I mean talk about *Alice in Wonderland,* they can't see what is in front of them."

Save for the alcohol and pills, which Adam had admitted to during previous testimony, the remainder of the statement was speculation and conjecture. Adam had never been charged with rape. VanNamee and the OCSO had not once rejected any theory or person of interest. In fact, they had gone after Bill Yoder before arriving at Katie as a suspect. It was the anonymous letter pointing to Adam, which investigators knew was replete with lies, that had made them even more interested in Katie, who then admitted to writing it.

Policelli found a groove and talked through how idiotic the prosecution's case felt on merit. Of all the poisons a killer might choose, he questioned, *"Colchicine?"* Then, quite brazen and insensitive, he offered a short tutorial, offering what might be a better poison to use if one wanted to commit murder: "Get your antifreeze and put it in somebody's drink and kill them. Well, she was researching poison on her phone, according to the prosecutor? Oh, really? Prove that. Prove that!"

Laurie Lisi and Stacey Scotti looked on, quiet and steady, knowing they had more than enough evidence to prove it.

Being clear about whom he was going after in this trial, Policelli said, "Ladies and gentlemen, it was Adam. It was Adam. And if you read this anonymous letter, which Katie admits she wrote it anonymously because she was scared of him . . . My God. He beat her. He'll admit that on the witness stand . . ."

Policelli went through the letter. He promised to prove the letters were Katie's way of protecting herself.

A lot of what came out of Policelli's mouth over the course of the next twenty minutes was, at best, gossip and rumor; at worst, ostentatious grandstanding, a lawyer taking a kernel of information and adding a speculative theory to it.

In her opening, ADA Laurie Lisi spent most of her time describing how colchicine had killed Mary. Then she finished by outlining the new evidence the state was about to present.

71

*T*ESTIMONY IN THE SECOND trial began on October 16, 2017. Katie wore a beige suit coat, a flamingo-pink blouse, her hair untied, flowing down over her shoulders. This time, an air of seriousness was visible on Katie's face. She was not the wholesome, apple-cheeked girl next door without a care in the world.

The state's narrative followed along the same path as the first trial; the only difference was that each witness added much more detail. Dozens of new exhibits (which would total in the hundreds) were introduced. The main witness for the state was Anthony Martino.

Director of Utica College's Northeast Cyber Forensics Center (NCFC), Martino had been employed there for close to five years leading up to trial. His department specialized in computer forensics, cyber security, and the examination of digital services. Martino's job on the stand was to enter in the record all of that evidence Stacey Scotti and the OCSO had uncovered in between the two trials, in addition to any evidence Martino's lab had found. Being so familiar with all of the material, Stacey Scotti took on Martino's direct examination.

Martino was a middle-aged, balding man; a horseshoe of black hair lay over his ears and ringed around his head. He had a professional seriousness about him. Before he worked at NCFC, he had been a police officer for the City of Utica for two decades, half that time a sergeant. As far as cybercrime and computer forensics, Martino held a master's in computer security and forensics. There was not a more qualified, intelligent, and unbiased expert around to analyze and comment on the mountain of computer/digital evidence the state was presenting.

Martino spoke articulately, without being condescending, which is an art form some witnesses cannot seem to grasp. He was able to communicate complicated computer forensic matters clearly, with the layperson always in mind. He came across charming and believable: an objective voice conveying incontrovertible evidence. The key was to boil down computer forensic information in an easy-to-understand vernacular that any computer-illiterate person could comprehend. On top of all his accomplishments, Martino had been deputized a member of the Secret Service Electronic Crime Task Force, helping the Secret Service with scores of computer forensic investigations. He had security clearance with the United States government.

After going through his long list of credentials and qualifications, Martino explained how an entire world—unseen by iPhone or computer users—exists behind the digital curtain on any device. There is an e-world churning in the background, storing, deleting, saving, and backing up whatever it is the user is doing on a device. Most people are unaware of this. Many think that by deleting something from an iPhone, computer, or tablet, the information is gone forever. Not always the case, Martino made clear. The information might be impossible for the user to retrieve again, or see, but the same information, in various forms, is forever stored somewhere—albeit unreadable data to the non–computer geek. It's not complicated, Martino insisted. It's how computers think and work.

Martino made another salient point about computer searches: "We can read information, we can extract data, [but] we cannot do anything back . . . toward the original device. We cannot write data back. We cannot make changes. We cannot delete. We cannot corrupt. We cannot alter."

In other words, the information computer forensic experts retrieve is absolute. It is either there as metadata or not.

"Is it fair to say that extensive skill and knowledge is required in order to hack something?" Stacey Scotti asked while standing at the prosecution's table, often looking down, referring to her notes.

One of the arguments Katie's team would make was that Adam—or someone else—had hacked into her iPhone and computers for months and months. This hacker made it appear as though Katie was ordering colchicine, creating a company, and doing all sorts of searching for how to kill with poison. The idea behind the hack was to frame her. Mind you, all of this supposedly occurred without her having any knowledge of it going on.

A ridiculous theory when put into perspective.

"In order to hack anything that is reasonably secured, it takes . . . someone with extreme knowledge of the systems, but also very significant experience and skills in the field," Martino said.

After a lunch break, Stacey Scotti asked Martino to talk about a device fingerprint address—the IP (Internet protocol)—which is assigned to each and every device on the planet.

As Martino spoke of how computers, servers, networks, software, and Web browsers are identified, the testimony became a slight bit technical. This was the essence of the state's evidence: its smoking gun. They tied all of the circumstantial evidence back to Katie and her devices, the computer she used in the office, and her home network of computers.

Following this trail, beginning in her iPhone and computers, adding the paperwork manufactured from the sale of the prepaid credit cards and colchicine purchase, the state contended that the evidence proved no one else could have been involved in this murder. If one was in the market for motive and opportunity, all one had to do was go into the *Notes* app on Katie's iPhone, her texts, e-mails, photos, screenshots, along with other personal Web searches. After bundling all of this together, her guilt became clear as water.

Martino talked about how he looked not only at Katie's devices and computers but Adam's and Bill's. Concluding those thoughts, he explained how it would have been impossible for Adam and Bill to delete any computer-related evidence entirely. Martino and his team would have found something connecting either of the men, if they were hackers, to the purchase of the toxin and to Katie's phone and computers.

It wasn't there.

In conducting his analysis, Martino used a host of keywords to search all devices, phrases, and words pertinent to the case: ArtChemicals, Spectrum, Copper Harbor, Letter of Intent, Chiro, Family Care, Mradamyoder1990@gmail.com, Adam is gay, Attention Rosa, Drugs.com, Hannaford grocery store, U.S Bank, Rape, Rape injuries, Bruises, Polygraph, Voice stress, DNA, DNA comparison, Transfer or touch DNA, Medical examiner, House, Netflix, Poison, Treatment, Antidote, Poison is a lady's weapon, Colchicine, C-O-L-C-H-I-C-I-N-E, Thallium, Arsenic oxide, Cyanide, Munchausen, Presumed innocent, Murder, Kill, Trial, Jail, Prison, Law, Legal, Innocent, Assault. Beyond these, there was another long list of additional words and phrases too boring and tedious to mention.

Explaining how he had looked inside Bill Yoder's iPhone and iPad, conducted a complete search, including memory extraction, Martino said he did not find anything of evidentiary value.

When searching Bill's phone for connections to marijuana, distribution, growing, Scotti wondered what was the result.

Martino said he uncovered nothing.

Colchicine?

Nothing.

The Mr. Adam Yoder 1990 e-mail address was nowhere to be found inside any of Bill's devices.

Martino ran the same tests on Adam's devices.

Again, he found nothing.

Martino looked at all of Mary's devices.

Nada.

When he went inside Katie's iPhone, personal computers, and the computer she used at the office, however, his search results lit up.

Hit after hit after hit. For example, Martino extracted data from Katie's devices showing e-mails sent from *kaconley@Utica.edu* to Mr. Adam Yoder 1990. He even located the *CamScanner* app Katie had downloaded from the username Mr. Adam Yoder 1990, with the password Adamisgay.

Any logical person, not living in denial, could look at this evidence and understand it was *impossible* for anyone to wipe out traces of those keywords and apps from Bill or Adam's devices and place that same information in *all* of Katie's devices. Even the most gifted computer expert, working months on it, could not have done what Katie's defense had suggested.

It was completely obvious Katie had committed this crime. To not see it was ignorant and prejudiced. All Martino did was point out the facts he had uncovered. And those facts—unchanged computer data that could not have been tampered with or altered—were more obvious as each hour passed. Stacey Scotti presented exhibits backing up Martino's testimony as the case against Katie grew.

Martino spent a total of five full days on the witness stand, and Scotti made it clear who had planned and carried out this crime. There could be no other suspect after one looked at all of the cyber/computer evidence.

When the photos of Katie's "bruises" from Adam's alleged sexual assault were discussed on the stand, the data proved Katie manipulated the entire exchange. These photos were not taken on the night of the assault, as Katie had told Adam in a series of texts Martino talked about. Photos are embedded with metadata generated by the device snapping the image—essentially time-stamping each one. There was no way to dispute the fact that these "bruising" photos were taken three months after the alleged rape. These images were generated on November 1, 2014.

The data on Katie's iPhone and computers proved she had repeatedly, pathologically, lied to Adam, Mary, Bill, her sisters, parents, friends, professors, and the school.

Nobody was immune from Katie Conley's tactical, manipulating deception.

72

As Anthony Martino testified into his fourth day, many in the gallery felt the mounting discomfort. The courtroom thinned out at times, filled up at others. Several people inside the courtroom later recalled that Katie coordinated "several emotional outbursts involving crying. These seemed to be orchestrated because everyone [Katie and her supporters] started at *exactly* the same time, as if on cue."

When Judge Dwyer announced there would not be a recess, despite the emotional outbursts, the crying stopped "instantly," one trial attendee remembered. "Especially noteworthy was not only did Katie stop her 'uncontrollable' sobbing immediately, but she was smiling afterward, right away."

Rumors of Bill and Adam conspiring to kill Mary were still circulating, making the rounds on social media and throughout courtroom hallway whispers. One of the latest wild accusations centered on Bill being able to perform mind control.

One of Mary's sisters who supported Katie was an outspoken voice on a pro-Katie website. She wrote:

I know the world at large didn't see what was behind the curtain, and I watched for almost forty years while Mary struggled to raise her children to be happy, but Bill was deeply self-serving and it is hard to

describe how cleverly he wields mental and emotional cruelty disguised
as concern.

Another sister, on the same website, berated Bill, and defamed both Adam and Bill. She wrote that she "firmly" believed that Kaitlyn Conley was innocent, and she believed that the "colchicine was ordered by the Yoders (whether by Bill and/or Adam and/or Mary)."

The remainder of her letter offered accusations and misinformation, speculation, and bizarre theories. She had nothing in the form of factual evidence or supporting documentation.

Murder victims and their families are generally—no, should always be!—off limits to such a bombardment of insults, intimidation, innuendoes, and taunts.

Not here.

There were several strange incidents, according to several eyewitnesses. At one point during a recess, Liana and another family member sat inside the courtroom looking at pictures of their mother on Liana's phone. It was, of course, a heartbreaking moment, with so much raw emotion swirling around the trial already.

As they sat marveling at those pictures of Mary, they cried. One of Katie's supporters and her boyfriend walked over and peered over their shoulders.

"Well, I guess there won't be any more family photos, will there?"

73

*T*HE DAY BEFORE HALLOWEEN, after a lengthy break to clear up several motions, Anthony Martino continued to testify for the state. Hour after hour, the state's expert provided detailed, factual evidence, proving how Katie Conley worked stealthily on her iPhone and other devices, including the Yoders' office computer. She was trying to figure out why colchicine was the best poison to use, how to use it, and where to purchase it.

As far back as December 2014, at 12:51 a.m., Katie's iPhone was searching for "some of the world's most toxic substances," Martino explained. He backed up his testimony by providing a screenshot of a website Katie had saved, deleted, but Martino had recovered. It was almost as though, when one looked inside Katie's phone at those thumbnails, images, and files she had deleted, a narrative of the entire murder presented itself. By November/December 2014, Katie had found the best possible poison to use; January/February she created a company—Chiro Family Care—and forged documents and Yoder signatures, while searching for the best place— and cheapest price—to order the colchicine; February into March she provided all the proper paperwork and documentation ArtChemicals had requested and Rosa Vargas was able to approve the order.

Moreover, throughout all those months, when one added in the *Notes* app evidence and texts to Adam, a clear picture emerged.

Her electronic digital trail tracked how Katie designed an alibi, calculated body weight versus amount of poison to achieve a lethal dose, and wrote notes to herself regarding what to say to police later. At the same time, she drafted several versions of the anonymous letter.

Martino withstood a day of questions from defense attorney Policelli, who tried to poke holes in everything the forensic examiner had to offer. Yet, in the end, what could one do to disprove impartial evidence, such as computer data and metadata? It either is or it isn't. There's no neutral territory within this type of evidence.

In what many described as a desperate move, Policelli did his best to go after Martino's motives as he set about searching for evidence. The defense attorney tried to insinuate that Martino was given a plan by the prosecution and he followed it.

The only other possible avenue Policelli had was to focus on who was on the other end of Katie's iPhone when some of what Martino had testified to was downloaded and later deleted. When that accusation was put to the test, however, it fell short. The problem was, if someone else had set Katie up, putting all of this evidence on her phone, how could that person know what to delete and when? Not to mention, how could they gain access to her phone for days at a time? There was no plausible explanation other than Katie.

Her mistake, which Katie's lawyer tried to walk back, had been plugging her iPhone into Adam's laptop. It was also proven that she was actually conducting many of these searches while group texting with friends and family. That mirror image of Katie's iPhone contents, which Martino pulled up, pointed directly to Katie planning, plotting, and carrying out the murder of Mary Yoder. There was zero reasonable doubt.

On November 2, 2017, and several days preceding, additional witnesses testified for the state. Then Laurie Lisi rested the state's case.

Katie's defense presented three witnesses of little value, Katie deciding again she didn't need to testify on her own behalf.

After that, closing arguments commenced.

The same day, Judge Dwyer gave the new jury its instructions and off they went into deliberations.

After two full days of deliberating, stepping out once to proclaim a divided verdict, on Monday, November 6, 2017, the jury sent word it was ready to announce its verdict. There would be no hung jury this time. No questions from the jury. No apprehension about its decision.

Katie, now twenty-four years old, sat in nervous expectation. She wore a white button-up coat, a purple shawl draped over her shoulders. She had a look of disinterest as she stared straight ahead at noting in particular.

As these things go, however, Katie had luck on her side. Jurors found her not guilty of second-degree murder, but guilty of the lesser charge, manslaughter in the first degree. As the jury answered with its guilty verdict, Katie's father and other family members broke out in tears and shrieks. Katie seemed indifferent, undaunted. Just another day. The stoic gaze she displayed said all there was to say about how she felt.

As Katie was escorted out of the courtroom, on her way to jail to await sentencing, she turned toward family, nodded her head yes, smiled, said nothing.

"I think it's a great verdict for us," Laurie Lisi explained to the media after. "I'm just glad that that's what they came back with. I think they really worked hard. I think they really spent time going over the evidence . . . It was an excellent verdict. I'm very happy with it. I know the family's very happy with it as well."

The Yoder family held one another as they left the courtroom in silence. They did not speak to anyone.

"I think they struggled with intent to harm versus intent to kill, and I think that's why we have the verdict we do," Lisi added.

Frank Policelli had an issue with the prosecution introducing the manslaughter option after the trial had already started. Outside the courtroom, he mentioned how the state's evidence focused on murder, not manslaughter.

"There was no evidence of any other intent but murder. You can't constructively amend an indictment in the middle of the trial and change your theory of prosecution. Can't do that," Policelli explained. "Not to mention there was *never* any evidence of her actually poisoning Mary Yoder."

He promised to appeal.

In January 2018, the judge called everyone back for sentencing.

"Every day I felt blessed and grateful that she was in my life and that she had chosen to share a life with me," Bill Yoder said before the court. Convicted murderer Katie Conley and her clan looked on. "And she often told me she felt the same. We felt like the two luckiest people in the world to have found each other. After forty years together, we were still deeply in love, still delighted just to spend time together."

In tears, his voice cracking, hands shaking, Adam Yoder stood up from his bench seat in the gallery and walked toward the lectern. He held several pages of a prepared victim's impact statement he'd written.

"I introduced Katie Conley to my family," Adam started, his voice already cracking with emotion. "And because I loved her, they all accepted her and treated her as family . . . as blood. I got her a job with my parents, and if I hadn't done those things"—he broke down, bowed his head, tears pouring out of him, barely able to get the words out—"my mother . . . would *still* be alive."

Katie sat, this time wearing an orange jumpsuit, her state-issued number stamped on the chest pocket, staring directly at the front of the room, Adam to her right, her face still, her demeanor apathetic. It appeared that the proceeding bored her.

"Make no mistake," Adam continued, "I *hate* the defendant with every bone in my body and every drop of blood in my veins. I hate Kaitlyn Ann Conley because Kaitlyn Ann Conley murdered my mother."

After Adam returned to his seat in the gallery, Katie stood and shuffled her way to the lectern.

"I am innocent!" she said before thanking her family, friends, and strangers. "[Thanks] for standing up in support of me, that's all. Thank you."

Katie never mentioned being sorry for the Yoders' loss, Mary's death, or acknowledged the pain they were going through.

Zero remorse.

Zero empathy.

Zero sense of the pain the Yoders felt.

One of Mary's sisters stood at the lectern and explained that she and her other two sisters support Katie and believe she is innocent, before asking the judge for leniency.

Dwyer sentenced Katie to twenty-three years. This was about the best the state could have hoped for. One law enforcement official, after sentencing, said she'd hoped the judge would give Katie enough time so that when she was released from prison, she would be too old to have children.

"We wanted to send her away long enough so that when she got out she was not of childbearing age, because she'd probably kill her own children if things didn't go the way she wanted."

EPILOGUE

*T*HIS BOOK WAS A project I had not imagined turning out the way in which it has. I don't mean the trumped-up "is she guilty or innocent" battle cry, and the prosecution having to go on and defend its work long after both verdicts. Almost immediately after I dug into the actual evidence, it was clear Katie Conley committed this crime. What interested me from the moment I started looking at it, instead, was the murder victim, Mary Yoder.

Mary's voice needed to be heard. Her life story needed to be made available to as many people as possible within a culture of instant gratification, social media hatred, divisiveness, disunity, and societal anxiety and fatigue. Her story needed to play out against the utter dissolution of the traditional family within a culture shoving celebrity, wealth, power, and materialistic success down our throats at a rate we cannot keep up with or avoid.

Mary Yoder was the antithesis to all of that toxicity. She was a person who delighted in family and worked her ass off to keep her family intact. She struggled to keep it as traditional as possible within the firestorm of the cultural insanity we experience today.

As you have read, Mary was passionate about gardening, pottery, and the arts. She enjoyed simple life pleasures—i.e., those small wonders we walk past without noticing: the smell and aesthetic grace of a flower, a blue sky, the sun beating on our face, the subtle (even spiritual) eloquence of a stream softly babbling by during a casual walk or hike. Dancing. Conversation. Sitting on a park bench and watching the world go by. Mary took the time to take such subtle, often overlooked gifts into her soul.

Yet, she also shared the serenity she had with the people around her. She gave of herself to her community. She helped people realize that the best was available within themselves. She loved (and lived) life. She adored people. She loved her grandchildren more than words could ever provide due diligence.

According to the *evidence* and *jury*, Katie Conley (because she felt scorned by a man?) took all of this away from the world. What's more, she deprived the community where Mary lived of experiencing the wonder of who she was.

That's the ripple effect of one murder: So many people still suffer from not having Mary Yoder in their lives.

In that regard, I need to mention I made multiple attempts—and made myself available on numerous occasions—to allow Katie Conley, her family, and her friends to speak with me and have a voice in this project. If, as they all claim, Katie is innocent, I wanted those explanations and any proof they had to offer, and would have been happy to publish what they had to say. One Conley family member agreed to meet me in Utica. We set a tentative day and time. I e-mailed her the day before I left Connecticut. She knew ahead of time I was coming. And that night, no surprise to me, she e-mailed and pulled out.

I get it. I really do. Yet what baffles me is how outspoken this family has been with certain people, in public, on the Internet, to *Dateline*. However, a lasting document, such as a book, was of no interest to any of them.

In my opinion, it says a lot.

Furthermore, I cannot end this book without sharing my opinion of Adam Yoder. We had long conversations about Katie, his mother, his life, the mistakes he's made, and how he continues to suffer long after the verdicts. Adam blames himself. He struggles with having brought Katie into the Yoder fold. I cannot pretend to place myself in his shoes.

What I can say, with absolute certainty, is that sometimes people arrive in our lives and, like black mold, create havoc and hell without us having a clue what is happening. Before we know it, we're doing things we never saw ourselves ever participating in. It is by no fault of our own. All the therapy and experience in the world cannot prepare us for allowing our judgment and choices to be clouded by what we *believe* is love disguised as codependency and toxicity.

Adam loved his mother. He is a good person, son, brother, and uncle. He stumbled. In my opinion, he fell into the web of a cunning sociopath. He did not see it. Breaking free from what was a Velcro-like, emotional clutch seemed impossible. Katie Conley manipulated and lied and tricked Adam into believing falsehoods. She played with his fragile and empathetic mind and heart, and ultimately wielded power over him during one of the weakest periods of his life.

One cannot blame himself for repeatedly trying—and perhaps needing—to save, or rescue, someone. There are soul-sucking humans in this world. We don't want to believe we can fall under their spell, because some of us want to see the good in everyone. But it happens. We're swept up before we realize it. And there really is nothing we could have done differently to see or stop it.

"People will say how strong I am that I made it through this," Adam told me during one of our final conversations, "but I never did. I'm not okay. I don't see myself *ever* being okay. People might think it's done because Katie is in prison. But she's not in prison forever. She will get out. My mother is gone!" He paused there. Emotion took over.

Concluding a moment after collecting himself, Adam said: "No chapter ended and no recovery ever happened . . . I don't know how to start that process yet."

I DIDN'T DWELL ON it in great detail during the actual narrative of the book. However, I need to say something about what several highly credible sources inside the courtroom, and beyond, told me about NBC's *Dateline* production while in Utica filming an episode about this case. Several expressed the opinion that as a whole the *Dateline* people were chummy with the Conley family during both trials. They ate lunch together, laughed, joked around, hugged each other, and cried together.

"Katie flirted with all the males in the crew, trying to work her charm on them," several sources observed.

I did not witness this myself. It hurts me, however, to have to report it was not just one or two individual sources who told me, and, mind you, these sources did not know one another. If half of what was reported to me about this activity is true, it is unsettling to hear. I have tremendous respect for NBC News and I know producers working on *Dateline* (none of whom were part of the production in Utica). I respect the work they do. To hear this sort of behavior from journalists was not what I would have expected.

Look, I understand television and what one must do at times to keep sources talking. I have executive-produced hours and hours of true-crime television. Again, I get it. However, when one digs into this case and places personal prejudice aside and looks at (and *accepts*) the actual evidence, the notion of anyone thinking Katie Conley is innocent is troubling.

No one else could have committed this crime.

No one.

This anecdotal information about *Dateline,* however, verifies for me the control Katie Conley was able employ, exercise, and maintain over some people—save for law enforcement and a few others in town. I won't claim to have armchair-diagnosed Katie, nor did I run into any professional diagnosis, but in my opinion sociopaths are expert charmers and con artists. Having written at least twenty-some books about confirmed, diagnosed psychopaths and sociopaths, I can say Katie exhibits all the same behaviors a sociopath would.

To this day, some residents in Utica (including several of Mary Yoder's own family members) support and believe Katie is innocent. That is beyond troubling and beyond my understanding. I cannot fathom how anyone studying this case, taking just the computer forensic evidence *alone,* cannot draw the conclusion—without *any* doubt—that Katie Conley is guilty. The idea that Bill or Adam Yoder committed this crime and framed Katie is laughable. Impossible. I implore anyone with a doubt to go online and find

Adam Yoder's statement during Katie's sentencing. Compare the raw emotion he exhibits to that of Katie's stoic, self-serving demeanor during her sentencing statement, on top of her overall performance throughout both trials. One cannot fake the type of visceral pain Adam Yoder was in as he read his impact statement.

"This is the most powerful circumstantial case I have *ever* seen," said a producer friend, who has, like me, looked at hundreds of murder cases, and has produced an episode of a popular true-crime series about this case.

All that being said, this book—and the mountain of evidence presented to prove no other person could have killed Mary Yoder—will do nothing to sway those who are still captured by Katie Conley's manipulating control. I'll get letters and e-mails and social media messages accusing me of not seeing the truth and siding with prosecutors and law enforcement. I'll be accused of favoring the prosecution and police while attacking Katie; not allowing myself to get to know the true Katie (I wrote her a letter asking her to participate, but she did not respond); not wanting to see the "real" evidence never allowed into trial; the made-up theories of super marijuana crops and Bill Yoder being some sort of computer savant and mind-controlling wizard; and how Katie was framed.

Yada yada yada.

Go ahead, send that BS. I have a delete key. I have no trouble using it.

KATIE CONLEY REMINDS ME of the cone snail, which is known for its brown-and-white, glossy, marble-like shell. You look at this beautiful gastropod found in the shallow waters of the tropics and believe it is harmless. It is, after all, only four to six inches long and has a ceramic-like sheen beckoning one to run a finger over. Yet, if you touch this seemingly harmless creature, you'll meet up with its concealed teeth, which "resemble tiny harpoons and contain a complex venom known as a conotoxin . . ."[5] If stung by the cone snail, you have about five minutes before the venom is working

5. https://www.cntraveler.com/stories/2016-06-21/the-10-most-dangerous-animals-in-the-world

through your body on a path toward your heart, subsequently killing you. There is no antivenin.

"People can say Katie is smart, and if she is intelligent at all, I don't know where this fucking idea came in that she had the intelligence to commit this crime and get away with it," Adam told me over the phone one morning. "Because the way she did it, people can say she's smart and clever, but in actuality she made really stupid mistakes that hurt her. She didn't get a lawyer when she spoke to the police those first few times, for one. And, number two, her not understanding technology and how it works."

Adam made a solid point that when Katie told Detective Mark VanNamee that "[Adam] hacked into my phone . . . Adam's name is on the e-mail accounts," it showed how computer illiterate she was. She unknowingly left behind all these additional electronic bread crumbs. When you consider the evidence from that context, it makes sense Katie would do what she did, without a concern for getting caught. She had no idea she would be.

"She attached one of the documents used to purchase the colchicine to her student e-mail account," Adam continued. "She made an account for the *CamScanner* app when she did not have to—because she didn't know or realize it could all be traced back to her . . . She just had no understanding of what she was doing."

As we spoke, I could hear the emotional strain, the constant pain, and self-hatred in Adam's voice. This case is still rooted—and festering—in the guy's soul. He is struggling to contend with all that had happened and the continued onslaught by his own family members to paint him as someone he is not.

"Katie is just a bad person. I think she's a really bad person who figured out how to manipulate people because she has no moral compass whatsoever."

Adam makes a valid point. Because once Katie figured out how vulnerable Adam was, the compassion he showed, the drinking and pills and depression, the way that he was willing to rescue her, once she figured *that* out, she realized it would be easy to control him. On the flip side, once she truly understood she had lost that control, watch out. It was payback time.

The respect and admiration Adam shared about his father, Bill Yoder, is commendable and sincere.

"I give my father a lot of credit for who I am and how I think about things," Adam said. "I do not want anyone to have the impression that I did not equally love and respect both of my parents. They were a huge, wonderful influence on me. I greatly credit my dad for the way I am able to critically think about things and be a good person . . . I want everyone to know how much I love and respect my dad throughout all this."

DENIAL IS A THICK fog clogging up and confusing the left cerebral hemisphere of the brain, which controls logical and rational thinking. Take that denial, sprinkle a cunning, manipulating liar (whose control and charm are effortlessly exercised) over it, and then add an additional layer of the girl-next-door, poor-me persona Katie has created for herself and worked with the degree of an Oscar-winning actress. When it's all merged together, you wind up with a toxic, dangerous personality.

Part of this, I understand, is ignorance.

Regarding those family members making wild claims about Adam and Bill, Adam said, "I genuinely don't know what happened to them . . . Conscious or subconscious, I believe the loss of my mother was too much for them."

I have studied cases where less evidence has sent men and women to prison for multiple life sentences. It's comical and inconceivable to me that when so much absolute evidence points in one particular direction—and the answer appears to be direct, simple, and clear—some will push all of that aside to hop aboard a conspiracy-theory train. They'll ride the rails to the rumor mill, and spin speculation into belief and credibility. True crime has become a cultural pillar, integrated into everyday life. As a result, some feel the need to dramatize and twist basic murder investigations into wild ideas and schemes in order to, I reckon, amp up the entertainment value. It's as though the actual answer, proven with concrete evidence beyond *any* reasonable doubt, is not enough anymore.

The fact is, a majority of murder cases are not the inspiration for, or equal to, a diabolical plot from a Netflix or a BBC limited, binge-worthy dramatic crime series. Solving murders generally follows an A-to-Z blueprint. There's no script. There's no criminal master-mind. There's no villainous prosecution, sitting back, dreaming up ways in which to coerce a confession or find an innocent person guilty in order to close a case. Of course, there *are* anomalies in any system, and it happens (very rarely). But that's Hollywood, my friends. In the real world, cops follow the evidence where it leads.

Closely look at and study conclusions, yes. Question the evidence and law enforcement integrity, ethics and tactics, always. Never, ever go into an investigation with tunnel vision, certainly. But do *not* allow ignorance or prejudice to cloud logic. If the answer is staring back at you, slapping you across the face, do the one thing we, as contemporary Americans, struggle so much with today: accept it.

I THINK A GOOD question regarding Katie is: Could there have been several different personalities she projected within her world in order to obtain what she wanted? In other words, various personalities she created and used to influence different people in her life.

"Intentional schizophrenia," Adam later called it, coining a term for what he believed was a condition Katie was not at all confused about. She knew what she was doing. It served a purpose in her life. She might not have feigned hearing voices and experiencing hallucinations—two factors in what is called "faked schizophrenia"—but her intent was to become a different person for a preconceived outcome around certain people.

"She's chosen to have different personalities of which she applies to different people and places," Adam concluded. "And that is scary shit."

The closest clinical term for what Adam described, on top of several behaviors Katie exhibited, is "malingered psychosis." Those who malinger do it for two reasons: to avoid pain or seek pleasure. Either way, it is a manipulative tactic devised to support the motives of the individual.

I believe Katie mastered this.

Katie has difficulty losing or being rejected. Lashing out stealthily after a defeat, she feels vindicated—a sense of pleasure and relief at getting back at the person who wronged her. We see this over and over in the narrative of her life with Adam. After the first big breakup, she faked an ectopic pregnancy to get him back. Second, she dreamed up this rape scenario and there she was, in bed with him the next day, eventually dropping those charges—and Adam went back to her. Third time, she poisoned Adam. When that did not work, she went after the one thing in Adam's life he loved more than anything else.

Mary Yoder.

ACKNOWLEDGMENTS

So MANY PEOPLE PARTICIPATE in the book-writing process in ways they do not realize, it is impossible for me to thank each of you individually. I believe you know who you are. In addition, please know how forever grateful I am for your contribution, however large or small, and your support.

My readers and fans: I bow to you. Thank you from the depths of my heart for continuing to support my career and interact with me on social media and share your love for what I do. Every complimentary note, comment, and hello is humbling. I read them all. I am honored. Truly.

It took some doing, but Bill Yoder opened up; he was honest, sincere, and willing to do whatever it took to get me the truth, whether it favored him and his son, Adam, or not. There is no doubt in my mind Mary Yoder was the love of Bill's life. I thank him for his honesty and commitment to the facts of the case.

Liana Hegde is an inspiration. A class act. A doctor, Liana has opted right now to take on the toughest job in the world, which she does without reservation and, I gather from talking to her, would have it no other way: raising a family. And those children, I know, were the light of Mary Yoder's life. Liana's help in understanding her mother and those days leading up to Mary's death was essential. I cannot thank Liana enough for carving out time from what is a busy-beyond-belief life to talk to me.

To all the Yoder family members who helped, I appreciate the sacrifice, along with the courage you showed in reliving what is the toughest and most painful moments of your lives. I am honored, grateful, and fortunate for your willingness to trust me. My hope is that I told your stories with accuracy, fairness, and integrity. None of you deserved the utter BS you put up with before, during, and after the trials. The lies and rumors printed and spread about you, the absolute drivel disguised as social media conversation, were reprehensible. Without reacting or responding to any of it, again, shows class and restraint. All you ever asked for was the public to objectively consider the evidence.

Laurie Lisi, Stacey Scotti, and the OCSO were incredibly helpful getting me documentation and explaining the evidence, making themselves available for interviews, going above and beyond to be certain I understood the entire case—again, whether or not it favored their side of the case. The countless e-mails all of you answered did not go without my utmost appreciation and gratitude.

On the investigation front, I need to say there were many instrumental players—investigators—involved in working countless hours on this case. To include all of you in the narrative would have confused the reader and I opted instead to tell most of the OCSO's story through Detective Mark VanNamee's point of view. But every single investigator and forensic expert (including those from the ME's office and PCC) deserve to be acknowledged for their professionalism and hard work. Without each and every one of you (I don't need to tell you), Mary Yoder and her family would not have received the justice they deserved.

Family, friends, and my literary agent/business manager/entertainment attorney, Matthew Valentinas, are always, of course, right there by my side encouraging and inspiring me in ways I could never explain here. You all know I love you because I tell you often. What I don't always share is how utterly grateful I am for your presence in my life.

Andrea Quick is someone I need to thank for changing my life and helping me realize there is light at the end of a dark and seemingly endless tunnel. Andrea is a special person in my life. Without her, I am not sure I would have been able to write this book or any that follow.

My good friend Paul Tieger has been someone who has both inspired and set me straight when I needed to hear it. I cannot thank Paul enough for his friendship, time, unconditional love, wisdom, and experience.

I would like to say how much I appreciate Jeremy Adair, my executive producing partner. Jeremy's friendship and creative genius has been a blessing in my life. An Australian by birth, I am so proud Jeremy is now and American citizen. I consider his presence in my life over the past 15 years an honor.

And last, if you are into true-crime podcasts, please search for M. William Phelps wherever you get your podcast fix. Download my investigative, narrative, episodic podcast *Paper Ghosts,* the first season of which focuses on a series of cold cases I've spent eleven years investigating: four missing girls and one confirmed murder in my hometown. It is available from iHeartRadio.